Locomotive built by Norris Brothers for the Syracuse & Utica Rail Road 1851.
with Septimus Norriss Patent Direct Action Variable Expansion Valves.

NORRIS'S HAND-BOOK

FOR

LOCOMOTIVE ENGINEERS

AND

MACHINISTS:

COMPRISING

THE PROPORTIONS AND CALCULATIONS FOR CONSTRUCTING LOCOMOTIVES, MANNER OF SETTING VALVES, TABLES OF SQUARES, CUBES, AREAS, &c. &c.

BY SEPTIMUS NORRIS,

CIVIL AND MECHANICAL ENGINEER.

"Knowledge is power."

PHILADELPHIA:
HENRY CAREY BAIRD,
SUCCESSOR TO E. L. CAREY.
1854.

STEREOTYPED BY L. JOHNSON AND CO.
PHILADELPHIA.
PRINTED BY T. K. AND P. G. COLLINS.

TO

WILLIAM NORRIS, ESQ.

AS A TESTIMONY OF

ESTEEM AND ADMIRATION OF HIS GREAT INTELLECTUAL ATTAINMENTS,

AND OF

HIS SCIENTIFIC AND CLASSICAL KNOWLEDGE;

This Volume,

DESCRIBING THE GREATEST WORK OF MAN,

The Locomotive Steam Engine,

IS AFFECTIONATELY INSCRIBED BY HIS BROTHER,

THE AUTHOR.

PREFACE.

In presenting this work to the Engineers of the United States, I beg they will study it with attention, as it is the result of many days' close application and research. I have taken care to present all formulas and rules in the most simple manner, so that there will be no danger of the young student being discouraged by unnecessary display of algebraical formulas, which the sight of frightens the timid. All may understand who are familiar with the simple rules of Arithmetic,—Addition, Subtraction, Multiplication, and Division. I give here the result of my experience after a study of twenty years, and for the last twelve years engaged with my senior brother, William Norris, to whom I am entirely indebted for all the information I have received relating to locomotives. *He* built the first locomotive in this country, and was the first engineer that ever attempted to surmount the Inclined Plane across the Schuylkill, where there is a rise of 1 in 14, for 1 mile equal to 377 feet ascent. This wonderful performance was made amid the shouts of thousands: no one has ever attempted such a feat since. In connection with my brothers, I have constructed and built some five hundred and thirty locomotives; one hundred and seventy of which are now successfully running on roads in England and the Continent, seventeen of which are running on the Birmingham and Gloucester Railway, England. Some builders, or perhaps foremen of the locomotive-shops of this country, may think it unwise in my giving to all mechanics the secrets (which they consider) of the business. My belief is, that all I can teach a man or apprentice, so much the better will be the success of my business; and the million should be learned in all things, as well as the few illiberal-minded. I give here every thing relating to the construction of locomotives; and I hope my feeble efforts may prove of value to many who seek after this great science, Mechanics. It is the greatest of all sciences, teaches the mind to think correctly, and produces that intellectual enjoyment which no other study can approach.

TABLE OF CONTENTS.

LOCOMOTIVE ENGINE

built by the

AMOSKEAG MANUFACTURING CO.

MANCHESTER N.H.

1851.

Lith. D. Chillas, Phila.

Scale ¼ in to a Foot.

NORRIS'S HAND-BOOK.

TROY WEIGHT.

grains

24 = 1 *dwt*

480 = 20 = 1 *oz*

5760 = 240 = 12 = 1 *lb*

AVOIRDUPOIS WEIGHT.

drachms

16 = 1 *oz*

256 = 16 = 1 *lb*

7168 = 448 = 28 = 1 *quarter*

286782 = 1792 = 112 = 4 = 1 *cwt*

573440 = 35840 = 2240 = 80 = 20 = 1 *ton*

1 lb. = 14 oz., 11 dwt., 15½ gr. *troy*.

1 oz. = 18 dwt., 5½ gr. *troy*.

N. B.—7000 troy grains make 1 pound avoirdupois; hence 175 pounds troy are equal to 144 pounds avoirdupois.

APOTHECARIES' WEIGHT.

grains

20 = 1 *scruple*

60 = 3 = 1 *drachm*

480 = 24 = 8 = 1 *oz*

5760 = 288 = 96 = 12 = 1 *lb*

LONG MEASURE.

inches						
12 =	1 *foot*					
36 =	3 =	1 *yard*				
72 =	6 =	2 =	1 *fathom*			
198 =	$16\frac{1}{2}$ =	$5\frac{1}{2}$ =	$2\frac{3}{4}$ =	1 *pole*		
7920 =	660 =	220 =	110 =	40 =	1 *furlong*	
63360 =	5280 =	1760 =	880 =	320 =	8 =	1 *mile*

A mile contains 80 chains, land measure; and a chain contains 100 links, or 22 yards. An inch contains 12 lines.

MEASURE OF THE CIRCLE.

seconds (″)				
60 =	1 *minute* (′)			
360 =	60 =	1 *degree* (°)		
32400 =	5400 =	90 =	1 *quadrant*	
129600 =	21600 =	360 =	4 =	1 *circumference*

WINE MEASURE.

pints							
2 =	1 *quart*						
8 =	4 =	1 *gallon*					
336 =	168 =	42 =	1 *tierce*				
504 =	257 =	63 =	$1\frac{1}{2}$ =	1 *hogshead*			
672 =	336 =	84 =	2 =	$1\frac{1}{3}$ =	1 *puncheon*		
1008 =	504 =	126 =	3 =	2 =	$1\frac{1}{2}$ =	1 *pipe*	
2016 =	1008 =	252 =	6 =	4 =	3 =	2 =	1 *tun*

ALE AND BEER MEASURE.

pints
2 = 1 *quart*
8 = 4 = 1 *gallon*
72 = 36 = 2 = 1 *firkin*
144 = 72 = 18 = 2 = 1 *kilderkin*
288 = 144 = 36 = 4 = 2 = 1 *barrel*
432 = 216 = 54 = 6 = 3 = 1½ = 1 *hogshead*
576 = 288 = 72 = 8 = 4 = 2 = 1½ = 1 *punch'n*
864 = 432 = 108 = 12 = 6 = 3 = 2 = 1½ = 1 *butt*

N. B.—The pint, quart, and gallon, for wine, ale, and beer, and grain or corn, measure the same with regard to their magnitude; 8 of these gallons make one bushel; and 1 gallon contains 277·274 cubic inches, or 10 lbs. of distilled water, at 62 degrees Fahrenheit.

DRY MEASURE.

pints
8 = 1 *gallon*
16 = 2 = 1 *peck*
64 = 8 = 4 = 1 *bushel*
256 = 32 = 16 = 4 = 1 *coom*
512 = 64 = 32 = 8 = 2 = 1 *quarter*
2560 = 320 = 160 = 40 = 10 = 5 = 1 *wey*
5120 = 640 = 320 = 80 = 20 = 10 = 2 = 1 *last*

CLOTH MEASURE.

inches				
$2\frac{1}{4}$	= 1 *nail*			
9	= 4	= 1 *quarter*		
36	= 16	= 4	= 1 *yard*	
27	= 12	= 3	= 1 *Flemish ell*	
45	= 20	= 5	= 1 *English ell*	
54	= 24	= 6	= 1 *French ell*	

SQUARE MEASURE.

inches					
144 =	1 *foot*				
1206 =	9 =	1 *yard*			
39204 =	$272\frac{1}{4}$ =	$30\frac{1}{4}$ =	1 *pole*		
1568160 =	10890 =	1210 =	40 =	1 *rood*	
6272640 =	43560 =	4840 =	160 =	4 =	1 *acre*

10 square chains make 1 acre; 640 acres make 1 square mile; 30 acres 1 yard of land; and 100 acres 1 hide of land.

SOLID MEASURE.

inches		
1728 =	1 *foot*	
46656 =	27 =	1 *yard*

1 cubic foot = 2200 cylindrical inches = 3300 spherical inches = 6600 conical inches.

MISCELLANEOUS.

1 Acre, Scotch, 1·271 acres English, or	6084 sq. yards.
1 Acre Irish, 1·638 acres English, or	7840 sq. yards.
1 Barrel, imperial measure	9981·86 cub. in.
" soap	256 lbs.
1 Bushel, imperial measure	2218·19 cub. in.
" Winchester measure	2150·42 cub. in.
" barley	50 lbs.
" coal	88 lbs.
" flour or salt	56 lbs.
" oats	40 lbs.
" wheat	60 lbs.
1 Chaldron coals, Newcastle	53 cwt.
1 Chain	100 links.
1 Clove of wool	7 lbs.
1 Fodder of lead, Stockton	22 cwt.
" at Newcastle	21 cwt.
" at London	19½ cwt.
1 Gallon, imperial measure	277·27 cub. in.
" distilled water, 62°	10 lbs.
" proof spirit or oil	9·3 lbs.
" former wine measure	231 cubic in.
" former ale measure	282 cubic in.
" Irish measure	217·6 cubic in.
1 Geographical mile	1·15 Eng. miles.
" degree	69·12 Eng. miles.
1 Gross	12 dozen.
1 Great gross	12 gross.
1 Hand	4 inches.
1 Hundred of deals	120 in number.
" nails	120 in number.
" salt	7 lasts.
1 Last of salt	18 barrels.

1 Last of gunpowder	24 barrels.
" potash, soap, pitch, or tar	12 barrels.
" flax or feathers	17 cwt.
" wool	4368 lbs.
1 Link	7·92 inches.
1 Load of boards, inch	600 square ft.
" bricks	500 in number.
" hay or straw	36 trusses.
" lime	32 bushels.
" planks, two-inch	300 square ft.
" sand	36 bushels.
" timber, squared	50 cubic feet.
" timber, unhewed	40 cubic feet.
1 Mile	80 chains.
1 Pack of wool	240 lbs.
1 Palm	3 inches.
1 Pole, Woodland	18 feet.
" Plantation	21 feet.
" Cheshire	24 feet.
1 Sack of coals	224 lbs.
" wool	364 lbs.
1 Seam of glass	124 lbs.
1 Span	9 inches.
1 Stone of meat or fish	8 lbs.
" horseman's weight	14 lbs.
" glass	5 lbs.
" wool	14 lbs.
1 Thousand of nails	1200.
1 Truss of new hay	60 lbs.
" old hay	56 lbs.
" straw	36 lbs.
1 Tun of vegetable oil	236 gallons.
" animal oil	252 gallons.
1 Tod of wool	28 lbs.
1 Wey of wool	182 lbs.

Relative Value of the Imperial and Old English Measures.

Wine Gallon.									
Imp. gallon . .	1	2	3	4	5	6	7	8	9
Old gallon . . .	1·200	2·401	3·601	4·801	6·002	7·202	9·402	9·602	10·803
Old gallon . . .	1	2	3	4	5	6	7	8	9
Imp. gallon . .	0·833	1·666	2·499	3·332	4·166	4·999	5·832	6·665	7·498
Ale Gallon.									
Imp. gallon . .	1	2	3	4	5	6	7	8	9
Old gallon . . .	0·983	1·966	2·950	3·933	4·916	5·899	6·883	7·866	8·849
Old gallon . . .	1	2	3	4	5	6	7	8	9
Imp. gallon . .	1·017	2·034	3·051	4·068	5·085	6·102	7·119	8·136	9·153
Corn Bushel.									
Imp. bushel . .	1	2	3	4	5	6	7	8	9
Old bushel . . .	1·031	2·063	3·095	4·126	5·158	6·189	7·221	8·252	9·284
Old bushel . . .	1	2	3	4	5	6	7	8	9
Imp. bushel . .	0·969	1·939	2·908	3·878	4·847	5·817	6·786	7·755	8·725

N. B.—The foregoing relative values are computed in whole numbers and decimal parts; they exhibit the value of units only, but the value for tens, hundreds, thousands, &c. may be found by changing as many of the decimals into integers as there are ciphers in the numbers sought.

EXAMPLE.—Required the number of imperial gallons in 4743 old wine gallons:—

4000 = 3332
700 = 583·2
40 = 33·32
3 = 2·490

3951·019 imperial gallons.

TROY WEIGHT.

Dec. parts of a lb.

Ozs.	*Decimals.*
11	·916666
10	·833333
9	·75
8	·666666
7	·583333
6	·5
5	·416666
4	·333333
3	·25
2	·166666
1	·083333

Dwts.	*Decimals.*
19	·079166
18	·075
17	·070833
16	·066666
15	·0625
14	·058333
13	·054166
12	·05
11	·045833
10	·041666
9	·0375
8	·033333
7	·029166
6	·025
5	·020833
4	·016666
3	·0125
2	·008333
1	·004166

Grs.	*Decimals.*
15	·002604
14	·002430
13	·002257
12	·002083
11	·001910
10	·001736
9	·001562
8	·001389
7	·001215
6	·001042
5	·000868
4	·000694
3	·000521
2	·000347
1	·000173

AVOIRDUPOIS WEIGHT.

Dec. parts of a cwt.

Qrs.	*Decimals.*
3	·75
2	·5
1	·25

Lbs.	*Decimals.*
27	·241071
26	·232142
25	·223214
24	·214286
23	·205357
22	·196428
21	·187500
20	·178572
19	·169643
18	·160714
17	·151785
16	·142856
15	·133928
14	·125
13	·116071
12	·107143
11	·098214
10	·089286
9	·080357
8	·071428
7	·0625
6	·053571
5	·044643
4	·035714
3	·026786
2	·017857
1	·008928

Ozs.	*Decimals.*
15	·008370
14	·007812
13	·007254
12	·006696
11	·006138
10	·005580
9	·005022
8	·004464
7	·003906
6	·003348
5	·002790
4	·002232
3	·001674
2	·001116
1	·000558

AVOIRDUPOIS WEIGHT.

Dec. parts of a lb.

Ozs.	*Decimals.*
15	·9375
14	·875
13	·8125
12	·75
11	·6875
10	·625
9	·5625
8	·5
7	·4375
6	·375
5	·3125
4	·25
3	·1875
2	·125
1	·0625

Drs.	*Decimals.*
15	·058593
14	·054686
13	·050780
12	·046874
11	·042968
10	·039062
9	·035156
8	·03125
7	·027343
6	·023437
5	·019531
4	·015625
3	·011718
2	·007812
1	·003906

LONG MEASURE.

Dec. parts of a foot.

Ins.	*Decimals.*
11	·916666
10	·833333
9	·75
8	·666666
7	·583333
6	·5
5	·416666
4	·333333
3	·25
2	·166666
1	·083333

ENGLISH MONEY.

Decimal parts of £1.

Sh.	*Dec.*	*Sh.*	*Dec.*
19	·95	9	·45
18	·9	8	·4
17	·85	7	·35
16	·8	6	·3
15	·75	5	·25
14	·7	4	·2
13	·65	3	·15
12	·6	2	·1
11	·55	1	·05
10	·5		

Pence.	*Decimals.*
11	·045833
10	·041666
9	·0375
8	·033333
7	·029166
6	·025
5	·020833
4	·016666
3	·0125
2	·008333
1	·004166

Farthing.	*Decimals.*
3	·003125
2	·0020833
1	·0010416

ENGLISH MONEY.

Decimal parts of 1*s*.

Pence.	*Decimals.*
11	·916666
10	·833333
9	·75
8	·666666
7	·583333
6	·5
5	·416666
4	·333333
3	·25
2	·166666
1	·083333

Farthing.	*Decimals.*
3	·0625
2	·041666
1	·020833

Relative Value of British and French Weights and Measures.

FRENCH DECIMAL, OR MODERN SYSTEM.

WEIGHTS.

French.	*British.*
GRAMME........	15·434 grains.
Decigramme ..	1·5434 "
Centigramme..	0·1543 "
Milligramme ..	0·0154 "
Decagramme..	154·34 "
Hectogramme.	3·2154 oz. troy.
or	3·527 oz. avoir.
Kilogramme ..	2·6795 lb. troy.
or	2·2048 lb. avoir.
Myriagramme	26·795 lb. troy.
or	22·048 lb. avoir.
Quintal	1 cwt. 3 qrs. 24½ lb.
Millier or Bar	9 tons, 16 cwt. 3 qrs. 12 lb.

MEASURES—OF CAPACITY.

French.	*British.*
LITRE*	61·028 cubic in.
or	1·761 imp. pint.
Decilitre........	6·1028 cubic in.
Centilitre	0·6103 "
Millilitre	0·0610 "
Decalitre	610·28 "
or	2·2 imp. gallons.
Hectolitre......	3·5317 cubic feet
or	2·75 imp. bush.
Kilolitre	35·317 cubic feet
Myrialitre......	353·17 "

MEASURES—OF LENGTH.

French.	*British.*
METRE	39·371 inches.
Decimetre..	3·9371 "
Centimetre.	0·3937 inch.
Millimetre .	0·0393 "
Decametre .	32·809 feet.
Hectometre	328·09 "
Kilometre...	1093·6 yards.
Myriametre	6·2138 miles.

OF SUPERFICIES.

French.	*British.*
ARE†.........	119·60 sq. yards.
Deciare......	11·960 "
Centiare	10·764 sq. feet.
Milliare.....	155·00 sq. inch.
Decare	1196·0 sq. yards.
Hectare	2·4712 acres.

OF SOLIDITY.

French.	*British.*
STERE‡......	35·317 cub. feet.
Decistere ...	3·5317 "
Centistere ..	610·28 cubic in.
Millistere...	61·028 "
Decastere...	13·080 cubic yds.
Hectostere .	130·80 "

* The Litre = a cubic decimetre.
† The Are = a square decimetre.
‡ The Stere = a cubic metre.

NOTE.—The decimetre, centimetre, and millimetre are respectively formed by dividing the metre by 10, 100, and 1000; and the decametre, hectometre, kilometre, and myriametre, by multiplying the metre by 10, 100, 1000, and 10,000: the other measures and weights of the decimal system are formed in a like manner from their respective units.

THE OLD SYSTEM, OR SYSTEME USUEL.

WEIGHTS.

French.	British.
Grain............	0·837 grain.
Gros (72 grains)	60·285 grains.
Once (8 gros)...	1·1024 oz. avoir.
Livre (16 onces)	1·1024 lb. avoir.

MEASURES OF CAPACITY.

Litron	1·376 imp. pints.
Boisseau.........	2·7515 imp. gal.

MEASURES OF LENGTH.

French.	British.
Ligne...............	0·091 inch.
Pouce (12 lignes)	1·093 "
Pied (12 pouces)	13·12 "
Aune (3⅗ pieds)..	3·937 feet.
Toise (6 pieds)...	6·562 "

The Livre is = 500 grammes.
The Boisseau is = 12·5 litres.
The Toise is = 2 metres.

British and Foreign Weights and Measures.

RELATIVE VALUE OF BRITISH AND FOREIGN COMMERCIAL WEIGHTS.

Country or Place.	Weights.	No. equal to 1 cwt. British.
Aleppo	Oke	40·10
Alexandria	Rottolo For.	119·84
Amsterdam	Pound Flem.	50·79
Algiers	Rottolo	94·12
Barcelona	Pound	126·97
Berlin	Pound	108·42
Bremen	Pound	101·95
Cairo	Rottolo	117·89
China	Catty	84·00
Cologne	Pound	108·64
Constantinople	Oke	39·53
Copenhagen	Pound	101·55
Cyprus	Rottolo	21·35
Damascus	Rottolo	28·44
Dantzic	Pound	108·42
Florence	Pound	149·61
France	Livre usuel	101·59
Frankfort	Pound	108·73
Geneva	Pound, heavy	92·25
Genoa	Pound, heavy	145·69
Hamburgh	Pound	104·86

Relative Value of British and Foreign Commercial Weights—continued.

Country or Place.	Weight.	No. equal to 1 cwt. British.
Hanover	Pound	104·37
Konigsberg	Pound	108·42
Japan	Catty	86·15
Leghorn	Pound	149·61
Leipsic	Pound	108·79
Lubec	Pound	104·82
Madeira	Pound	110·79
Malta	Rottolo	64·17
Milan	Pound, new	50·79
Naples	Cantaro gro.	56·99
Nuremberg	Pound	99·61
Persia	Batman	88·31
Poland	Pound	125·72
Portugal	Pound	110·68
Prussia	Pound	108·60
Riga	Pound	121·51
Rome	Pound	149·79
Rostock	Pound	99·84
Rotterdam	Pound	102·82
Russia	Pound	124·08
Sardinia	Pound	128·00
Sicily	Pound	160·00
Smyrna	Oke	39·53
Spain	Pound	110·40
Sweden	Pound	149·33
Trieste	Pound	90·75
Tripoli	Rottolo	100·00
Tunis	Rotul	100·85
Venice	Pound, new	50·79
Vienna	Pound	90·68
Zurich	Pound, heavy	96·33

Relative Value of British and Foreign Corn or Dry Measures.

Country or Place.	Name of Measure.	No. equal to 1 quarter, or 8 bush. English.
Alexandria	rebebe	1·85
Algiers	zarrie	14·54
Amsterdam	mudde	2·61
Ancona	rubbio	1·01
Antwerp	mudde	2·91
Barcelona	quartera	4·25
Berlin	scheffel	5·58
Bruges	hoed	1·74
Cologne	malter	1·79
Constantinople	killow	8·77
Copenhagen	toende	2·09
Cyprus	medimno	3·87
Dantzic	scheffel	5·32
Dunkirk	rasiere	2·18
Embden	tonne	1·51
Florence	staja	11·95
France	boisseau	23·32
Frankfort	malter	2·69
Genoa	mina	2·40
Groningen	mudde	3·19
Hague	sack	2·71
Hamburgh	scheffel	2·76
Hanover	himten	9·35
Leghorn	sacco	4·00
Leipsic	scheffel	2·09
Lisbon	alquiere	21·50
Lubec	scheffel	8·70
Majorca	quartera	4·13
Malaga	fanega	5·16
Malta	salma	1·00
Munich	scheffel	0·80
Naples	zomolo	5·69
Netherlands	mudde	2·91
Persia	artaba	4·42
Poland	korzec	5·69
Prague	strick	2·72
Prussia	scheffel	5·29
Riga	loop	4·26
Rome	rubbio	0·98

Relative Value of British and Foreign Corn or Dry Measures—continued.

Country or Place.	Name of Measure.	No. equal to 1 quarter or 8 bush. English.
Rostock	scheffel	7·48
Rotterdam	sack	2·80
Russia	chetwert	1·38
Sardinia	starello	5·94
Sicily	salma	1·05
Smyrna	killow	5·67
Spain	fanega	5·16
Sweden	tunna	1·98
Texel	loop	4·64
Trieste	metzen	4·79
Tunis	caffice	0·55
Venice	stajo	3·6[illegible]
Vienna	metze	4·73
Utrecht	sack	3·22
Wirtemberg	scheffel	1·61
Zante	misura	13·84
Zealand	sack	3·89
Zurich	mutt	3·51

Relative Value of British and Foreign Wine or Liquid Measures.

Country or Place.	Name of Measure.	Content in British Imp. Gallons.
Amsterdam	wine stekan	4·27
Antwerp	stoop	0·60
Barcelona	carga	27·24
Berlin	anker	8·24
Bordeaux	velte	1·58
Burgundy	quartant	22·63
Canaries	arroba	3·53
Champagne	quartant	19·82
Cognac	brandy velte	1·60
Cologne	viertel	1·31
Constantinople	almud	1·15

Relative Value of British and Foreign Wine or Liquid Measures—continued.

Country or Place.	Name of Measure.	Content in British Imp. Gallons.
Copenhagen	viertel	1·70
Cyprus	cass	1·04
Dantzic	ohm	32·96
Dresden	eimer	14·88
Florence	wine barile	10·03
France	setier	1·63
Frankfort	viertel	1·60
Geneva	setier	9·95
Genoa	wine barile	16·33
Hamburgh	ahm	31·86
Hanover	ahm	34·23
Heidelberg	maas	0·51
Leghorn	wine barile	10 03
Leipsic	eimer	16·74
Lisbon	almude	3·64
Lucca	oil coppo	21·97
Malaga	arroba	2·49
Malta	oil caffiso	4·58
Marseilles	millerolle	14·15
Naples	wine barile	9·17
Netherlands	vat	22·01
Oporto	almude	5·61
Poland	garniec	0·35
Prussia	eimer	15·12
Riga	anker	8·61
Rome	wine barile	12·84
Rostock	anker	7·96
Rotterdam	ahm	33·32
Rouen	barrique	43·06
Russia	vedro	2·09
Spain	wine arroba	3·53
Strasburg	ohm	10·14
Sweden	kann	0·57
Trieste	eimer	12·45
Venice	secchio	2·37
Vienna	eimer	12·42
Zante	barile	14·68
Zurich	maas	0·36

Relative Value of British and Foreign Measures of Length.

Country or Place.	Name of Measure.	No. of each equal to 100 English Feet.
Amsterdam	Foot	107·71
Antwerp	Foot	106·76
Augsburg	Foot	103·00
Berlin	Foot	98·44
Berne	Foot	103·98
Bremen	Foot	105·44
Brunswick	Foot	106·85
Carrara	Palmo	125·13
China	Foot	94·41
Cologne	Foot	110·80
Copenhagen	Foot	97·16
Cracow	Foot	85·53
Dantzic	Foot	106·19
Dresden	Foot	107·71
France	Foot	91·46
Frankfort	Foot	106·38
Geneva	Foot	62·46
Genoa	Palmo	123·45
Gottingen	Foot	104·80
Hamburg	Foot	106·38
Hanover	Foot	104·80
Leipsic	Foot	108·01
Leyden	Foot	97·24
Liege	Foot	106·00
Lisbon	Foot	92·73
Malta	Foot	107·52
Mecklenburg	Foot	104·80
Milan	Foot	76·82
Moscow	Foot	91·11
Munich	Foot	105·54
Naples	Palmo	115·60
Neufchatel	Foot	101·60
Nuremberg	Foot	100·33
Padua	Foot	86·14
Pisa	Palmo	102·21
Prague	Foot	101·52
Prussia	Foot	97·16
Riga	Foot	111·21

Relative Value of British and Foreign Measures of Length—continued.

Country or Place.	Name of Measure.	No. of each equal to 100 English Feet.
Rome	Foot	102·38
Rostock	Foot	105·44
Russia	Foot	87·27
Sardinia	Palmo	122·69
Sicily	Palmo	125·91
Spain	Foot	107·91
Sweden	Foot	102·73
Venice	Foot	87·71
Vienna	Foot	96·38
Ulm	Foot	105·35
Wirtemberg	Foot	106·57
Zurich	Foot	101·60

Relative Value of British and Foreign Square and Cubic Measures.

Country or Place.	Square Foot in English Sq. Inches.	Cubic Foot in English Cubic Inches.
Amsterdam	124·255	1385·070
Antwerp	126·337	1420·027
Augsberg	135·722	1581·161
Berlin	148·693	1813·162
Berne	133·287	1538·798
Bremen	129·504	1473·755
Cologne	117·288	1270·229
Dantzic	127·690	1442·897
Dresden	124·099	1382·463
France	163·558	2091·743
Geneva	369·024	7088·951
Hamburg	127·441	1438·684
Hanover	131·194	1502·696
Leipsic	123·432	1371·329
Liege	128·142	1450·577
Lisbon	167·547	2168·728
Milan	243·984	3811·030

Relative Value of British and Foreign Square and Cubic Measures—continued.

Country or Place.	Square Foot in English Sq. Inches.	Cubic Foot in English Cubic Inches.
Munich	129·390	1471·811
Nuremberg	143·041	1710·770
Prussia	152·670	1886·390
Rhineland	152·670	1886·390
Riga	116·424	1256·215
Rome	137·358	1609·835
Spain	123·832	1378·002
Sweden	136·515	1595·041
Venice	187·142	2560·102
Vienna	155·002	1929·774
Zurich	139·476	1647·211

Relative Value of British and Foreign Land Measures.

Country or Place.	Name of Measure.	English Square Yards.	No. of each equal to 10 English Acres.
Amsterdam	Morgen	9722	4·978
Berlin	Great Morgen	6786	7·132
Dantzic	Morgen	6650	7·278
France	Hectare	11960	4·046
Geneva	Arpent	6179	7·833
Hamburg	Morgen	11545	4·192
Hanover	Morgen	3100	15·613
Naples	Moggia	3998	12·106
Portugal	Geira	6970	6·944
Prussia	Morgen	3053	15·853
Rhineland	Morgen	10185	4·752
Rome	Pezza	3158	15·196
Russia	Dessetina	13066	3·704
Saxony	Acre	6590	7·344
Spain	Fanegada	5500	8·800
Sweden	Tunneland	5900	8·203
Switzerland	Faux	7855	6·161
Vienna	Jock	6889	7·025
Zurich	Common Acre	3875	12·488

Relative Value of British and Foreign Road Measures.

Country or Place.	Name of Measure.	English Yards.	No. of each equal to 100 English Miles.
Arabia	Mile	2148	81·936
Brabant	League	6077	28·966
China	Li	632	278·481
Denmark	Mile	8244	21·348
Flanders	League	6864	25·641
France	League of 2000 Toises	4263	41·285
Germany	Mile, long	10126	17·381
Hamburg	Mile	8244	21·348
Hanover	Mile	11559	15·226
Holland	Mile	8103	21·725
Hungary	Mile	9113	19·313
Netherlands	Mile, metrical	1093	161·024
Persia	Parasang	6086	28·918
Poland	Mile, long	8103	21·725
Portugal	League	6760	26·035
Prussia	Mile	8237	21·367
Rome	Mile	1628	108·108
Russia	Werst	1067	150·814
Spain	League, common	7416	23·732
Sweden	Mile	11700	15·042
Switzerland	Mile	9153	19·228
Turkey	Berri	1826	96·385

A TABLE

Of the Reciprocals of Numbers; or the Decimal Fractions corresponding to Vulgar Fractions of which the Numerator is unity or 1.

[In the following tables, the decimal fractions are reciprocals of the denominators of those opposite to them; and their product is = unity.

To find the decimal corresponding to a fraction having a higher numerator than 1, multiply the decimal opposite to the given denominator, by the given numerator. Thus, the decimal corresponding to $\frac{1}{64}$ being ·015625, the decimal to $\frac{15}{64}$ will be ·015625 × 15 = ·234375.]

Fraction or Numb.	Decimal or Reciprocal.	Fraction or Numb.	Decimal or Reciprocal.	Fraction or Numb.	Decimal or Reciprocal.
1/2	·5	1/20	·05	1/38	·026315789
1/3	·333333333	1/21	·047619048	1/39	·025641026
1/4	·25	1/22	·045454545	1/40	·025
1/5	·2	1/23	·043478261	1/41	·024390244
1/6	·166666667	1/24	·041666667	1/42	·023809524
1/7	·142857143	1/25	·04	1/43	·023255814
1/8	·125	1/26	·038461538	1/44	·022727273
1/9	·111111111	1/27	·037037037	1/45	·022222222
1/10	·1	1/28	·035714286	1/46	·02173913
1/11	·090909091	1/29	·034482759	1/77	·0212766
1/12	·083333333	1/30	·033333333	1/48	·020833333
1/13	·076923077	1/31	·032258065	1/49	·020408163
1/14	·071428571	1/32	·03125	1/50	·02
1/15	·066666667	1/33	·030303030	1/51	·019607843
1/16	·0625	1/34	·029411765	1/52	·019230769
1/17	·058823529	1/35	·028571429	1/53	·018867925
1/18	·055555556	1/36	·027777778	1/54	·018518519
1/19	·052631579	1/37	·027027027	1/55	·018181818

Fraction or Numb.	Decimal or Reciprocal.	Fraction or Numb.	Decimal or Reciprocal.	Fraction or Numb.	Decimal or Reciprocal.
1/56	·017857143	1/98	·010204082	1/140	·007142857
1/57	·01754386	1/99	·01010101	1/141	·007092199
1/58	·017241379	1/100	·01	1/142	·007042254
1/59	·016949153	1/101	·00990099	1/143	·006993007
1/60	·016666667	1/102	·009803922	1/144	·006944444
1/61	·016393443	1/103	·009708738	1/145	·006896552
1/62	·016129032	1/104	·009615385	1/146	·006849315
1/63	·015873016	1/105	·00952381	1/147	·006802721
1/64	·015625	1/106	·009433962	1/148	·006756757
1/65	·015384615	1/107	·009345794	1/149	·006711409
1/66	·015151515	1/108	·009259259	1/150	·006666667
1/67	·014925373	1/109	·009174312	1/151	·006622517
1/68	·014705882	1/110	·009090909	1/152	·006578947
1/69	·014492754	1/111	·009009009	1/153	·006535948
1/70	·014285714	1/112	·008928571	1/154	·006493506
1/71	·014084517	1/113	·008849558	1/155	·006451613
1/72	·013888889	1/114	·00877193	1/156	·006410256
1/73	·01369863	1/115	·008695652	1/157	·006369427
1/74	·013513514	1/116	·00802069	1/158	·006329114
1/75	·013333333	1/117	·008547009	1/159	·006289308
1/76	·013157895	1/118	·008474576	1/160	·00625
1/77	·012987013	1/119	·008403361	1/161	·00621118
1/78	·012820513	1/120	·008333333	1/162	·00617284
1/79	·012658228	1/121	·008264463	1/163	·006134969
1/80	·0125	1/122	·008196721	1/164	·006097561
1/81	·012345679	1/123	·008130081	1/165	·006060606
1/82	·012195122	1/124	·008064516	1/166	·006024096
1/83	·012048193	1/125	·008	1/167	·005988024
1/84	·011904762	1/126	·007936508	1/168	·005952381
1/85	·011764706	1/127	·007874016	1/169	·00591716
1/86	·011627907	1/128	·0078125	1/170	·005882353
1/87	·011494253	1/129	·007751938	1/171	·005847953
1/88	·011363636	1/130	·007692308	1/172	·005813953
1/89	·011235955	1/131	·007633588	1/173	·005780347
1/90	·011111111	1/132	·007575758	1/174	·005747126
1/91	·010989011	1/133	·007518797	1/175	·005714286
1/92	·010869565	1/134	·007462687	1/176	·005681818
1/93	·010752688	1/135	·007407407	1/177	·005649718
1/94	·010638298	1/136	·007352941	1/178	·005617978
1/95	·010526316	1/137	·00729927	1/179	·005586592
1/96	·010416667	1/138	·007246377	1/180	·005555556
1/97	·010309278	1/139	·007194245	1/181	·005524862

Fraction or Numb.	Decimal or Reciprocal.	Fraction or Numb.	Decimal or Reciprocal.	Fraction or Numb.	Decimal or Reciprocal.
1/182	·005494505	1/224	·004464286	1/266	·003759398
1/183	·005464481	1/225	·004444444	1/267	·003745318
1/184	·005434783	1/226	·004424779	1/268	·003731343
1/185	·005405405	1/227	·004405286	1/269	·003717472
1/186	·005376344	1/228	·004385965	1/270	·003703704
1/187	·005347594	1/229	·004366812	1/271	·003690037
1/188	·005319149	1/230	·004347826	1/272	·003676471
1/189	·005291005	1/231	·004329004	1/273	·003663004
1/190	·005263158	1/232	·004310345	1/274	·003649635
1/191	·005235602	1/233	·004291845	1/275	·003636364
1/192	·005208333	1/234	·004273504	1/276	·003623188
1/193	·005181347	1/235	·004255319	1/277	·003610108
1/194	·005154639	1/236	·004237288	1/278	·003597122
1/195	·005128205	1/237	·004219409	1/279	·003584229
1/196	·005102041	1/238	·004201681	1/280	·003571429
1/197	·005076142	1/239	·0041841	1/281	·003558719
1/198	·005050505	1/240	·004166667	1/282	·003546099
1/199	·005025126	1/241	·004149378	1/283	·003533569
1/200	·005	1/242	·004132231	1/284	·003522127
1/201	·004975124	1/243	·004115226	1/285	·003508772
1/202	·004950495	1/244	·004098361	1/286	·003496503
1/203	·004926108	1/245	·004081633	1/287	·003484321
1/204	·004901961	1/246	·004065041	1/288	·003472222
1/205	·004878049	1/247	·004048583	1/289	·003460208
1/206	·004854369	1/248	·004032258	1/290	·003448276
1/207	·004830918	1/249	·004016064	1/291	·003436426
1/208	·004807692	1/250	·004	1/292	·003424658
1/209	·004784689	1/251	·003984064	1/293	·003412969
1/210	·004761905	1/252	·003968254	1/294	·003401261
1/211	·004739336	1/253	·003952569	1/295	·003389831
1/212	·004716981	1/254	·003937008	1/296	·003378378
1/213	·004694836	1/255	·003921569	1/297	·003367003
1/214	·004672897	1/256	·00390625	1/298	·003355705
1/215	·004651163	1/257	·003891051	1/299	·003344482
1/216	·00462963	1/258	·003875969	1/300	·003333333
1/217	·004608295	1/259	·003861004	1/301	·003322259
1/218	·004587156	1/260	·003846154	1/302	·003311258
1/219	·00456621	1/261	·003831418	1/303	·00330133
1/220	·004545455	1/262	·003816794	1/304	·003289474
1/221	·004524887	1/263	·003802281	1/305	·003278689
1/222	·004504505	1/264	·003787879	1/306	·003267974
1/223	·004484305	1/265	·003773585	1/307	·003257329

Fraction or Numb.	Decimal or Reciprocal.	Fraction or Numb.	Decimal or Reciprocal.	Fraction or Numb.	Decimal or Reciprocal.
1/308	·003246753	1/350	·002857143	1/392	·00255102
1/309	·003236246	1/351	·002849003	1/393	·002544529
1/310	·003225806	1/352	·002840909	1/394	·002538071
1/311	·003215434	1/353	·002832861	1/395	·002531646
1/312	·003205128	1/354	·002824859	1/396	·002525253
1/313	·003194888	1/355	·002816901	1/397	·002518892
1/314	·003184713	1/356	·002808989	1/398	·002512563
1/315	·003174603	1/357	·00280112	1/399	·002506266
1/316	·003164557	1/358	·002793296	1/400	·0025
1/317	·003154574	1/359	·002785515	1/401	·002493766
1/318	·003144654	1/360	·002777778	1/402	·002487562
1/319	·003134796	1/361	·002770083	1/403	·00248139
1/320	·003125	1/362	·002762431	1/404	·002475248
1/321	·003115265	1/363	·002754821	1/405	·002469136
1/322	·00310559	1/364	·002747253	1/406	·002463054
1/323	·003095975	1/365	·002739726	1/407	·002457002
1/324	·00308642	1/366	·00273224	1/408	·00245098
1/325	·003076923	1/367	·002724796	1/409	·002444988
1/326	·003067485	1/368	·002717391	1/410	·002439024
1/327	·003058104	1/369	·002710027	1/411	·00243309
1/328	·00304878	1/370	·002702703	1/412	·002427184
1/329	·003039514	1/371	·002695418	1/413	·002421308
1/330	·003030303	1/372	·002688172	1/414	·002415459
1/331	·003021148	1/373	·002680965	1/415	·002409639
1/332	·003012048	1/374	·002673797	1/416	·002403846
1/333	·003003003	1/375	·002666667	1/417	·002398082
1/334	·002994012	1/376	·002659574	1/418	·002392344
1/335	·002985075	1/377	·00265252	1/419	·002386635
1/336	·00297619	1/378	·002645503	1/420	·002380952
1/337	·002967359	1/379	·002638521	1/421	002375297
1/338	·00295858	1/380	·002631579	1/422	·002369668
1/339	·002949853	1/381	·002624672	1/423	·002364066
1/340	·002941176	1/382	·002617801	1/424	·002358491
1/341	·002932551	1/383	·002610966	1/425	·002352941
1/342	·002923977	1/384	·002604167	1/426	·002347418
1/343	·002915452	1/385	·002597403	1/427	·00234192
1/344	·002906977	1/386	·002590674	1/428	·002336449
1/345	·002898551	1/387	·002583979	1/429	·002331002
1/346	·002890173	1/388	·00257732	1/430	·002325581
1/347	·002881844	1/389	·002570694	1/431	·002320186
1/348	·002873563	1/390	·002564103	1/432	·002314815
1/349	·00286533	1/391	·002557545	1/433	·002309469

Fraction or Numb.	Decimal or Reciprocal.	Fraction or Numb.	Decimal or Reciprocal.	Fraction or Numb.	Decimal or Reciprocal.
1/434	·002304147	1/476	·00210084	1/518	·001930502
1/435	·002298851	1/477	·002096486	1/519	·001926782
1/436	·002293578	1/478	·00209205	1/520	·001923077
1/437	·00228833	1/479	·002087683	1/521	·001919386
1/438	·002283105	1/480	·002083333	1/522	·001915709
1/439	·002277904	1/481	·002079002	1/523	·001912046
1/440	·002272727	1/482	·002074689	1/524	·001908397
1/441	·002267574	1/483	·002070393	1/525	·001904762
1/442	·002262443	1/484	·002066116	1/526	·001901141
1/443	·002257336	1/485	·002061856	1/527	·001897533
1/444	·002252252	1/486	·002057613	1/528	·001893939
1/445	·002247191	1/487	·002053388	1/529	·001890359
1/446	·002242152	1/488	·00204918	1/530	·001886792
1/447	·002237136	1/489	·00204499	1/531	·001883239
1/448	·002232143	1/490	·002040816	1/532	·001879699
1/449	·002227171	1/491	·00203666	1/533	·001876173
1/450	·002222222	1/492	·00203252	1/534	·001872659
1/451	·002217295	1/493	·002028398	1/535	·001869159
1/452	·002212389	1/494	·002024291	1/536	·001865672
1/453	·002207506	1/495	·002020202	1/537	·001862197
1/454	·002202643	1/496	·002016129	1/538	·001858736
1/455	·002197802	1/497	·002012072	1/539	·001855288
1/456	·002192982	1/498	·002008032	1/540	·001851852
1/457	·002188184	1/499	·002004008	1/541	·001848429
1/458	·002183406	1/500	·002	1/542	·001845018
1/459	·002178649	1/501	·001996008	1/543	·001841621
1/460	·002173913	1/502	·001992032	1/544	·001838235
1/461	·002169197	1/503	·001988072	1/545	·001834862
1/462	·002164502	1/504	·001984127	1/546	·001831502
1/463	·002159827	1/505	·001980198	1/547	·001828154
1/464	·002155172	1/506	·001976285	1/548	·001824818
1/465	·002150538	1/507	·001972387	1/549	·001821494
1/466	·002145923	1/508	·001968504	1/550	·001818182
1/467	·002141328	1/509	·001964637	1/551	·001814882
1/468	·002136752	1/510	·001960784	1/552	·001811594
1/469	·002132196	1/511	·001956947	1/553	·001808318
1/470	·00212766	1/512	·001953125	1/554	·001805054
1/471	·002123142	1/513	·001949318	1/555	·001801802
1/472	·002118644	1/514	·001945525	1/556	·001798561
1/473	·002114165	1/515	·001941748	1/557	·001795332
1/474	·002109705	1/516	·001937984	1/558	·001792115
1/475	·002105263	1/517	·001934236	1/559	·001788909

Fraction or Numb.	Decimal or Reciprocal.	Fraction or Numb.	Decimal or Reciprocal.	Fraction or Numb.	Decimal or Reciprocal.
1/560	·001785714	1/602	·00166113	1/644	·001552795
1/561	·001782531	1/603	·001658375	1/645	·001550388
1/562	·001779359	1/604	·001655629	1/646	·001547988
1/563	·001776199	1/605	·001652893	1/647	·001545595
1/564	·00177305	1/606	·001650165	1/648	·00154321
1/565	·001769912	1/607	·001647446	1/649	·001540832
1/566	·001766784	1/608	·001644737	1/650	·001538462
1/567	·001763668	1/609	·001642036	1/651	·001536098
1/568	·001760563	1/610	·001639344	1/652	·001533742
1/569	·001757469	1/611	·001636661	1/653	·001531394
1/570	·001754386	1/612	·001633987	1/654	·001529052
1/571	·001751313	1/613	·001631321	1/655	·001526718
1/572	·001748252	1/614	·001628664	1/656	·00152439
1/573	·001745201	1/615	·001626016	1/657	·00152207
1/574	·00174216	1/616	·001623377	1/658	·001519751
1/575	·00173913	1/617	·001620746	1/659	·001517451
1/576	·001736111	1/618	·001618123	1/660	·001515152
1/577	·001733102	1/619	·001615509	1/661	·001512859
1/578	·001730104	1/620	·001612903	1/662	·001510574
1/579	·001727116	1/621	·001610306	1/663	·001508296
1/580	·001724138	1/622	·001607717	1/664	·001506024
1/581	·00172117	1/623	·001605136	1/665	·001503759
1/582	·001718213	1/624	·001602564	1/666	·001501502
1/583	·001715266	1/625	·0016	1/667	·00149925
1/584	·001712329	1/626	·001597444	1/668	·001497006
1/585	·001709402	1/627	·001594896	1/669	·001494768
1/586	·001706485	1/628	·001592357	1/670	·001492537
1/587	·001703578	1/629	·001589825	1/671	·001490313
1/588	·00170068	1/630	·001587302	1/672	·001488095
1/589	·001697793	1/631	·001584786	1/673	·001485884
1/590	·001694915	1/632	·001582278	1/674	·00148368
1/591	·001692047	1/633	·001579779	1/675	·001481481
1/592	·001689189	1/634	·001577287	1/676	·00147929
1/593	·001686341	1/635	·001574803	1/677	·001477105
1/594	·001683502	1/636	·001572327	1/678	·001474926
1/595	·001680672	1/637	·001569859	1/679	·001472754
1/596	·001677852	1/638	·001567398	1/680	·001470588
1/597	·001675042	1/639	·001564945	1/681	·001468429
1/598	·001672241	1/640	·0015625	1/682	·001466276
1/599	·001669449	1/641	·001560062	1/683	·001464129
1/600	·001666667	1/642	·001557632	1/684	·001461988
1/601	·001663894	1/643	·00155521	1/685	·001459854

Fraction or Numb.	Decimal or Reciprocal.	Fraction or Numb.	Decimal or Reciprocal.	Fraction or Numb.	Decimal or Reciprocal.
1/686	·001457726	1/728	·001373626	1/770	·001298701
1/687	·001455604	1/729	·001371742	1/771	·001297017
1/688	·001453488	1/730	·001369863	1/772	·001295337
1/689	·001451379	1/731	·001367989	1/773	·001293661
1/690	·001449275	1/732	·00136612	1/774	·00129199
1/691	·001447178	1/733	·001364256	1/775	·001290323
1/692	·001445087	1/734	·001362398	1/776	·00128866
1/693	·001443001	1/735	·001360544	1/777	·001287001
1/694	·001440922	1/736	·001358696	1/778	·001285347
1/695	·001438849	1/737	·001356852	1/779	·001283697
1/696	·001436782	1/738	·001355014	1/780	·001282051
1/697	·00143472	1/739	·00135318	1/781	·00128041
1/698	·001432665	1/740	·001351351	1/782	·001278772
1/699	·001430615	1/741	·001349528	1/783	·001277139
1/700	·001428571	1/742	·001347709	1/784	·00127551
1/701	·001426534	1/743	·001345895	1/785	·001273885
1/702	·001424501	1/744	·001344086	1/786	·001272265
1/703	·001422475	1/745	·001342282	1/787	·001270648
1/704	·001420455	1/746	·001340483	1/788	·001269036
1/705	·00141844	1/747	·001338688	1/789	·001267427
1/706	·001416431	1/748	·001336898	1/790	·001265823
1/707	·001414427	1/749	·001335113	1/791	·001264223
1/708	·001412429	1/750	·001333333	1/792	·001262626
1/709	·001410437	1/751	·001331558	1/793	·001261034
1/710	·001408451	1/752	·001329787	1/794	·001259446
1/711	·00140647	1/753	·001328021	1/795	·001257862
1/712	·001404494	1/754	·00132626	1/796	·001256281
1/713	·001402525	1/755	·001324503	1/797	·001254705
1/714	·00140056	1/756	·001322751	1/798	·001253133
1/715	·001398601	1/757	·001321004	1/799	·001251364
1/716	·001396648	1/758	·001319261	1/800	·00125
1/717	·0013947	1/759	·001317523	1/801	·001248439
1/718	·001392758	1/760	·001315789	1/802	·001246883
1/719	·001390821	1/761	·00131406	1/803	·00124533
1/720	·001388889	1/762	·001312336	1/804	·001243781
1/721	·001386963	1/763	·001310616	1/805	·001242236
1/722	·001385042	1/764	·001308901	1/806	·001240695
1/723	·001383126	1/765	·00130719	1/807	·001239157
1/724	·001381215	1/766	·001305483	1/808	·001237624
1/725	·00137931	1/767	·001303781	1/809	·001236094
1/726	·00137741	1/768	·001302083	1/810	·001234568
1/727	·001375516	1/769	·00130039	1/811	·001233046

4

Fraction or Numb.	Decimal or Reciprocal.	Fraction or Numb.	Decimal or Reciprocal.	Fraction or Numb.	Decimal or Reciprocal.
1/812	·001231527	1/854	·00117096	1/896	·001116071
1/813	·001230012	1/855	·001169591	1/897	·001114827
1/814	·001228501	1/856	·001168224	1/898	·001113586
1/815	·001226994	1/857	·001166861	1/899	·001112347
1/816	·001225499	1/858	·001165501	1/900	·001111111
1/817	·00122399	1/859	·001164144	1/901	·001109878
1/818	·001222494	1/860	·001162791	1/902	·001108647
1/819	·001221001	1/861	·00116144	1/903	·00110742
1/820	·001219512	1/862	·001160093	1/904	·001106195
1/821	·001218027	1/863	·001158749	1/905	·001104972
1/822	·001216545	1/864	·001157407	1/906	·001103753
1/823	·001215067	1/865	·001156069	1/907	·001102536
1/824	·001213592	1/866	·001154734	1/908	·001101322
1/825	·001212121	1/867	·001153403	1/909	·00110011
1/826	·001210654	1/868	·001152074	1/910	·001098901
1/827	·00120919	1/869	·001150748	1/911	·001091695
1/828	·001207729	1/870	·001149425	1/912	·001096491
1/829	·001206273	1/871	·001148106	1/913	·00109529
1/830	·001204819	1/872	·001146789	1/914	·001094092
1/831	·001203369	1/873	·001145475	1/915	·001092896
1/832	·001201923	1/874	·001144165	1/916	·001091703
1/833	·00120048	1/875	·001142857	1/917	·001090513
1/834	·001199041	1/876	·001141553	1/918	·001089325
1/835	·001197605	1/877	·001140251	1/919	·001088139
1/836	·001196172	1/878	·001138952	1/920	·001086957
1/837	·001194743	1/879	·001137656	1/921	·001085776
1/838	·001193317	1/880	·001136364	1/922	·001084599
1/839	·001191895	1/881	·001135074	1/923	·001083423
1/840	·001190476	1/882	·001133787	1/924	·001082251
1/841	·001189061	1/883	·001132503	1/925	001081081
1/842	·001187648	1/884	·001131222	1/926	·001079914
1/843	·00118624	1/885	·001129944	1/927	·001078749
1/844	·001184834	1/886	·001128668	1/928	·001077586
1/845	·001183432	1/887	·001127396	1/929	·001076426
1/846	·001182033	1/888	·001126126	1/930	·001075269
1/847	·001180638	1/889	·001124859	1/931	·001074114
1/848	·001179245	1/890	·001123596	1/932	·001072961
1/849	·001177856	1/891	·001122334	1/933	·001071811
1/850	·001176471	1/892	·001121076	1/934	·001070664
1/851	·001175088	1/893	·001119821	1/935	·001069519
1/852	·001173709	1/894	·001118568	1/936	·001068376
1/853	·001172333	1/895	·001117818	1/937	·001067236

Fraction or Numb.	Decimal or Reciprocal.	Fraction or Numb.	Decimal or Reciprocal.	Fraction or Numb.	Decimal or Reciprocal.
1/938	·001066098	1/959	·001042753	1/980	·001020408
1/939	·001064963	1/960	·001041667	1/981	·001019168
1/940	·00106383	1/961	·001040583	1/982	·00101833
1/941	·001062699	1/962	·001039501	1/983	·001017294
1/942	·001061571	1/963	·001038422	1/984	·00101626
1/943	·001060445	1/964	·001037344	1/985	·001015228
1/944	·001059322	1/965	·001036269	1/986	·001014199
1/945	·001058201	1/966	·001035197	1/987	·001013171
1/946	·001057082	1/967	·001034126	1/988	·001012146
1/947	·001055966	1/968	·001033058	1/989	·001011122
1/948	·001054852	1/969	·001031992	1/990	·001010101
1/949	·001053741	1/970	·001030928	1/991	·001009082
1/950	·001052632	1/971	·001029866	1/992	·001008065
1/951	·001051525	1/972	·001028807	1/993	·001007049
1/952	·00105042	1/973	·001027749	1/994	·001006036
1/953	·001049318	1/974	·001026694	1/995	·001005025
1/954	·001048218	1/975	·001025641	1/996	·001004016
1/955	·00104712	1/976	·00102459	1/997	·001003009
1/956	·001046025	1/977	·001023541	1/998	·001002004
1/957	·001044932	1/978	·001022495	1/999	·001001001
1/958	·001043841	1/979	·00102145	1/1000	·001

TABLE

Of the Diameters, Circumferences, and Areas of Circles, in Inches.

Diameter in Inches.	Circumference in Inches.	Area in Square Inches.	Diameter in Inches.	Circumference in Inches.	Area in Square Inches.	Diameter in Inches.	Circumference in Inches.	Area in Square Inches.
1/16	·1963	·00306	4	12·566	12·566	9	28·274	63·617
1/8	·3927	·01227	1/8	12·959	13·364	1/8	28·667	65·396
3/16	·5890	·02761	1/4	13·351	14·186	1/4	29·059	67·200
1/4	·7854	·04909	3/8	13·744	15·033	3/8	29·452	69·029
5/16	·9817	·07670	1/2	14·137	15·904	1/2	29·845	70·882
3/8	1·1781	·11044	5/8	14·529	16·800	5/8	30·237	72·759
7/16	1.3744	·15033	3/4	14·922	17·720	3/4	30·630	74·662
1/2	1·5708	·19635	7/8	15·315	18·665	7/8	31·023	76·588
9/16	1·7671	·24850	5	15·708	19·635	10	31·416	78·540
5/8	1·9635	·30680	1/8	16·100	20·629	1/8	31·808	80·515
11/16	2·1598	·37122	1/4	16·493	21·647	1/4	32·201	82·516
3/4	2·3562	·44172	3/8	16·886	22·690	3/8	32·594	84·540
13/16	2·5525	·51849	1/2	17·278	23·758	1/2	32·986	86·590
7/8	2·7489	·60132	5/8	17·671	24·850	5/8	33·379	88·664
15/16	2·9452	·69030	3/4	18·064	25·967	3/4	33·772	90·762
			7/8	18·457	27·108	7/8	34·164	92·885
1	3·141	·785	6	18·849	28·274	11	34·557	95·033
1/8	3·534	·994	1/8	19·242	29·464	1/8	34·950	97·205
1/4	3·927	1·227	1/4	19·635	30·679	1/4	35·343	99·402
3/8	4·319	1·484	3/8	20·027	31·919	3/8	35·735	101·623
1/2	4·712	1·767	1/2	20·420	33·183	1/2	36·128	103·869
5/8	5·105	2·073	5/8	20·813	34·471	5/8	36·521	106·139
3/4	5·497	2·405	3/4	21·205	35·784	3/4	36·913	108·434
7/8	5·890	2·761	7/8	21·598	37·122	7/8	37·306	110·753
2	6·283	3·141	7	21·991	38·484	12	37·699	113·097
1/8	6·675	3·546	1/8	22·383	39·871	1/8	38·091	115·466
1/4	7·068	3·976	1/4	22·776	41·282	1/4	38·484	117·859
3/8	7·461	4·430	3/8	23·169	42·718	3/8	38·877	120·276
1/2	7·854	4·908	1/2	23·562	44·178	1/2	39·270	122·718
5/8	8·246	5·411	5/8	23·954	45·663	5/8	39·662	125·184
3/4	8·639	5·939	3/4	24·347	47·173	3/4	40·055	127·676
7/8	9·032	6·491	7/8	24·740	48·707	7/8	40·448	130·192
3	9·424	7·068	8	25·132	50·265	13	40·840	132·732
1/8	9·817	7·669	1/8	25·525	51·848	1/8	41·233	135·297
1/4	10·210	8·295	1/4	25·918	53·456	1/4	41·626	137·886
3/8	10·602	8·946	3/8	26·310	55·088	3/8	42·018	140·500
1/2	10·995	9·621	1/2	26·703	56·745	1/2	42·411	143·139
5/8	11·388	10·320	5/8	27·096	58·426	5/8	42·804	145·802
3/4	11·781	11·044	3/4	27·489	60·132	3/4	43·197	148·489
7/8	12·173	11·793	7/8	27·881	61·862	7/8	43·589	151·201

Diam.	Circum.	Area.	Diam.	Circum.	Area.	Diam.	Circum.	Area.
14	43·98	153·93	20	62·83	314·16	26	81·68	530·93
⅛	44·37	156·69	⅛	63·22	318·09	⅛	82·07	536·04
¼	44·76	159·48	¼	63·61	322·06	¼	82·46	541·18
⅜	45·16	162·29	⅜	64·01	326·05	⅜	82·85	546·35
½	45·55	165·13	½	64·40	330·06	½	83·25	551·54
⅝	45·94	167·98	⅝	64·79	334·10	⅝	83·64	556·76
¾	46·33	170·87	¾	65·18	338·16	¾	84·03	562·00
⅞	46·73	173·78	⅞	65·58	342·25	⅞	84·43	567·26
15	47·12	176·71	21	65·97	346·36	27	84·82	572·55
⅛	47·51	179·67	⅛	66·36	350·49	⅛	85·21	577·87
¼	47·90	182·65	¼	66·75	354·65	¼	85·60	583·20
⅜	48·30	185·66	⅜	67·15	358·84	⅜	86·00	588·57
½	48·69	188·69	½	67·54	363·05	½	86·39	593·95
⅝	49·08	191·74	⅝	67·93	367·28	⅝	86·78	599·37
¾	49·48	194·82	¾	68·32	371·54	¾	87·17	604·80
⅞	49·87	197·93	⅞	68·72	375·82	⅞	87·57	610·26
16	50·26	201·06	22	69·11	380·13	28	87·96	615·75
⅛	50·65	204·21	⅛	69·50	384·46	⅛	88·35	621·26
¼	51·05	207·39	¼	69·90	388·82	¼	88·75	626·79
⅜	51·44	210·59	⅜	70·29	393·20	⅜	89·14	632·35
½	51·83	213·82	½	70·68	397·60	½	89·53	637·94
⅝	52·22	217·07	⅝	71·07	402·03	⅝	89·92	643·54
¾	52·62	220·35	¾	71·47	406·49	¾	90·32	649·18
⅞	53·01	223·65	⅞	71·86	410·97	⅞	90·71	654·83
17	53·40	226·98	23	72·25	415·47	29	91·10	660·52
⅛	53·79	230·33	⅛	72·64	420·00	⅛	91·49	666·22
¼	54·19	233·70	¼	73·04	424·55	¼	91·89	671·95
⅜	54·58	237·10	⅜	73·43	429·13	⅜	92·28	677·71
½	54·97	240·52	½	73·82	433·73	½	92·67	683·49
⅝	55·37	243·97	⅝	74·21	438·36	⅝	93·06	689·29
¾	55·76	247·45	¾	74·61	443·01	¾	93·46	695·12
⅞	56·15	250·94	⅞	75·00	447·69	⅞	93·85	700·98
18	56·54	254·46	24	75·39	452·39	30	94·24	706·86
⅛	56·94	258·01	⅛	75·79	457·11	⅛	94·64	712·76
¼	57·33	261·58	¼	76·18	461·86	¼	95·03	718·69
⅜	57·72	265·18	⅜	76·57	466·63	⅜	95·42	724·64
½	58·11	268·80	½	76·96	471·43	½	95·81	730·61
⅝	58·51	272·44	⅝	77·36	476·25	⅝	96·21	736·61
¾	58·90	276·11	¾	77·75	481·10	¾	96·60	742·64
⅞	59·29	279·81	⅞	78·14	485·97	⅞	96·99	748·69
19	59·69	283·52	25	78·53	490·87	31	97·38	754·76
⅛	60·08	287·27	⅛	78·93	495·79	⅛	97·78	760·86
¼	60·47	291·03	¼	79·32	500·74	¼	98·17	766·99
⅜	60·86	294·83	⅜	79·71	505·71	⅜	98·56	773·14
½	61·26	298·64	½	80·10	510·70	½	98·96	779·31
⅝	61·65	302·48	⅝	80·50	515·72	⅝	99·35	785·51
¾	62·04	306·35	¾	80·89	520·76	¾	99·74	791·73
⅞	62·43	310·24	⅞	81·28	525·83	⅞	100·13	797·97

Diam.	Circum.	Area.	Diam.	Circum.	Area.	Diam.	Circum.	Area.
32	100·5	804·24	38	119·3	1134·11	44	138·2	1520·53
⅛	100·9	810·54	⅛	119·7	1141·50	⅛	138·6	1529·18
¼	101·3	816·86	¼	120·1	1149·08	¼	139·0	1537·86
⅜	101·7	823·21	⅜	120·5	1156·61	⅜	139·4	1546·55
½	102·1	829·57	½	120·9	1164·15	½	139·8	1555·28
⅝	102·4	835·97	⅝	121·3	1171·73	⅝	140·1	1564·03
¾	102·8	842·39	¾	121·7	1179·32	¾	140·5	1572·81
⅞	103·2	848·83	⅞	122·1	1186·94	⅞	140·9	1581·61
33	103·6	855·30	39	122·5	1194·59	45	141·3	1590·43
⅛	104·0	861·79	⅛	122·9	1202·26	⅛	141·7	1599·28
¼	104·4	868·30	¼	123·3	1209·95	¼	142·1	1608·15
⅜	104·8	874·84	⅜	123·7	1217·67	⅜	142·5	1617·04
½	105·2	881·41	½	124·0	1225·42	½	142·9	1625·97
⅝	105·6	888·00	⅝	124·4	1233·18	⅝	143·3	1634·92
¾	106·0	894·61	¾	124·8	1240·98	¾	143·7	1643·89
⅞	106·4	901·25	⅞	125·2	1248·79	⅞	144·1	1652·88
34	106·8	907·92	40	125·6	1256·64	46	144·5	1661·90
⅛	107·2	914·61	⅛	126·0	1264·50	⅛	144·9	1670·95
¼	107·5	921·32	¼	126·4	1272·39	¼	145·2	1680·01
⅜	107·9	928·06	⅜	126·8	1280·31	⅜	145·6	1689·10
½	108·3	934·82	½	127·2	1288·25	½	146·0	1698·23
⅝	108·7	941·60	⅝	127·6	1296·21	⅝	146·4	1707·37
¾	109·1	948·41	¾	128·0	1304·20	¾	146·8	1716·54
⅞	109·5	955·25	⅞	128·4	1312·21	⅞	147·2	1725·73
35	109·9	962·11	41	128·8	1320·25	47	147·6	1734·94
⅛	110·3	968·99	⅛	129·1	1328·32	⅛	148·0	1744·18
¼	110·7	975·90	¼	129·5	1336·40	¼	148·4	1753·45
⅜	111·1	982·84	⅜	129·9	1344·51	⅜	148·8	1762·73
½	111·5	989·80	½	130·3	1352·65	½	149·2	1772·05
⅝	111·9	996·78	⅝	130·7	1360·81	⅝	149·6	1781·39
¾	112·3	1003·71	¾	131·1	1369·00	¾	150·0	1790·76
⅞	112·7	1010·81	⅞	131·5	1377·21	⅞	150·4	1800·14
36	113·0	1017·87	42	131·9	1385·44	48	150·7	1809·56
⅛	113·4	1024·95	⅛	132·3	1393·70	⅛	151·1	1818·99
¼	113·8	1032·06	¼	132·7	1401·98	¼	151·5	1828·46
⅜	114·2	1039·19	⅜	133·1	1410·29	⅜	151·9	1837·93
½	114·6	1046·39	½	133·5	1418·62	½	152·3	1847·45
⅝	115·0	1053·52	⅝	133·9	1426·98	⅝	152·7	1856·99
¾	115·4	1060·73	¾	134·3	1435·36	¾	153·1	1866·55
⅞	115·8	1067·95	⅞	134·6	1443·77	⅞	153·5	1876·13
37	116·2	1075·21	43	135·0	1452·20	49	153·9	1885·74
⅛	116·6	1082·48	⅛	135·4	1460·65	⅛	154·3	1895·37
¼	117·0	1089·79	¼	135·8	1469·13	¼	154·7	1905·03
⅜	117·4	1097·11	⅜	136·2	1477·63	⅜	155·1	1914·70
½	117·8	1104·46	½	136·6	1486·17	½	155·5	1924·42
⅝	118·2	1111·84	⅝	137·0	1494·72	⅝	155·9	1934·15
¾	118·5	1119·24	¾	137·4	1503·30	¾	156·2	1943·91
⅞	118·9	1126·66	⅞	137·8	1511·90	⅞	156·6	1953·69

Diam. Inches.	Circum. Inches.	Area in Square Inches.	Area in Square Feet.	Diam. Inches.	Circum. Inches.	Area in Square Inches.	Area in Square Feet.
50	157.0	1963.5	13·63	61	191·6	2922·4	20·29
¼	157·8	1983·1	13·77	¼	192·4	2946·4	20·46
½	158·6	2002·9	13·90	½	193·2	2970·5	20·62
¾	159·4	2022·8	14·04	¾	193·9	2994·7	20·79
51	160·2	2042·8	14·18	62	194·7	3019·0	20·96
¼	161·0	2062·9	14·32	¼	195·5	3043·4	21·13
½	161·7	2083·0	14·46	½	196·3	3067·9	21·20
¾	162·5	2103·3	14·60	¾	197·1	3092·5	21·47
52	163·3	2123·7	14·74	63	197·9	3117·2	21·64
¼	164·1	2144·1	14·89	¼	198·7	3142·0	21·81
½	164·9	2164·7	15·03	½	199·4	3166·9	21·98
¾	165·7	2185·4	15·17	¾	200·2	3191·9	22·16
53	166·5	2206·1	15·32	64	201·0	3216·9	22·34
¼	167·2	2227·0	15·46	¼	201·8	3242·1	22·51
½	168·0	2248·0	15·61	½	202·6	3267·4	22·68
¾	168·8	2269·0	15·75	¾	203·4	3292·8	22·86
54	169·6	2290·2	15·90	65	204·2	3318·3	23·04
¼	170·4	2311·4	16·05	¼	204·9	3343·8	23·22
½	171·2	2332·8	16·20	½	205·7	3369·5	23·39
¾	172·0	2354·2	16·34	¾	206·5	3395·3	23·57
55	172·7	2375·8	16·49	66	207·3	3421·2	23·75
¼	173·5	2397·4	16·64	¼	208·1	3447·1	23·93
½	174·3	2419·2	16·80	½	208·9	3473·2	24·11
¾	175·1	2441·0	16·95	¾	209·7	3499·3	24·30
56	175·9	2463·0	17·10	67	210·4	3525·6	24·48
¼	176·7	2485·0	17·25	¼	211·2	3552·0	24·66
½	177·5	2507·1	17·41	½	212·0	3578·4	24·84
¾	178·2	2529·4	17·56	¾	212·8	3605·0	25·03
57	179·0	2551·7	17·72	68	213·6	3631·6	25·22
¼	179·8	2574·1	17·87	¼	214·4	3658·4	25·40
½	180·6	2596·7	18·03	½	215·1	3685·2	25·59
¾	181·4	2619·3	18·19	¾	215·9	3712·2	25·77
58	182·2	2642·0	18·34	69	216·7	3739·2	25·96
¼	182·9	2664·9	18·50	¼	217·5	3766·4	26·15
½	183·7	2687·8	18·68	½	218·3	3793·6	26.34
¾	184·5	2710·8	18·82	¾	219·1	3821·0	26·53
59	185·3	2733·9	18·98	70	219·9	3848·4	26·72
¼	186·1	2757·1	19·14	¼	220·6	3875·9	26·91
½	186·9	2780·5	19·30	½	221·4	3903·6	27·10
¾	187·7	2803·9	19·47	¾	222·2	3931·3	27·30
60	188·4	2827·4	19·63	71	223·0	3959·2	27·49
¼	189·2	2851·0	19·79	¼	223·8	3987·1	27·68
½	190·0	2874·7	19·96	½	224·6	4015·1	27·87
¾	190·8	2898·5	20·12	¾	225·4	4043·2	28·07

Diam. Inches.	Circum. Inches.	Area in Square Inches.	Area in Square Feet.	Diam. Inches.	Circum. Inches.	Area in Square Inches.	Area in Square Feet.
72	226·1	4071·5	28·27	83	260·7	5410·6	37·57
¼	226·9	4099·8	28·47	¼	261·5	5443·2	37·79
½	227·7	4128·2	28·66	½	262·3	5476·0	38·02
¾	228·5	4156·7	28·86	¾	263·1	5508·8	38·25
73	229·3	4185·3	29·06	84	263·8	5541·7	38·48
¼	230·1	4214·1	29·26	¼	264·6	5574·8	38·71
½	230·9	4242·9	29·46	½	265·4	5607·9	38·94
¾	231·6	4271·8	29·66	¾	266·2	5641·1	39·07
74	232·4	4300·8	29·86	85	267·0	5674·5	39·40
¼	233·2	4329·9	30·06	¼	267·8	5707·9	39·63
½	234·0	4359·1	30·26	½	268·6	5741·4	39·87
¾	234·8	4388·4	30·47	¾	269·3	5775·0	40·10
75	235·6	4417·8	30·67	86	270·1	5808·8	40·33
¼	236·4	4447·3	30·88	¼	270·9	5842·6	40·57
½	237·1	4476·9	31·09	½	271·7	5876·5	40·80
¾	237·9	4506·6	31·30	¾	272·5	5910·5	41·04
76	238·7	4536·4	31·50	87	273·3	5944·6	41·28
¼	239·5	4566·3	31·71	¼	274·1	5978·9	41·52
½	240·3	4596·3	31·91	½	274·8	6013·2	41·75
¾	241·1	4626·4	32·12	¾	275·6	6047·6	41·99
77	241·9	4656·6	32·33	88	276·4	6082·1	42·23
¼	242·6	4686·9	32·54	¼	277·2	6116·7	42·47
½	243·4	4717·3	32·75	½	278·0	6151·4	42·71
¾	244·2	4747·7	32·96	¾	278·8	6186·2	42·95
78	245·0	4778·3	33·18	89	279·6	6221·1	43·20
¼	245·8	4809·0	33·39	¼	280·3	6256·1	43·44
½	246·6	4839·8	33·60	½	281·1	6291·2	43·68
¾	247·4	4870·7	33·81	¾	281·9	6326·4	43·92
79	248·1	4901·6	34·03	90	282·7	6361·7	44·17
¼	248·9	4932·7	34·24	¼	283·5	6397·1	44·42
½	249·7	4963·9	34·46	½	284·3	6432·6	44·66
¾	250·5	4995·1	34·68	¾	285·1	6468·2	44·81
80	251·3	5026·5	34·90	91	285·8	6503·8	45·16
¼	252·1	5058·0	35·12	¼	286·6	6539·6	45·41
½	252·8	5089·5	35·34	½	287·4	6575·5	45·66
¾	253·6	5121·2	35·56	¾	288·2	6611·5	45·91
81	254·4	5153·0	35·78	92	289·0	6647·6	46·16
¼	255·2	5184·8	36·00	¼	289·8	6683·8	46·41
½	256·0	5216·8	36·22	½	290·5	6720·0	46·66
¾	256·8	5248·8	36·44	¾	291·3	6756·4	46·91
82	257.6	5281·0	36·67	93	292·1	6792·9	47·17
¼	258·3	5313·2	36·90	¼	292·9	6829·4	47·43
½	259·1	5345·6	37·12	½	293·7	6866·1	47·68
¾	259·9	5378·0	37·34	¾	294·5	6902·9	47·93

Diam. Inches.	Circum. Inches.	Area in Square Inches.	Area in Square Feet.	Diam. Inches.	Circum. Inches.	Area in Square Inches.	Area in Square Feet.
94	295·3	6939·7	48·19	121	380·1	11499·0	79·85
¼	296·0	6976·7	48·45	122	383·2	11689·9	81·18
½	296·8	7013·8	48·70	123	386·4	11882·3	82·51
¾	297·6	7050·9	48·96	124	389·5	12076·3	83·86
95	298·4	7088·2	49·22	125	392·7	12271·8	85·22
¼	299·2	7125·5	49·48	126	395·8	12469·0	86·59
½	300·0	7163·0	49·64	127	398·9	12667·7	87·97
¾	300·8	7200·5	50·00	128	402·1	12867·9	89·36
96	301·5	7238·2	50·26	129	405·2	13069·8	90·76
¼	302·3	7275·9	50·52	130	408·4	13273·2	92·17
½	303·1	7313·8	50·78	131	411·5	13478·2	93·59
¾	303·9	7351·7	51·05	132	414·6	13684·8	95·03
97	304·7	7389·8	51·31	133	417·8	13892·9	96·47
¼	305·5	7427·9	51·57	134	420·9	14102·6	97·93
½	306·3	7466·2	51·84	135	424·1	14313·9	99·40
¾	307·0	7504·5	52·11	136	427·2	14526·7	100·88
98	307·8	7542·9	52·38	137	430·3	14741·1	102·36
¼	308·6	7581·5	52·65	138	433·5	14957·1	103·87
½	309·4	7620·1	52·91	139	436·6	15174·7	105·37
¾	310·2	7658·8	53·18	140	439·8	15393·8	106·90
99	311·0	7697·7	53·45	141	442·9	15614·5	108·43
¼	311·8	7736·6	53·72	142	446·1	15836·8	109·97
½	312·5	7775·6	53·99	143	449·2	16060·6	111·53
¾	313·3	7814·7	54·26	144	452·3	16286·0	113·09
100	314·1	7854·0	54·54	145	455·5	16513·0	114·67
101	317·3	8011·7	55·63	146	458·6	16741·5	116·26
102	320·4	8091·2	56·74	147	461·8	16971·7	117·86
103	323·5	8332·3	57·86	148	464·9	17203·4	119·46
104	326·7	8494·9	58·99	149	468·0	17436·6	121·08
105	329·8	8659·0	60·13	150	471·2	17671·5	122·71
106	333·0	8824·7	61·28	151	474·3	17907·9	124·36
107	336·1	8992·0	62·44	152	477·5	18145·9	126·01
108	339·2	9160·9	63·61	153	480·6	18385·4	127·67
109	342·4	9331·1	64·80	154	483·8	18626·5	129·35
110	345·5	9503·3	65·99	155	486·9	18869·2	131·03
111	348·7	9676·9	67·20	156	490·0	19113·5	132·73
112	351·8	9852·0	68·41	157	493·2	19359·3	134·44
113	355·0	10028·7	69·64	158	496·3	19606·7	136·15
114	358·1	10207·0	70·88	159	499·5	19855·7	137·88
115	361·2	10386·9	72·13	160	502·6	20106·2	139·62
116	364·4	10568·3	73·39	161	505·7	20358·3	141·37
117	367·5	10751·3	74·66	162	508·9	20612·0	143·13
118	370·7	10935·9	75·94	163	512·0	20867·3	144·91
119	373·8	11122·0	77·23	164	515·2	21124·1	146·69
120	376·6	11309·7	78·54	165	518·3	21382·5	148·48

Areas *of the Segments and Zones of a Circle, of which the* Diameter *is Unity, and supposed to be divided into* 1000 *equal parts.*

Height.	Area of Segment.	Area of Zone.	Height.	Area of Segment.	Area of Zone.
·001	·000042	·001000	·036	·009008	·035969
·002	·000119	·002000	·037	·009383	·036967
·003	·000219	·003000	·038	·009763	·037965
·004	·000337	·004000	·039	·010148	·038962
·005	·000470	·005000	·040	·010537	·039958
·006	·000618	·006000	·041	·010931	·040954
·007	·000779	·007000	·042	·011330	·041951
·008	·000951	·008000	·043	·011734	·042947
·009	·001135	·009000	·044	·012142	·043944
·010	·001329	·010000	·045	·012554	·044940
·011	·001533	·011000	·046	·012971	·045935
·012	·001746	·011999	·047	·013392	·046931
·013	·001968	·012999	·048	·013818	·047927
·014	·002199	·013998	·049	·014247	·048922
·015	·002438	·014998	·050	·014681	·049917
·016	·002685	·015997	·051	·015119	·050912
·017	·002940	·016997	·052	·015561	·051906
·018	·003202	·017996	·053	·016007	·052901
·019	·003471	·018996	·054	·016457	·053895
·020	·003748	·019995	·055	·016911	·054890
·021	·004031	·020994	·056	·017369	·055883
·022	·004322	·021993	·057	·017831	·056877
·023	·004618	·022992	·058	·018296	·057870
·024	·004921	·023991	·059	·018766	·058863
·025	·005230	·024990	·060	·019239	·059856
·026	·005546	·025989	·061	·019716	·060849
·027	·005867	·026987	·062	·020196	·061841
·028	·006194	·027986	·063	·020680	·062833
·029	·006527	·028984	·064	·021168	·063825
·030	·006865	·029982	·065	·021659	·064817
·031	·007209	·030980	·066	·022154	·065807
·032	·007558	·031978	·067	·022652	·066799
·033	·007913	·032976	·068	·023154	·067790
·034	·008273	·033974	·069	·023659	·068782
·035	·008638	·034972	·070	·024168	·069771

Height.	Area of Segment.	Area of Zone.	Height.	Area of Segment.	Area of Zone.
·071	·024680	·070761	·111	·047632	·110082
·072	·025195	·071751	·112	·048262	·111057
·073	·025714	·072740	·113	·048894	·112031
·074	·026236	·073729	·114	·049528	·113005
·075	·026761	·074718	·115	·050167	·113978
·076	·027289	·075707	·116	·050804	·114951
·077	·027821	·076695	·117	·051446	·115924
·078	·028356	·077683	·118	·052090	·116896
·079	·028894	·078670	·119	·052736	·117867
·080	·029435	·079658	·120	·053385	·118838
·081	·029979	·080645	·121	·054036	·119809
·082	·030526	·081631	·122	·054689	·120779
·083	·031076	·082618	·123	·055345	·121748
·084	·031629	·083604	·124	·056003	·122717
·085	·032186	·084589	·125	·056663	·123686
·086	·032745	·085574	·126	·057326	·124654
·087	·033307	·086559	·127	·057991	·125621
·088	·033872	·087544	·128	·058658	·126588
·089	·034441	·088528	·129	·059327	·127555
·090	·035011	·089512	·130	·059999	·128521
·091	·035585	·090496	·131	·060672	·129486
·092	·036162	·091479	·132	·061348	·130451
·093	·036741	·092461	·133	·062026	·131415
·094	·037323	·093444	·134	·062707	·132379
·095	·037909	·094426	·135	·063389	·133342
·096	·038496	·095407	·136	·064074	·134304
·097	·039087	·096388	·137	·064760	·135266
·098	·039680	·097369	·138	·065449	·136228
·099	·040276	·098350	·139	·066140	·137189
·100	·040875	·099330	·140	·066833	·138149
·101	·041476	·100309	·141	·067528	·139109
·102	·042080	·101288	·142	·068225	·140068
·103	·042687	·102267	·143	·068924	·141026
·104	·043296	·103246	·144	·069625	·141984
·105	·043908	·104223	·145	·070328	·142942
·106	·044522	·105201	·146	·071033	·143898
·107	·045139	·106178	·147	·071741	·144854
·108	·045759	·107155	·148	·072450	·145810
·109	·046381	·108131	·149	·073161	·146765
·110	·047005	·109107	·150	·073874	·147719

Height.	Area of Segment.	Area of Zone.	Height.	Area of Segment.	Area of Zone.
·151	·074589	·148673	·191	·104685	·186248
·152	·075306	·149625	·192	·105472	·187172
·153	·076026	·150578	·193	·106261	·188094
·154	·076747	·151530	·194	·107051	·189016
·155	·077469	·152481	·195	·107842	·189938
·156	·078194	·153431	·196	·108636	·190858
·157	·078921	·154381	·197	·109430	·191777
·158	·079649	·155330	·198	·110226	·192696
·159	·080380	·156278	·199	·111024	·193614
.160	·081112	·157226	·200	·111823	·194531
·161	·081846	·158173	·201	·112624	·195447
·162	·082582	·159119	·202	·113426	·196362
·163	·083320	·160065	·203	·114230	·197277
·164	·084059	·161010	·204	·115035	·198190
·165	·084801	·161954	·205	·115842	·199103
·166	·085544	·162898	·206	·116650	·200015
·167	·086289	·163841	·207	·117460	·200924
·168	·087036	·164784	·208	·118271	·201835
·169	·087785	·165725	·209	·119083	·202744
·170	·088535	·166666	·210	·119897	·203652
·171	·089287	·167606	·211	·120712	·204559
·172	·090041	·168549	·212	·121529	·205465
·173	·090797	·160484	·213	·122347	·206370
·174	·091554	·170422	·214	·123167	·207274
·175	·092313	·171359	·215	·123988	·208178
·176	·093074	·172295	·216	·124810	·209080
·177	·093836	·173231	·217	·125634	·209981
·178	·094601	·174166	·218	·126459	·210882
·179	·095366	·175100	·219	·127285	·211782
·180	·096134	·176033	·220	·128113	·212680
·181	·096903	·176966	·221	·128942	·213577
·182	·097674	·177897	·222	·129773	·214474
·183	·098447	·178828	·223	·130605	·215369
·184	·099221	·179759	·224	·131438	·216264
·185	·099997	·180688	·225	·132272	·217157
·186	·100774	·181617	·226	·133108	·218050
·187	·101553	·182545	·227	·133945	·218941
·188	·102334	·183472	·228	·134784	·219832
·189	·103116	·184398	·229	·135624	·220721
·190	·103900	·185323	·230	·136465	·221610

Height.	Area of Segment.	Area of Zone.	Height.	Area of Segment.	Area of Zone.
·231	·137307	·222497	·271	·171978	·257075
·232	·138150	·223354	·272	·172867	·257915
·233	·138995	·224269	·273	·173758	·258754
·234	·139841	·225153	·274	·174649	·259591
·235	·140688	·226036	·275	·175542	·260427
·236	·141537	·226919	·276	·176435	·261261
·237	·142387	·227800	·277	·177330	·262094
·238	·143238	·228680	·278	·178225	·262926
·239	·144091	·229559	·279	·179122	·263757
·240	·144944	·230439	·280	·180019	·264586
·241	·145799	·231313	·281	·180918	·265414
·242	·146655	·232189	·282	·181817	·266240
·243	·147512	·233063	·283	·182718	·267065
·244	·148371	·233937	·284	·183619	·267889
·245	·149230	·234809	·285	·184521	·268711
·246	·150091	·235680	·286	·185425	·269532
·247	·150953	·236550	·287	·186329	·270252
·248	·151816	·237419	·288	·187234	·271170
·249	·152680	·238287	·289	·188140	·271987
·250	·153546	·239153	·290	·189047	·272802
·251	·154412	·240019	·291	·189955	·273616
·252	·155280	·240883	·292	·190864	·274428
·253	·156149	·241746	·293	·191775	·275239
·254	·157019	·242608	·294	·192684	·276049
·255	·157890	·243469	·295	·193596	·276857
·256	·158762	·244328	·296	·194509	·277664
·257	·159636	·245187	·297	·195422	·278469
·258	·160510	·246044	·298	·196337	·279273
·259	·161386	·246900	·299	·197252	·280075
·260	·162263	·247755	·300	·198168	·280876
·261	·163140	·248608	·301	·199085	·281675
·262	·164019	·249461	·302	·200003	·282473
·263	·164899	·250212	·303	·200922	·283269
·264	·165780	·251162	·304	·201841	·284063
·265	·166663	·252011	·305	·202761	·284857
·266	·167546	·252851	·306	·203683	·285648
·267	·168430	·253704	·307	·204605	·286438
·268	·169315	·254549	·308	·205527	·287227
·269	·170202	·255392	·309	·206451	·288014
·270	·171089	·256235	·310	·207376	·288799

Height.	Area of Segment.	Area of Zone.	Height.	Area of Segment.	Area of Zone.
·311	·208301	·289583	·351	·245934	·319538
·312	·209227	·290365	·352	·246889	·320249
·313	·210154	·291146	·353	·247845	·320958
·314	·211082	·291925	·354	·248801	·321666
·315	·212011	·292702	·355	·249757	·322371
·316	·212940	·293478	·356	·250715	·323075
·317	·213871	·294252	·357	·251673	·323775
·318	·214802	·295025	·358	·252631	·324474
·319	·215733	·295796	·359	·253590	·325171
·320	·216666	·296565	·360	·254550	·325866
·321	·217599	·297333	·361	·255510	·326559
·322	·218533	·298098	·362	·256471	·327250
·323	·219468	·298863	·363	·257433	·327939
·324	·220404	·299625	·364	·258395	·328625
·325	·221340	·300386	·365	·259357	·329310
·326	·222277	·301145	·366	·260320	·329992
·327	·223215	·301902	·367	·261284	·330673
·328	·224154	·302658	·368	·262248	·331351
·329	·225093	·303412	·369	·263213	·332027
·330	·226033	·304164	·370	·264178	·332700
·331	·226974	·304914	·371	·265144	·333372
·332	·227915	·305663	·372	·266111	·334041
·333	·228858	·306410	·373	·267078	·334708
·334	·229801	·307155	·374	·268045	·335373
·335	·230745	·307898	·375	·269013	·336036
·336	·231689	·308640	·376	·269982	·336696
·337	·232634	·309379	·377	·270951	·337354
·338	·233580	·310117	·378	·271920	·338010
·339	·234526	·310853	·379	·272890	·338663
·340	·235473	·311588	·380	·273861	·339314
·341	·236421	·312319	·381	·274832	·339963
·342	·237369	·313050	·382	·275803	·340609
·343	·238318	·313778	·383	·276775	·341253
·344	·239268	·314505	·384	·277748	·341895
·345	·240218	·315230	·385	·278721	·342534
·346	·241169	·315952	·386	·279694	·343171
·347	·242121	·316673	·387	·280668	·343805
·348	·243074	·317393	·388	·281642	·344437
·349	·244026	·318110	·389	·282617	·345067
·350	·244980	·318825	·390	·283592	·345694

Height.	Area of Segment.	Area of Zone.	Height.	Area of Segment.	Area of Zone.
·391	·284568	·346318	·431	·323918	·369040
·392	·285544	·346940	·432	·324909	·369545
·393	·286521	·347560	·433	·325900	·370047
·394	·287498	·348177	·434	·326892	·370545
·395	·288476	·348791	·435	·327882	·371040
·396	·289453	·349403	·436	·328874	·371531
·397	·290432	·350012	·437	·329866	·372019
·398	·291411	·350619	·438	·330858	·372503
·399	·292390	·351223	·439	·331850	·372983
·400	·293369	·351824	·440	·332843	·373460
·401	·294349	·352423	·441	·333836	·373933
·402	·295330	·353019	·442	·334829	·374403
·403	·296311	·353612	·443	·335822	·374868
·404	·297292	·354202	·444	·336816	·375330
·405	·298273	·354790	·445	·337810	·375788
·406	·299255	·355376	·446	·338804	·376242
·407	·300238	·355958	·447	·339798	·376692
·408	·301220	·356537	·448	·340793	·377138
·409	·302203	·357114	·449	·341787	·377580
·410	·303187	·357688	·450	·342782	·378018
·411	·304171	·358258	·451	·343777	·378452
·412	·305155	·858827	·452	·344772	·378881
·413	·306140	·359392	·453	·345768	·379307
·414	·307125	·359954	·454	·346764	·379728
·415	·308110	·360513	·455	·347759	·380145
·416	·309095	·361070	·456	·348755	·380557
·417	·310081	·361623	·457	·349752	·380965
·418	·311068	·362173	·458	·350748	·381369
·419	·312054	·362720	·459	·351745	·381768
·420	·313041	·363264	·460	·352742	·382162
·421	·314029	·363805	·461	·353739	·382551
·422	·315016	·364343	·462	·354736	·382936
·423	·316004	·364878	·463	·355732	·383316
·424	·316992	·365410	·464	·356730	·383691
·425	·317981	·365939	·465	·357727	·384061
·426	·318970	·366463	·466	·358725	·384426
·427	·319959	·366985	·467	·359723	·384786
·428	·320948	·367504	·468	·360721	·385144
·429	·321938	·368019	·469	·361719	·385490
·430	·322928	·368531	·470	·362717	·385834

Height.	Area of Segment.	Area of Zone.	Height.	Area of Segment.	Area of Zone.
·471	·363715	·386172	·486	·378701	·390500
·472	·364713	·386505	·487	·379700	·390730
·473	·365712	·386832	·488	·380700	·390953
·474	·366710	·387153	·489	·381699	·391166
·475	·367709	·387469	·490	·382699	·391370
·476	·368708	·387778	·491	·383699	·391564
·477	·369707	·388081	·492	·384699	·391748
·478	·370706	·388377	·493	·385699	·391920
·479	·371704	·388669	·494	·386699	·392081
·480	·372704	·388951	·495	·387699	·392229
·481	·373703	·389228	·496	·388699	·392362
·482	·374702	·389497	·497	·389699	·392480
·483	·375702	·389759	·498	·390699	·392580
·484	·376702	·390014	·499	·391699	·392657
·485	·377701	·390261	·500	·392699	·392699

To find the Area of the Segment of a Circle.

Rule.—Divide the height, or versed sine, by the diameter of the circle, and find the quotient in the column of heights.

Then take out the corresponding area, in the column of areas, and multiply it by the square of the diameter; this will give the area of the segment.

Example.—Required the area of a segment of a circle, whose height is 3¼ feet, and the diameter of the circle 50 feet.

$3\frac{1}{4} = 3{\cdot}25$; and $3{\cdot}25 \div 50 = {\cdot}065$.

·065, as per Table, $= {\cdot}021659$; and $\cdot021659 \times 50^2 = 54{\cdot}147500$, the area required.

To find the Area of a Circular Zone.

RULE 1.—When the zone is less than a semicircle, divide the height by the longest chord, and seek the quotient in the column of heights. Take out the corresponding area, in the next column on the right hand, and multiply it by the square of the longest chord; the product will be the area of the zone.

EXAMPLE.—Required the area of a zone whose longest chord is 50, and height 15.

$15 \div 50 = \cdot 300$; and $\cdot 300$, as per Table, $= \cdot 280876$. Hence $\cdot 280876 \times 50^2 = 702 \cdot 19$, the area of the zone.

RULE 2.—When the zone is greater than a semicircle, take the height on each side of the diameter of the circle, and find, by Rule 1, their respective areas; the areas of these two portions, added together, will be the area of the zone.

EXAMPLE.—Required the area of a zone, the diameter of the circle being 50, and the height of the zone on each side of the line which passes through the diameter of the circle 20 and 15 respectively.

$20 \div 50 = \cdot 400$; $\cdot 400$, as per Table, $= \cdot 351824$; and $\cdot 351824 \times 50^2 = 879 \cdot 56$.

$15 \div 50 = \cdot 300$; $\cdot 300$, as per Table, $= \cdot 280876$; and $\cdot 280876 \times 50^2 = 702 \cdot 19$.

Hence $879 \cdot 56 + 702 \cdot 19 = 1581 \cdot 75$.

Approximating Rule to find the Area of a Segment of a Circle.

RULE.—Multiply the chord of the segment by the versed sine, divide the product by 3, and multiply the remainder by 2.

Cube the height, or versed sine, find how often twice the length of the chord is contained in it, and add the quotient to the former product: this will give the area of the segment very nearly.

EXAMPLE.—Required the area of the segment of a circle, the chord being 12, and the versed sine 2.

$$12 \times 2 = 24; \ \frac{24}{3} = 8; \text{ and } 8 \times 2 = 16.$$

$$2^3 \div 24 \ (12 \times 2) = \cdot 3333.$$

Hence $16 + \cdot 3333 = 16 \cdot 3333$, the area of the segment very nearly.

TABLE V.

Proportions of the Lengths of Circular Arcs.

Height of Arc.	Length of Arc.	Height of Arc.	Length of Arc.	Height of Arc.	Length of Arc.	Height of Arc.	Length of Arc.
·100	1·02645	·135	1·04792	·170	1·07537	·205	1·10855
·101	1·02698	·136	1·04862	·171	1·07624	·206	1·10958
·102	1·02752	·137	1·04932	·172	1·07711	·207	1·11062
·103	1·02806	·138	1·05003	·173	1·07799	·208	1·11165
·104	1·02860	·139	1·05075	·174	1·07888	·209	1·11269
·105	1·02914	·140	1·05147	·175	1·07977	·210	1·11374
·106	1·02970	·141	1·05220	·176	1·08066	·211	1·11479
·107	1·03026	·142	1·05293	·177	1·08156	·212	1·11584
·108	1·03082	·143	1·05367	·178	1·08246	·213	1·11692
·109	1·03139	·144	1·05441	·179	1·08337	·214	1·11796
·110	1·03196	·145	1·05516	·180	1·08428	·215	1·11904
·111	1·03254	·146	1·05591	·181	1·08519	·216	1·12011
·112	1·03312	·147	1·05667	·182	1·08611	·217	1·12118
·113	1·03371	·148	1·05743	·183	1·08704	·218	1·12225
·114	1·03430	·149	1·05819	·184	1·08797	·219	1·12334
·115	1·03490	·150	1·05896	·185	1·08890	·220	1·12445
·116	1·03551	·151	1·05973	·186	1·08984	·221	1·12556
·117	1·03611	·152	1·06051	·187	1·09079	·222	1·12663
·118	1·03672	·153	1·06130	·188	1·09174	·223	1·12774
·119	1·03734	·154	1·06209	·189	1·09269	·224	1·12885
·120	1·03797	·155	1·06288	·190	1·09365	·225	1·12997
·121	1·03860	·156	1·06368	·191	1·09461	·226	1·13108
·122	1·03923	·157	1·06449	·192	1·09557	·227	1·13219
·123	1·03987	·158	1·06530	·193	1·09654	·228	1·13331
·124	1·04051	·159	1·06611	·194	1·09752	·229	1·13444
·125	1·04116	·160	1·06693	·195	1·09850	·230	1·13557
·126	1·04181	·161	1·06775	·196	1·09949	·231	1·13671
·127	1·04247	·162	1·06858	·197	1·10048	·232	1·13786
·128	1·04313	·163	1·06941	·198	1·10147	·233	1·13903
·129	1·04380	·164	1·07025	·199	1·10247	·234	1·14020
·130	1·04447	·165	1·07109	·200	1·10348	·235	1·14136
·131	1·04515	·166	1·07194	·201	1·10447	·236	1·14247
·132	1·04584	·167	1·07279	·202	1·10548	·237	1·14363
·133	1·04652	·168	1·07365	·203	1·10650	·238	1·14480
·134	1·04722	·169	1·07451	·204	1·10752	·239	1·14597

Height of Arc.	Length of Arc.	Height of Arc.	Length of Arc.	Height of Arc.	Length of Arc.	Height of Arc.	Length of Arc.
·240	1·14714	·283	1·20146	·326	1·26286	·369	1·33069
·241	1·14831	·284	1·20282	·327	1·26437	·370	1·33234
·242	1·14949	·285	1·20419	·328	1·26588	·371	1·33399
·243	1·15067	·286	1·20558	·329	1·26740	·372	1·33564
·244	1·15186	·287	1·20696	·330	1·26892	·373	1·33730
·245	1·15308	·288	1·20828	·331	1·27044	·374	1·33896
·246	1·15429	·289	1·20967	·332	1·27196	·375	1·34063
·247	1·15549	·290	1·21202	·333	1·27349	·376	1·34229
·248	1·15670	·291	1·21239	·334	1·27502	·377	1·34396
·249	1·15791	·292	1·21381	·335	1·27656	·378	1·34563
·250	1·15912	·293	1·21520	·336	1·27810	·379	1·34731
·251	1·16033	·294	1·21658	·337	1·27864	·380	1·34899
·252	1·16157	·295	1·21794	·338	1·28118	·381	1·35068
·253	1·16279	·296	1·21926	·339	1·28273	·382	1·35237
·254	1·16402	·297	1·22061	·340	1·28428	·383	1·35406
·255	1·16526	·298	1·22203	·341	1·28583	·384	1·35575
·256	1·16649	·299	1·22347	·342	1·28739	·385	1·35744
·257	1·16774	·300	1·22495	·343	1·28895	·386	1·35914
·258	1·16899	·301	1·22635	·344	1·29052	·387	1·36084
·259	1·17024	·302	1·22776	·345	1·29209	·388	1·36254
·260	1·17150	·303	1·22918	·346	1·29366	·389	1·36425
·261	1·17275	·304	1·23061	·347	1·29523	·390	1·36596
·262	1·17401	·305	1·23205	·348	1·29681	·391	1·36767
·263	1·17527	·306	1·23349	·349	1·29839	·392	1·36939
·264	1·17655	·307	1·23494	·350	1·29997	·393	1·37111
·265	1·17784	·308	1·23636	·351	1·30156	·394	1·37283
·266	1·17912	·309	1·23780	·352	1·30315	·395	1·37455
·267	1·18040	·310	1·23925	·353	1·30474	·396	1·37628
·268	1·18162	·311	1·24070	·354	1·30634	·397	1·37801
·269	1·18294	·312	1·24216	·355	1·30794	·398	1·37974
·270	1·18428	·313	1·24360	·356	1·30954	·399	1·38148
·271	1·18557	·314	1·24506	·357	1·31115	·400	1·38322
·272	1·18688	·315	1·24654	·358	1·31276	·401	1·38496
·273	1·18819	·316	1·24801	·359	1·31437	·402	1·38671
·274	1·18969	·317	1·24946	·360	1·31599	·403	1·38846
·275	1·19082	·318	1·25095	·361	1·31761	·404	1·39021
·276	1·19214	·319	1·25243	·362	1·31923	·405	1·39196
·277	1·19345	·320	1·25391	·363	1·32086	·406	1·39372
·278	1·19477	·321	1·25539	·364	1·32249	·407	1·39548
·279	1·19610	·322	1·25686	·365	1·32413	·408	1·39724
·280	1·19743	·323	1·25836	·366	1·32577	·409	1·39900
·281	1·19887	·324	1·25987	·367	1·32741	·410	1·40077
·282	1·20011	·325	1·26137	·368	1·32905	·411	1·40254

Height of Arc.	Length of Arc.	Height of Arc.	Length of Arc.	Height of Arc.	Length of Arc.	Height of Arc.	Length of Arc.
·412	1·40432	·435	1·44589	·457	1·48699	·479	1·52931
·413	1·40610	·436	1·44773	·458	1·48889	·480	1·53126
·414	1·40788	·437	1·44957	·459	1·49079	·481	1·53322
·415	1·40966	·438	1·45142	·460	1·49269	·482	1·53518
·416	1·41145	·439	1·45327	·461	1·49460	·483	1·53714
·417	1·41324	·440	1·45512	·462	1·49651	·484	1·53910
·418	1·41503	·441	1·45697	·463	1·49842	·485	1·54106
·419	1·41682	·442	1·45883	·464	1·50033	·486	1·54302
·420	1·41861	·443	1·46069	·465	1·50224	·487	1·54499
·421	1·42041	·444	1·46255	·466	1·50416	·488	1·54696
·422	1·42222	·445	1·46441	·467	1·50608	·489	1·54893
·423	1·42402	·446	1·46628	·468	1·50300	·490	1·55090
·424	1·42583	·447	1·46815	·469	1·50992	·491	1·55288
·425	1·42764	·448	1·47002	·470	1·51185	·492	1·55486
·426	1·42945	·449	1·47189	·471	1·51378	·493	1·55685
·427	1·43127	·450	1·47377	·472	1·51571	·494	1·55854
·428	1·43309	·451	1·47565	·473	1·51764	·495	1·56083
·429	1·43491	·452	1·47753	·474	1·51958	·496	1·56282
·430	1·43673	·453	1·47942	·475	1·52152	·497	1·56481
·431	1·43856	·454	1·48131	·476	1·52346	·498	1·56680
·432	1·44039	·455	1·48320	·477	1·52541	·499	1·56879
·433	1·44222	·456	1·48509	·478	1·52736	·500	1·57079
·434	1·44405						

TABLE VI.

Proportions of the Lengths of Semi-Elliptic Arcs.

Height of Arc.	Length of Arc.	Height of Arc.	Length of Arc.	Height of Arc.	Length of Arc.	Height of Arc.	Length of Arc.
·100	1·04162	·135	1·07726	·170	1·11569	·205	1·15602
·101	1·04262	·136	1·07831	·171	1·11682	·206	1·15720
·102	1·04362	·137	1·07937	·172	1·11795	·207	1·15838
·103	1·04462	·138	1·08043	·173	1·11908	·208	1·15957
·104	1·04562	·139	1·08149	·174	1·12021	·209	1·16076
·105	1·04662	·140	1·08255	·175	1·12134	·210	1·16196
·106	1·04762	·141	1·08362	·176	1·12247	·211	1·16316
·107	1·04862	·142	1·08469	·177	1·12360	·212	1·16436
·108	1·04962	·143	1·08576	·178	1·12473	·213	1·16557
·109	1·05063	·144	1·08684	·179	1·12586	·214	1·16678
·110	1·05164	·145	1·08792	·180	1·12699	·215	1·16799
·111	1·05265	·146	1·08901	·181	1·12813	·216	1·16920
·112	1·05366	·147	1·09010	·182	1·12927	·217	1·17041
·113	1·05467	·148	1·09119	·183	1·13041	·218	1·17163
·114	1·05568	·149	1·09228	·184	1·13155	·219	1·17285
·115	1·05669	·150	1·09330	·185	1·13269	·220	1·17407
·116	1·05770	·151	1·09448	·186	1·13383	·221	1·17529
·117	1·05872	·152	1·09558	·187	1·13497	·222	1·17651
·118	1·05974	·153	1·09669	·188	1·13611	·223	1·17774
·119	1·06076	·154	1·09780	·189	1·13726	·224	1·17897
·120	1·06178	·155	1·09891	·190	1·13841	·225	1·18020
·121	1·06280	·156	1·10002	·191	1·13956	·226	1·18143
·122	1·06382	·157	1·10113	·192	1·14071	·227	1·18266
·123	1·06484	·158	1·10224	·193	1·14186	·228	1·18390
·124	1·06586	·159	1·10335	·194	1·14301	·229	1·18514
·125	1·06689	·160	1·10447	·195	1·14416	·230	1·18638
·126	1·06792	·161	1·10560	·196	1·14531	·231	1·18762
·127	1·06895	·162	1·10672	·197	1·14646	·232	1·18886
·128	1·06998	·163	1·10784	·198	1·14762	·233	1·19010
·129	1·07001	·164	1·10896	·199	1·14888	·234	1·19134
·130	1·07204	·165	1·11008	·200	1·15014	·235	1·19258
·131	1·07308	·166	1·11120	·201	1·15131	·236	1·19382
·132	1·07412	·167	1·11232	·202	1·15248	·237	1·19506
·133	1·07516	·168	1·11344	·203	1·15366	·238	1·19630
·134	1·07621	·169	1·11456	·204	1·15484	·239	1·19755

Height of Arc.	Length of Arc.	Height of Arc.	Length of Arc.	Height of Arc.	Length of Arc.	Height of Arc.	Length of Arc.
·240	1·19880	·283	1·25406	·326	1·31198	·369	1·37268
·241	1·20005	·284	1·25538	·327	1·31335	·370	1·37414
·242	1·20130	·285	1·25670	·328	1·31472	·371	1·37662
·243	1·20255	·286	1·25803	·329	1·31610	·372	1·37708
·244	1·20380	·287	1·25936	·330	1·31748	·373	1·37854
·245	1·20506	·288	1·26069	·331	1·31886	·374	1·38000
·246	1·20632	·289	1·26202	·332	1·32024	·375	1·38146
·247	1·20758	·290	1·26335	·333	1·32162	·376	1·38292
·248	1·20884	·291	1·26468	·334	1·32300	·377	1·38439
·249	1·21010	·292	1·26601	·335	1·32438	·378	1·38585
·250	1·21136	·293	1·26734	·336	1·32576	·379	1·38732
·251	1·21263	·294	1·26867	·337	1·32715	·380	1·38879
·252	1·21390	·295	1·27000	·338	1·32854	·381	1·39024
·253	1·21517	·296	1·27133	·339	1·32993	·382	1·39169
·254	1·21644	·297	1·27267	·340	1·33132	·383	1·39314
·255	1·21772	·298	1·27401	·341	1·33272	·384	1·39459
·256	1·21900	·299	1·27535	·342	1·33412	·385	1·39605
·257	1·22028	·300	1·27669	·343	1·33552	·386	1·39751
·258	1·22156	·301	1·27803	·344	1·33692	·387	1·39897
·259	1·22284	·302	1·27937	·345	1·33833	·388	1·40043
·260	1·22412	·303	1·28071	·346	1·33974	·389	1·40189
·261	1·22541	·304	1·28205	·347	1·34115	·390	1·40335
·262	1·22670	·305	1·28339	·348	1·34256	·391	1·40481
·263	1·22799	·306	1·28474	·349	1·34397	·392	1·40627
·264	1·22928	·307	1·28609	·350	1·34539	·393	1·40773
·265	1·23057	·308	1·28744	·351	1·34681	·394	1·40919
·266	1·23186	·309	1·28879	·352	1·34823	·395	1·41065
·267	1·23315	·310	1·29014	·353	1·34965	·396	1·41211
·268	1·23445	·311	1·29149	·354	1·35108	·397	1·41357
·269	1·23575	·312	1·29285	·355	1·35251	·398	1·41504
·270	1·23705	·313	1·29421	·356	1·35394	·399	1·41651
·271	1·23835	·314	1·29557	·357	1·35537	·400	1·41798
·272	1·23966	·315	1·29603	·358	1·35680	·401	1·41945
·273	1·24097	·316	1·29829	·359	1·35823	·402	1·42092
·274	1·24228	·317	1·29965	·360	1·35967	·403	1·42239
·275	1·24359	·318	1·30102	·361	1·36111	·404	1·42386
·276	1·24480	·319	1·30239	·362	1·36255	·405	1·42533
·277	1·24612	·320	1·30376	·363	1·36399	·406	1·42681
·278	1·24744	·321	1·30513	·364	1·36543	·407	1·42829
·279	1·24876	·322	1·30650	·365	1·36688	·408	1·42977
·280	1·25010	·323	1·30787	·366	1·36833	·409	1·43125
·281	1·25142	·324	1·30924	·367	1·36978	·410	1·43273
·282	1·25274	·325	1·31061	·368	1·37123	·411	1·43421

Height of Arc.	Length of Arc.	Height of Arc.	Length of Arc.	Height of Arc.	Length of Arc.	Height of Arc.	Length of Arc.
·412	1·43569	·455	1·50077	·498	1·56763	·541	1·63465
·413	1·43718	·456	1·50230	·499	1·56921	·542	1·63623
·414	1·43867	·457	1·50383	·500	1·57089	·543	1·63780
·415	1·44016	·458	1·50536	·501	1·57234	·544	1·63937
·416	1·44165	·459	1·50689	·502	1·57389	·545	1·64094
·417	1·44314	·460	1·50842	·503	1·57544	·546	1·64251
·418	1·44463	·461	1·50996	·504	1·57699	·547	1·64408
·419	1·44613	·462	1·51150	·505	1·57854	·548	1·64565
·420	1·44763	·463	1·51304	·506	1·58009	·549	1·64722
·421	1·44913	·464	1·51458	·507	1·58164	·550	1·64879
·422	1·45064	·465	1·51612	·508	1·58319	·551	1·65036
·423	1·45214	·466	1·51766	·509	1·58474	·552	1·65193
·424	1·45364	·467	1·51920	·510	1·58629	·553	1·65350
·425	1·45515	·468	1·52074	·511	1·58784	·554	1·65507
·426	1·45665	·469	1·52229	·512	1·58940	·555	1·65665
·427	1·45815	·470	1·52384	·513	1·59096	·556	1·65823
·428	1·45966	·471	1·52539	·514	1·59252	·557	1·65981
·429	1·46167	·472	1·52691	·515	1·59408	·558	1·66139
·430	1·46268	·473	1·52849	·516	1·59564	·559	1·66297
·431	1·46419	·474	1·53004	·517	1·59720	·560	1·66455
·432	1·46570	·475	1·53159	·518	1·59876	·561	1·66613
·433	1·46721	·476	1·53314	·519	1·60032	·562	1·66771
·434	1·46872	·477	1·53469	·520	1·60188	·563	1·66929
·435	1·47023	·478	1·53625	·521	1·60344	·564	1·67087
·436	1·47174	·479	1·53781	·522	1·60500	·565	1·67245
·437	1·47326	·480	1·53937	·523	1·60656	·566	1·67403
·438	1·47478	·481	1·54093	·524	1·60812	·567	1·67561
·439	1·47630	·482	1·54249	·525	1·60968	·568	1·67719
·440	1·47782	·483	1·54405	·526	1·61124	·569	1·67877
·441	1·47934	·484	1·54561	·527	1·61280	·570	1·68036
·442	1·48086	·485	1·54718	·528	1·61436	·571	1·68195
·443	1·48238	·486	1·54875	·529	1·61592	·572	1·68354
·444	1·48391	·487	1·55032	·530	1·61748	·573	1·68513
·445	1·48544	·488	1·55189	·531	1·61904	·574	1·68672
·446	1·48697	·489	1·55346	·532	1·62060	·575	1·68831
·447	1·48850	·490	1·55503	·533	1·62216	·576	1·68990
·448	1·49003	·491	1·55660	·534	1·62372	·577	1·69149
·449	1·49157	·492	1·55817	·535	1·62528	·578	1·69308
·450	1·49311	·493	1·55974	·536	1·62684	·579	1·69467
·451	1·49465	·494	1·56131	·537	1·62840	·580	1·69626
·452	1·49618	·495	1·56289	·538	1·62996	·581	1·69785
·453	1·49771	·496	1·56447	·539	1·63152	·582	1·69945
·454	1·49924	·497	1·56605	·540	1·63309	·583	1·70105

Height of Arc.	Length of Arc.	Height of Arc.	Length of Arc.	Height of Arc.	Length of Arc.	Height of Arc.	Length of Arc.
·584	1·70264	·627	1·77197	·670	1·84226	·713	1·91355
·585	1·70424	·628	1·77359	·671	1·84391	·714	1·91523
·586	1·70584	·629	1·77521	·672	1·84556	·715	1·91691
·587	1·70745	·630	1·77684	·673	1·84720	·716	1·91859
·588	1·70905	·631	1·77847	·674	1·84885	·717	1·92027
·589	1·71065	·632	1·78009	·675	1·85050	·718	1·92195
·590	1·71225	·633	1·78172	·676	1·85215	·719	1·92363
·591	1·71286	·634	1·78335	·677	1·85379	·720	1·92531
·592	1·71546	·635	1·78498	·678	1·85544	·721	1·92700
·593	1·71707	·636	1·78660	·679	1·85709	·722	1·92868
·594	1·71868	·637	1·78823	·680	1·85874	·723	1·93036
·595	1·72029	·638	1·78986	·681	1·86039	·724	1·93204
·596	1·72190	·639	1·79149	·682	1·86205	·725	1·93373
·597	1·72350	·640	1·79312	·683	1·86370	·726	1·93541
·598	1·72511	·641	1·79475	·684	1·86535	·727	1·93710
·599	1·72672	·642	1·79638	·685	1·86700	·728	1·93878
·600	1·72833	·643	1·79801	·686	1·86866	·729	1·94046
·601	1·72994	·644	1·79964	·687	1·87031	·730	1·94215
·602	1·73155	·645	1·80127	·688	1·87196	·731	1·94383
·603	1·73316	·646	1·80290	·689	1·87362	·732	1·94552
·604	1·73477	·647	1·80454	·690	1·87527	·733	1·94721
·605	1·73638	·648	1·80617	·691	1·87693	·734	1·94890
·606	1·73799	·649	1·80780	·692	1·87859	·735	1·95059
·607	1·73960	·650	1·80943	·693	1·88024	·736	1·95228
·608	1·74121	·651	1·81107	·694	1·88190	·737	1·95397
·609	1·74283	·652	1·81271	·695	1·88356	·738	1·95566
·610	1·74444	·653	1·81435	·696	1·88522	·739	1·95735
·611	1·74605	·654	1·81599	·697	1·88688	·740	1·95994
·612	1·74767	·655	1·81763	·698	1·88854	·741	1·96074
·613	1·74929	·656	1·81928	·699	1·89020	·742	1·96244
·614	1·75091	·657	1·82091	·700	1·89186	·743	1·96414
·615	1·75252	·658	1·82255	·701	1·89352	·744	1·96583
·616	1·75414	·659	1·82419	·702	1·89519	·745	1·96753
·617	1·75576	·660	1·82583	·703	1·89685	·746	1·96923
·618	1·75738	·661	1·82747	·704	1·89851	·747	1·97093
·619	1·75900	·662	1·82911	·705	1·90017	·748	1·97262
·620	1·76062	·663	1·83075	·706	1·90184	·749	1·97432
·621	1·76224	·664	1·83240	·707	1·90350	·750	1·97602
·622	1·76386	·665	1·83404	·708	1·90517	·751	1·97772
·623	1·76548	·666	1·83568	·709	1·90684	·752	1·97943
·624	1·76710	·667	1·83733	·710	1·90852	·753	1·98113
·625	1·76872	·668	1·83897	·711	1·91019	·754	1·98283
·626	1·77034	·669	1·84061	·712	1·91187	·755	1·98453

Height of Arc.	Length of Arc.	Height of Arc.	Length of Arc.	Height of Arc.	Length of Arc.	Height of Arc.	Length of Arc.
·756	1·98623	·799	2·06027	·842	2·13618	·885	2·21388
·757	1·98794	·800	2·06202	·843	2·13797	·886	2·21571
·758	1·98964	·801	2·06377	·844	2·13976	·887	2·21754
·759	1·99134	·802	2·06552	·845	2·14155	·888	2·21937
·760	1·99305	·803	2·06727	·846	2·14334	·889	2·22120
·761	1·99476	·804	2·06901	·847	2·14513	·890	2·22303
·762	1·99647	·805	2·07076	·848	2·14692	·891	2·22486
·763	1·99818	·806	2·07251	·849	2·14871	·892	2·22670
·764	1·99989	·807	2·07427	·850	2·15050	·893	2·22854
·765	2·00160	·808	2·07602	·851	2·15229	·894	2·23038
·766	2·00331	·809	2·07777	·852	2·15409	·895	2·23222
·767	2·00502	·810	2·07953	·853	2·15589	·896	2·23406
·768	2·00673	·811	2·08128	·854	2·15770	·897	2·23590
·769	2·00844	·812	2·08304	·855	2·15950	·898	2·23774
·770	2·01016	·813	2·08480	·856	2·16130	·899	2·23958
·771	2·01187	·814	2·08656	·857	2·16309	·900	2·24142
·772	2·01359	·815	2·08832	·858	2·16489	·901	2·24325
·773	2·01531	·816	2·09008	·859	2·16668	·902	2·24508
·774	2·01702	·817	2·09198	·860	2·16848	·903	2·24691
·775	2·01874	·818	2·09360	·861	2·17028	·904	2·24874
·776	2·02045	·819	2·09536	·862	2·17209	·905	2·25057
·777	2·02217	·820	2·09712	·863	2·17389	·906	2·25240
·778	2·02389	·821	2·09888	·864	2·17570	·907	2·25423
·779	2·02561	·822	2·10065	·865	2·17751	·908	2·25606
·780	2·02733	·823	2·10242	·866	2·17932	·909	2·25789
·781	2·02907	·824	2·10419	·867	2·18113	·910	2·25972
·782	2·03080	·825	2·10596	·868	2·18294	·911	2·26155
·783	2·03252	·826	2·10773	·869	2·18475	·912	2·26338
·784	2·03425	·827	2·10950	·870	2·18656	·913	2·26521
·785	2·03598	·828	2·11127	·871	2·18837	·914	2·26704
·786	2·03771	·829	2·11304	·872	2·19018	·915	2·26888
·787	2·03944	·830	2·11481	·873	2·19200	·916	2·27071
·788	2·04117	·831	2·11659	·874	2·19382	·917	2·27254
·789	2·04290	·832	2·11837	·875	2·19564	·918	2·27437
·790	2·04462	·833	2·12015	·876	2·19746	·919	2·27620
·791	2·04635	·834	2·12193	·877	2·19928	·920	2·27803
·792	2·04809	·835	2·12371	·878	2·20110	·921	2·27987
·793	2·04983	·836	2·12549	·879	2·20292	·922	2·28170
·794	2·05157	·837	2·12727	·880	2·20474	·923	2·28354
·795	2·05331	·838	2·12905	·881	2·20656	·924	2·28537
·796	2·05505	·839	2·13083	·882	2·20839	·925	2·28720
·797	2·05679	·840	2·13261	·883	2·21022	·926	2·28903
·798	2·05853	·841	2·13439	·884	2·21205	·927	2·29086

Height of Arc.	Length of Arc.	Height of Arc.	Length of Arc.	Height of Arc.	Length of Arc.	Height of Arc.	Length of Arc.
·928	2·29270	·947	2·32785	·965	2·36191	·983	2·39631
·929	2·29453	·948	2·32972	·966	2·36381	·984	2·39823
·930	2·29636	·949	2·33160	·967	2·36571	·985	2·40016
·931	2·29820	·950	2·33348	·968	2·36762	·986	2·40208
·932	2·30004	·951	2·33537	·969	2·36952	·987	2·40400
·933	2·30188	·952	2·33726	·970	2·37143	·988	2·40592
·934	2·30373	·953	2·33915	·971	2·37334	·989	2·40784
·935	2·30557	·954	2·34104	·972	2·37525	·990	2·40976
·936	2·30741	·955	2·34293	·973	2·37716	·991	2·41169
·937	2·30926	·956	2·34483	·974	2·37908	·992	2·41362
·938	2·31111	·957	2·34673	·975	2·38100	·993	2·41556
·939	2·31295	·958	2·34862	·976	2·38291	·994	2·41749
·940	2·31479	·959	2·35051	·977	2·38482	·995	2·41943
·941	2·31666	·960	2·35241	·978	2·38673	·996	2·42136
·942	2·31852	·961	2·35431	·979	2·38864	·997	2·42329
·943	2·32038	·962	2·35621	·980	2·39055	·998	2·42522
·944	2·32224	·963	2·35810	·981	2·39247	·999	2·42715
·945	2·32411	·964	2·36000	·982	2·39439	1·000	2·42908
·946	2·32598						

To find the Length of an Arc of a Circle, or the Curve of a Right Semi-Ellipse.

Rule.—Divide the height by the base, and the quotient will be the height of an arc of which the base is unity. Seek, in the Table of Circular or Semi-elliptical arcs, as the case may be, for a number corresponding to this quotient, and take the length of the arc from the next right-hand column. Multiply the number thus taken out by the base of the arc, and the product will be the length of the arc or curve required.

Example 1.—In Southwark Bridge, London, the profiles of the arches are the arcs of circles; the span of the middle arch is 240 feet, and the height 24 feet; required the length of the arc.

24 ÷ 240 = ·100; and ·100, as per Table V., is 1·02645.

Hence 1·02645 × 240 = 246·34800 feet, the length required.

EXAMPLE 2.—The profiles of the arches of Waterloo Bridge are all equal and similar semi-ellipses; the span of each is 120 feet, and the rise 28 feet; required the length of the curve.

28 ÷ 120 = ·233; and ·233, as per Table VI., is 1·19040.

Hence 1·19010 × 120 = 142·81200 feet, the length required.

In this example there is, in the division of 28 by 120, a remainder of 40, or one-third part of the divisor; consequently the answer, 142·81200, is rather less than the truth. But this difference, in even so large an arch, is little more than half an inch; therefore, except where extreme accuracy is required, it is not worth computing.

These Tables are equally useful in estimating works which may be carried into practice, and the quantity of work to be executed from drawings to a scale.

As the Tables do not afford the means of finding the lengths of the curves of elliptic arcs which are less than half of the entire figure, the following geometrical method is given to supply the defect.

Let the curve, of which the length is required to be found, be A B C.

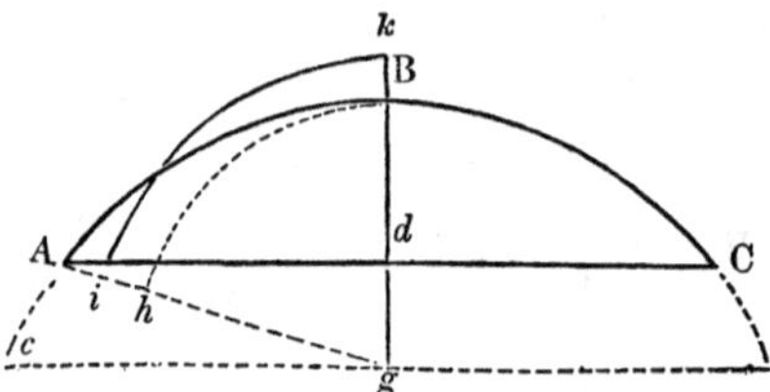

Produce the height line, B *d*, to meet the centre of the curve, in *g*. Draw the right line, A *g*, and from the centre, *g*, with the distance, *g* B, describe an arc, B *h*, meeting A *g* in *h*. Bisect A *h* in *i*, and from the centre, *g*, with the radius, *g i*, describe the arc *i k*, meeting *d* B, produced to *k*; then *i k* is half the arc A B C.

The following TABLES of Areas and Solidities will be found considerably to diminish the labour of calculation.

The numbers in the *first* column after the names represent the areas or solidities, when the length of the side or edge is 1, or unity; and the numbers in the other columns are multiples of those in the first, by the unit over each.

To find, therefore, the area of a Polygon, take the square of the length of the side, and seek in the proper columns the multipliers, which are to be ranged under each other as in common multiplication. The sum of these will be the area required.

EXAMPLE.—To find the area of a Pentagon, whose side is 18 inches, the multiplier being the square of 18 = 324.

The number in the Table under 4 is	6·8 8 1 9
" " " " " 2 "	3·4 4 0 9
" " " " " 3 "	5·1 6 1 4
Answer, the last four figures being decimals - - - - (the Area,)	5 5 7·4 3 0 9.

The same RULE is applicable to Table X., of the Solidities of Regular Bodies, using the *cube* instead of the square.

To find the Areas of Regular Polygons.

Rule.—Square the length of side of the Polygon, and take the products from the subjoined Table, as directed in page 66.

	1	2	3	4	5	6	7	8	9
Trigon............	·4330	·8660	1·2990	1·7320	2·1651	2·5981	3·0311	3·4641	3·8971
Pentagon	1·7204	3·4409	5·1614	6·8819	8·6024	10·3229	12·0433	13·7638	15·4843
Hexagon..........	2·5981	5·1961	7·7942	10·3923	12·9903	15·5884	18·1865	20·7846	23·3826
Heptagon.........	3·6339	7·2678	10·9017	14·5356	18·1695	21·8035	25·4374	29·0713	32·7052
Octagon...........	4·8284	9·6568	14·4852	19·3137	24·1421	28·9706	33·7990	38·6274	43·4558
Nonagon..........	6·1818	12·3636	18·5455	24·7273	30·9091	37·0909	43·2728	49·4546	55·6364
Decagon...........	7·6942	15·3884	23·0826	30·7768	38·4710	46·1652	53·8595	61·5537	69·2479
Undecagon.......	9·3656	18·7313	28·0969	37·4626	46·8282	56·1938	65·5595	74·9251	84·2908
Dodecagon........	11·1961	22·3923	33·5884	44·7846	55·9808	67·1769	78·3731	89·5692	100·7654

To find the Areas of Circles and Spheres.

Rule.—Square the diameter, and take the products from the subjoined Table, as directed in page 66. To find the circumference of a circle, take the products of the diameter only.

	1	2	3	4	5	6	7	8	9
Area of Circle...	·7854	1·5708	2·3562	3·1416	3·9270	4·7124	5·4978	6·2832	7·0686
Area of Sphere..	3·1416	6·2832	9·4248	12·5664	15·7080	18·8496	21·9912	25·1328	28·2744
Circumference of Circle.....	3·1416	6·2832	9·4248	12·5664	15·7080	18·8496	21·9912	25·1328	28·2744

To find the Areas of the Regular Bodies.

Rule.—Square the length of one of the edges, and take the products from the subjoined Table, as directed in page 66.

	1	2	3	4	5	6	7	8	9
Tetrahedron	1·7320	3·4641	5·1962	6·9282	8·6603	10·3923	12·1244	13·8564	15·5885
Hexahedron......	6·0000	12·0000	18·0000	24·0000	30·0000	36·0000	42·0000	48·0000	54·0000
Octahedron	3·4641	6·9282	10·3923	13·8564	17·3205	20·7846	24·2487	27·7128	31·1769
Dodecahedron ...	20·6457	41·2915	61·9372	82·5829	103·2287	123·8744	144·5201	165·1658	185·8116
Icosahedron......	8·6603	17·3205	25·9808	34·6410	43·3013	51·9615	60·6218	69·2820	77·9423

To find the Solidities of the Regular Bodies.

Rule.—Cube the length of one of the edges, and take the products from the subjoined Table, as directed in page 66.

	1	2	3	4	5	6	7	8	9
Tetrahedron	·1178	·2357	·3536	·4714	·5893	·7071	·8250	·9428	1·0607
Hexahedron......	1·0000	2·0000	3·0000	4·0000	5·0000	6·0000	7·0000	8·0000	9·0000
Octahedron	·4714	·9428	1·4142	1·8856	2·3570	2·8284	3·2998	3·7712	4·2426
Dodecahedron ...	7·6631	15·3262	22·9894	30·6525	38·3156	45·9787	53·6418	61·3050	68·9681
Icosahedron......	2·1817	4·3634	6·5451	8·7268	10·9085	13·0901	15·2718	17·4535	19·6352

TABLE *of Squares, Cubes, Square Roots, and Cube Roots.*

Number.	Square.	Cube.	Square Root.	Cube Root.	Number.
1	1	1	1·0	1·0	1
2	4	8	1·4142136	1·2599210	2
3	9	27	1·7320508	1·4422496	3
4	16	64	2·0	1·5874011	4
5	25	125	2·2360680	1·7099759	5
6	36	216	2·4494897	1·8171206	6
7	49	343	2·6457513	1·9129312	7
8	64	512	2·8284271	2·0	8
9	81	729	3·0	2·0800837	9
10	100	1000	3·1622777	2·1544347	10
11	121	1331	3·3166248	2·2239801	11
12	144	1728	3·4641016	2·2894286	12
13	169	2197	3·6055513	2·3513347	13
14	196	2744	3·7416574	2·4101422	14
15	225	3375	3·8729833	2·4662121	15
16	256	4096	4·0	2·5198421	16
17	289	4913	4·1231056	2·5712816	17
18	324	5832	4·2426407	2·6207414	18
19	361	6859	4·3588989	2·6684016	19
20	400	8000	4·4721360	2·7144177	20
21	441	9261	4·5825757	2·7589243	21
22	484	10648	4·6904158	2·8020393	22
23	529	12167	4·7958315	2·8438670	23
24	576	13824	4·8989795	2·8844991	24
25	625	15625	5·0	2·9240177	25
26	676	17576	5·0990195	2·9624960	26
27	729	19683	5·1961524	3·0	27
28	784	21952	5·2915026	3·0365889	28
29	841	24389	5·3851648	3·0723168	29
30	900	27000	5·4772256	3·1072325	30
31	961	29791	5·5677644	3·1413806	31
32	1024	32768	5·6568542	3·1748021	32
33	1089	35937	5·7445626	3·2075343	33
34	1156	39304	5·8309519	3·2396118	34
35	1225	42875	5·9160798	3·2710663	35
36	1296	46656	6·0	3·3019272	36
37	1369	50653	6·0827625	3·3322218	37
38	1444	54872	6·1644140	3·3619754	38
39	1521	59319	6·2449980	3·3912114	39
40	1600	64000	6·3245553	3·4199519	40

Number.	Square.	Cube.	Square Root.	Cube Root.	Number.
41	1681	68921	6·4031242	3·4482172	41
42	1764	74088	6·4807407	3·4760266	42
43	1849	79507	6·5574385	3·5033981	43
44	1936	85184	6·6332496	3·5303483	44
45	2025	91125	6·7082039	3·5568933	45
46	2116	97336	6·7823300	3·5830479	46
47	2209	103823	6·8556546	3·6088261	47
48	2304	110592	6·9282032	3·6342411	48
49	2401	117649	7·0	3·6593057	49
50	2500	125000	7·0710678	3·6840314	50
51	2601	132651	7·1414284	3·7084298	51
52	2704	140608	7·2111026	3·7325111	52
53	2809	148877	7·2801099	3·7562858	53
54	2916	157464	7·3484692	3·7797631	54
55	3025	166375	7·4161985	3·8029525	55
56	3136	175616	7·4833148	3·8258624	56
57	3249	185193	7·5498344	3·8485011	57
58	3364	195112	7·6157731	3·8708766	58
59	3481	205379	7·6811457	3·8929965	59
60	3600	216000	7·7459667	3·9148676	60
61	3721	226981	7·8102497	3·9364972	61
62	3844	238328	7·8740079	3·9578915	62
63	3969	250047	7·9372539	3·9790571	63
64	4096	262144	8·0	4·0	64
65	4225	274625	8·0622577	4·0207256	65
66	4356	287496	8·1240384	4·0412401	66
67	4489	300763	8·1853528	4·0615480	67
68	4624	314432	8·2462113	4·0816551	68
69	4761	328509	8·3066239	4·1015661	69
70	4900	343000	8·3666003	4·1212853	70
71	5041	357911	8·4261498	4·1408178	71
72	5184	373248	8·4852814	4·1601676	72
73	5329	389017	8·5440037	4·1793392	73
74	5476	405224	8·6023253	4·1983364	74
75	5625	421875	8·6602540	4·2171633	75
76	5776	438976	8·7177979	4·2358236	76
77	5929	456533	8·7749644	4·2543210	77
78	6084	474552	8·8317609	4·2726586	78
79	6241	493039	8·8881944	4·2908404	79
80	6400	512000	8·9442719	4·3088695	80

Number.	Square.	Cube.	Square Root.	Cube Root.	Number.
81	6561	531441	9·0	4·3267487	81
82	6724	551368	9·0553851	4·3444815	82
83	6889	571787	9·1104336	4·3620707	83
84	7056	592704	9·1651514	4·3795191	84
85	7225	614125	9·2195445	4·3968296	85
86	7396	636056	9·2736185	4·4140049	86
87	7569	658503	9·3273791	4·4310476	87
88	7744	681472	9·3808315	4·4479602	88
89	7921	704969	9·4339811	4·4647451	89
90	8100	729000	9·4868330	4·4814047	90
91	8281	753571	9·5393920	4·4979414	91
92	8464	778688	9·5916630	4·5143574	92
93	8649	804357	9·6436508	4·5306549	93
94	8836	830584	9·6953597	4·5468359	94
95	9025	857375	9·7467943	4·5629026	95
96	9216	884736	9·7979590	4·5788570	96
97	9409	912673	9·8488578	4·5947009	97
98	9604	941192	9·8994949	4·6104363	98
99	9801	970299	9·9498744	4·6260650	99
100	10000	1000000	10·0	4·6415888	100
101	10201	1030301	10·0498756	4·6570095	101
102	10404	1061208	10·0995049	4·6723287	102
103	10609	1092727	10·1488916	4·6875482	103
104	10816	1124864	10·1980390	4·7026694	104
105	11025	1157625	10·2469508	4·7176940	105
106	11236	1191016	10·2956301	4·7326235	106
107	11449	1225043	10·3440804	4·7474594	107
108	11664	1259712	10·3923048	4·7622032	108
109	11881	1295029	10·4403065	4·7768562	109
110	12100	1331000	10·4880885	4·7914199	110
111	12321	1367631	10·5356538	4·8058955	111
112	12544	1404928	10·5830052	4·8202845	112
113	12769	1442897	10·6301458	4·8345881	113
114	12996	1481544	10·6770783	4·8488076	114
115	13225	1520875	10·7238053	4·8629442	115
116	13456	1560896	10·7703296	4·8769990	116
117	13689	1601613	10·8166538	4·8909732	117
118	13924	1643032	10·8627805	4·9048681	118
119	14161	1685159	10·9087121	4·9186847	119
120	14400	1728000	10·9544512	4·9324242	120

Number.	Square.	Cube.	Square Root.	Cube Root.	Number.
121	14641	1771561	11·0	4·9460874	121
122	14884	1815848	11·0453610	4·9596757	122
123	15129	1860867	11·0905365	4·9731898	123
124	15376	1906624	11·1355287	4·9866310	124
125	15625	1953125	11·1803399	5·0	125
126	15876	2000376	11·2249722	5·0132979	126
127	16129	2048383	11·2694277	5·0265257	127
128	16384	2097152	11·3137085	5·0396842	128
129	16641	2146689	11·3578167	5·0527743	129
130	16900	2197000	11·4017543	5·0657970	130
131	17161	2248091	11·4455231	5·0787531	131
132	17424	2299968	11·4891253	5·0916434	132
133	17689	2352637	11·5325626	5·1044687	133
134	17956	2406104	11·5758369	5·1172299	134
135	18225	2460375	11·6189500	5·1299278	135
136	18496	2515456	11·6619038	5·1425632	136
137	18769	2571353	11·7046999	5·1551367	137
138	19044	2628072	11·7473401	5·1676493	138
139	19321	2685619	11·7898261	5·1801015	139
140	19600	2744000	11·8321596	5·1924941	140
141	19881	2803221	11·8743422	5·2048279	141
142	20164	2863288	11·9163753	5·2171034	142
143	20449	2924207	11·9582607	5·2293215	143
144	20736	2985984	12·0	5·2414828	144
145	21025	3048625	12·0415946	5·2535879	145
146	21316	3112136	12·0830460	5·2656374	146
147	21609	3176523	12·1243557	5·2776321	147
148	21904	3241792	12·1655251	5·2895725	148
149	22201	3307949	12·2065556	5·3014592	149
150	22500	3375000	12·2474487	5·3132928	150
151	22801	3442951	12·2882057	5·3250740	151
152	23104	3511808	12·3288280	5·3368033	152
153	23409	3581577	12·3693169	5·3484812	153
154	23716	3652264	12·4096736	5·3601084	154
155	24025	3723875	12·4498996	5·3716854	155
156	24336	3796416	12·4899960	5·3832126	156
157	24649	3869893	12·5299641	5·3946907	157
158	24964	3944312	12·5698051	5·4061202	158
159	25281	4019679	12·6095202	5·4175015	159
160	25600	4096000	12·6491106	5·4288352	160

Number.	Square.	Cube.	Square Root.	Cube Root.	Number.
161	25921	4173281	12·6885775	5·4401218	161
162	26244	4251528	12·7279221	5·4513618	162
163	26569	4330747	12·7671453	5·4625556	163
164	26896	4410944	12·8062485	5·4737037	164
165	27225	4492125	12·8452326	5·4848066	165
166	27556	4574296	12·8840987	5·4958647	166
167	27889	4657463	12·9228480	5·5068784	167
168	28224	4741632	12·9614814	5·5178484	168
169	28561	4826809	13·0	5·5287748	169
170	28900	4913000	13·0384048	5·5396583	170
171	29241	5000211	13·0766968	5·5504991	171
172	29584	5088448	13·1148770	5·5612978	172
173	29929	5177717	13·1529464	5·5720546	173
174	30276	5268024	13·1909060	5·5827702	174
175	30625	5359375	13·2287566	5·5934447	175
176	30976	5451776	13·2664992	5·6040787	176
177	31329	5545233	13·3041347	5·6146724	177
178	31684	5639752	13·3416641	5·6252263	178
179	32041	5735339	13·3790882	5·6357408	179
180	32400	5832000	13·4164079	5·6462162	180
181	32761	5929741	13·4536240	5·6566528	181
182	33124	6028568	13·4907376	5·6670511	182
183	33489	6128487	13·5277493	5·6774114	183
184	33856	6229504	13·5646600	5·6877340	184
185	34225	6331625	13·6014705	5·6980192	185
186	34596	6434856	13·6381817	5·7082675	186
187	34969	6539203	13·6747943	5·7184791	187
188	35344	6644672	13·7113092	5·7286543	188
189	35721	6751269	13·7477271	5·7387936	189
190	36100	6859000	13·7840488	5·7488971	190
191	36481	6967871	13·8202750	5·7589652	191
192	36864	7077888	13·8564065	5·7689982	192
193	37249	7189097	13·8924440	5·7789966	193
194	37636	7301384	13·9283883	5·7889604	194
195	38025	7414875	13·9642400	5·7988900	195
196	38416	7529536	14·0	5·8087857	196
197	38809	7645373	14·0356688	5·8186479	197
198	39204	7762392	14·0712473	5·8284767	198
199	39601	7880599	14·1067360	5·8382725	199
200	40000	8000000	14·1421356	5·8480355	200

Number.	Square.	Cube.	Square Root.	Cube Root.	Number.
201	40401	8120601	14·1774469	5·8577660	201
202	40804	8242408	14·2126704	5·8674643	202
203	41209	8365427	14·2478068	5·8771307	203
204	41616	8489664	14·2828569	5·8867653	204
205	42025	8615125	14·3178211	5·8963685	205
206	42436	8741816	14·3527001	5·9059406	206
207	42849	8869743	14·3874946	5·9154817	207
208	43264	8998912	14·4222051	5·9249921	208
209	43681	9129329	14·4568323	5·9344721	209
210	44100	9261000	14·4913767	5·9439220	210
211	44521	9393931	14·5258390	5·9533418	211
212	44944	9528128	14·5602198	5·9627320	212
213	45369	9663597	14·5945195	5·9720926	213
214	45796	9800344	14·6287388	5·9814240	214
215	46225	9938375	14·6628783	5·9907264	215
216	46656	10077696	14·6969385	6·0	216
217	47089	10218313	14·7309199	6·0092450	217
218	47524	10360232	14·7648231	6·0184617	218
219	47961	10503459	14·7986486	6·0276502	219
220	48400	10648000	14·8323970	6·0368107	220
221	48841	10793861	14·8660687	6·0459435	221
222	49284	10941048	14·8996644	6·0550489	222
223	49729	11089567	14·9331845	6·0641270	223
224	50176	11239424	14·9666295	6·0731779	224
225	50625	11390625	15·0	6·0822020	225
226	51076	11543176	15·0332964	6·0911994	226
227	51529	11697083	15·0665192	6·1001702	227
228	51984	11852352	15·0996689	6·1091147	228
229	52441	12008989	15·1327460	6·1180332	229
230	52900	12167000	15·1657509	6·1269257	230
231	53361	12326391	15·1986842	6·1357924	231
232	53824	12487168	15·2315462	6·1446337	232
233	54289	12649337	15·2643375	6·1534495	233
234	54756	12812904	15·2970585	6·1622401	234
235	55225	12977875	15·3297097	6·1710058	235
236	55696	13144256	15·3622915	6·1797466	236
237	56169	13312053	15·3948043	6·1884628	237
238	56644	13481272	15·4272486	6·1971544	238
239	57121	13651919	15·4596248	6·2058218	239
240	57600	13824000	15·4919334	6·2144650	240

Number.	Square.	Cube.	Square Root.	Cube Root.	Number.
241	58081	13997521	15·5241747	6·2230843	241
242	58564	14172488	15·5563492	6·2316797	242
243	59049	14348907	15·5884573	6·2402515	243
244	59536	14526784	15·6204994	6·2487998	244
245	60025	14706125	15·6524758	6·2573248	245
246	60516	14886936	15·6843871	6·2658266	246
247	61009	15069223	15·7162336	6·2743054	247
248	61504	15252992	15·7480157	6·2827613	248
249	62001	15438249	15·7797338	6·2911946	249
250	62500	15625000	15·8113883	6·2996053	250
251	63001	15813251	15·8429795	6·3079935	251
252	63504	16003008	15·8745079	6·3163596	252
253	64009	16194277	15·9059737	6·3247035	253
254	64516	16387064	15·9373775	6·3330256	254
255	65025	16581375	15·9687194	6·3413257	255
256	65536	16777216	16·0	6·3496042	256
257	66049	16974593	16·0312195	6·3578611	257
258	66564	17173512	16·0623784	6·3660968	258
259	67081	17373979	16·0934769	6·3743111	259
260	67600	17576000	16·1245155	6·3825043	260
261	68121	17779581	16·1554944	6·3906765	261
262	68644	17984728	16·1864141	6·3988279	262
263	69169	18191447	16·2172747	6·4069585	263
264	69696	18399744	16·2480768	6·4150687	264
265	70225	18609625	16·2788206	6·4231583	265
266	70756	18821096	16·3095064	6·4312276	266
267	71289	19034163	16·3401346	6·4392767	267
268	71824	19248832	16·3707055	6·4473057	268
269	72361	19465109	16·4012195	6·4553148	269
270	72900	19683000	16·4316767	6·4633041	270
271	73441	19902511	16·4620776	6·4712736	271
272	73984	20123648	16·4924225	6·4792236	272
273	74529	20346417	16·5227116	6·4871541	273
274	75076	20570824	16·5529454	6·4950653	274
275	75625	20796875	16·5831240	6·5029572	275
276	76176	21024576	16·6132477	6·5108300	276
277	76729	21253933	16·6433170	6·5186839	277
278	77284	21484952	16·6733320	6·5265189	278
279	77841	21717639	16·7032931	6·5343351	279
280	78400	21952000	16·7332005	6·5421326	280

Number.	Square.	Cube.	Square Root.	Cube Root.	Number.
281	78961	22188041	16·7630546	6·5499116	281
282	79524	22425768	16·7928556	6·5576722	282
283	80089	22665187	16·8226038	6·5654144	283
284	80656	22906304	16·8522995	6·5731385	284
285	81225	23149125	16·8819430	6·5808443	285
286	81796	23393656	16·9115345	6·5885323	286
287	82369	23639903	16·9410743	6·5962023	287
288	82944	23887872	16·9705627	6·6038545	288
289	83521	24137569	17·0	6·6114890	289
290	84100	24389000	17·0293864	6·6191060	290
291	84681	24642171	17·0587221	6·6267054	291
292	85264	24897088	17·0880075	6·6342874	292
293	85849	25153757	17·1172428	6·6418522	293
294	86436	25412184	17·1464282	6·6493998	294
295	87025	25672375	17·1755640	6·6569302	295
296	87616	25934336	17·2046505	6·6644437	296
297	88209	26198073	17·2336879	6·6719403	297
298	88804	26463592	17·2626765	6·6794200	298
299	89401	26730899	17·2916165	6·6868831	299
300	90000	27000000	17·3205081	6·6943295	300
301	90601	27270901	17·3493516	6·7017593	301
302	91204	27543608	17·3781472	6·7091729	302
303	91809	27818127	17·4068952	6·7165700	303
304	92416	28094464	17·4355958	6·7239508	304
305	93025	28372625	17·4642492	6·7313155	305
306	93636	28652616	17·4928557	6·7386641	306
307	94249	28934443	17·5214155	6·7459967	307
308	94864	29218112	17·5499288	6·7533134	308
309	95481	29503629	17·5783958	6·7606143	309
310	96100	29791000	17·6068169	6·7678995	310
311	96721	30080231	17·6351921	6·7751690	311
312	97344	30371328	17·6635217	6·7824229	312
313	97969	30664297	17·6918060	6·7896613	313
314	98596	30959144	17·7200451	6·7968844	314
315	99225	31255875	17·7482393	6·8040921	315
316	99856	31554496	17·7763888	6·8112847	316
317	100489	31855013	17·8044938	6·8184620	317
318	101124	32157432	17·8325545	6·8256242	318
319	101761	32461759	17·8605711	6·8327714	319
320	102400	32768000	17·8885438	6·8399037	320

Number.	Square.	Cube.	Square Root.	Cube Root.	Number.
321	103041	33076161	17·9164729	6·8470213	321
322	103684	33386248	17·9443584	6·8541240	322
323	104329	33698267	17·9722008	6·8612120	323
324	104976	34012224	18·0	6·8682855	324
325	105625	34328125	18·0277564	6·8753443	325
326	106276	34645976	18·0554701	6·8823888	326
327	106929	34965783	18·0831413	6·8894188	327
328	107584	35287552	18·1107703	6·8964345	328
329	108241	35611289	18·1383571	6·9034359	329
330	108900	35937000	18·1659021	6·9104232	330
331	109561	36264691	18·1934054	6·9173964	331
332	110224	36594368	18·2208672	6·9243556	332
333	110889	36926037	18·2482876	6·9313008	333
334	111556	37259704	18·2756669	6·9382321	334
335	112225	37595375	18·3030052	6·9451496	335
336	112896	37933056	18·3303028	6·9520533	336
337	113569	38272753	18·3575598	6·9589434	337
338	114244	38614472	18·3847763	6·9658198	338
339	114921	38958219	18·4119526	6·9726826	339
340	115600	39304000	18·4390889	6·9795321	340
341	116281	39651821	18·4661853	6·9863681	341
342	116964	40001688	18·4932420	6·9931906	342
343	117649	40353607	18·5202592	7·0	343
344	118336	40707584	18·5472370	7·0067962	344
345	119025	41063625	18·5741756	7·0135791	345
346	119716	41421736	18·6010752	7·0203490	346
347	120409	41781923	18·6279360	7·0271058	347
348	121104	42144192	18·6547581	7·0338497	348
349	121801	42508549	18·6815417	7·0405806	349
350	122500	42875000	18·7082869	7·0472987	350
351	123201	43243551	18·7349940	7·0540041	351
352	123904	43614208	18·7616630	7·0606967	352
353	124609	43986977	18·7882942	7·0673767	353
354	125316	44361864	18·8148877	7·0740440	354
355	126025	44738875	18·8414437	7·0806988	355
356	126736	45118016	18·8679623	7·0873411	356
357	127449	45499293	18·8944436	7·0939709	357
358	128164	45882712	18·9208879	7·1005885	358
359	128881	46268279	18·9472953	7·1071937	359
360	129600	46656000	18·9736660	7·1137866	360

Number.	Square.	Cube.	Square Root.	Cube Root.	Number.
361	130321	47045881	19·0	7·1203674	361
362	131044	47437928	19·0262976	7·1269360	362
363	131769	47832147	19·0525589	7·1334925	363
364	132496	48228544	19·0787840	7·1400370	364
365	133225	48627125	19·1049732	7·1465695	365
366	133956	49027896	19·1311265	7·1530901	366
367	134689	49430863	19·1572441	7·1595988	367
368	135424	49836032	19·1833261	7·1660957	368
369	136161	50243409	19·2093727	7·1725809	369
370	136900	50653000	19·2353841	7·1790544	370
371	137641	51064811	19·2613603	7·1855162	371
372	138384	51478848	19·2873015	7·1919663	372
373	139129	51895117	19·3132079	7·1984050	373
374	139876	52313624	19·3390796	7·2048322	374
375	140625	52734375	19·3649167	7·2112479	375
376	141376	53157376	19·3907194	7·2176522	376
377	142129	53582633	19·4164878	7·2240450	377
378	142884	54010152	19·4422221	7·2304268	378
379	143641	54439939	19·4679223	7·2367972	379
380	144400	54872000	19·4935887	7·2431565	380
381	145161	55306341	19·5192213	7·2495045	381
382	145924	55742968	19·5448203	7·2558415	382
383	146689	56181887	19·5703858	7·2621675	383
384	147456	56623104	19·5959179	7·2684824	384
385	148225	57066625	19·6214169	7·2747864	385
386	148996	57512456	19·6468827	7·2810794	386
387	149769	57960603	19·6723156	7·2873617	387
388	150544	58411072	19·6977156	7·2936330	388
389	151321	58863869	19·7230829	7·2998936	389
390	152100	59319000	19·7484177	7·3061436	390
391	152881	59776471	19·7737199	7·3123828	391
392	153664	60236288	19·7989899	7·3186114	392
393	154449	60698457	19·8242276	7·3248295	393
394	155236	61162984	19·8494332	7·3310369	394
395	156025	61629875	19·8746069	7·3372339	395
396	156816	62099136	19·8997487	7·3434205	396
397	157609	62570773	19·9248588	7·3495966	397
398	158404	63044792	19·9499373	7·3557624	398
399	159201	63521199	19·9749844	7·3619178	399
400	160000	64000000	20·0	7·3680630	400

Number.	Square.	Cube.	Square Root.	Cube Root.	Number.
401	160801	64481201	20·0249844	7·3721979	401
402	161604	64964808	20·0499377	7·3803227	402
403	162409	65450827	20·0748599	7·3864373	403
404	163216	65939264	20·0997512	7·3925419	404
405	164025	66430125	20·1246118	7·3986363	405
406	164836	66923416	20·1494417	7·4047206	406
407	165649	67419143	20·1742410	7·4107950	407
408	166464	67917312	20·1990099	7·4168595	408
409	167281	68417929	20·2237484	7·4229142	409
410	168100	68921000	20·2484567	7·4289589	410
411	168921	69426531	20·2731349	7·4349938	411
412	169744	69934528	20·2977831	7·4410189	412
413	170569	70444997	20·3224014	7·4470342	413
414	171396	70957944	20·3469899	7·4530399	414
415	172225	71473375	20·3715488	7·4590359	415
416	173056	71991296	20·3960781	7·4650223	416
417	173889	72511713	20·4205779	7·4709991	417
418	174724	73034632	20·4450483	7·4769664	418
419	175561	73560059	20·4694895	7·4829242	419
420	176400	74088000	20·4939015	7·4888724	420
421	177241	74618461	20·5182845	7·4948113	421
422	178084	75151448	20·5426486	7·5007406	422
423	178929	75686967	20·5669638	7·5066607	423
424	179776	76225024	20·5912603	7·5125715	424
425	180625	76765625	20·6155281	7·5184730	425
426	181476	77308776	20·6397674	7·5243652	426
427	182329	77854483	20·6639783	7·5302482	427
428	183184	78402752	20·6881609	7·5361221	428
429	184041	78953589	20·7123152	7·5419867	429
430	184900	79507000	20·7364414	7·5478423	430
431	185761	80062991	20·7605395	7·5536888	431
432	186624	80621568	20·7846097	7·5595263	432
433	187489	81182737	20·8086520	7·5653548	433
434	188356	81746504	20·8326667	7·5711743	434
435	189225	82312875	20·8566536	7·5769849	435
436	190096	82881856	20·8806130	7·5827865	436
437	190969	83453453	20·9045450	7·5885793	437
438	191844	84027672	20·9284495	7·5943633	438
439	192721	84604519	20·9523268	7·6001385	439
440	193600	85184000	20·9761770	7·6059049	440

Number.	Square.	Cube.	Square Root.	Cube Root.	Number.
441	194481	85766121	21·0	7·6116626	441
442	195364	86350888	21·0237960	7·6174116	442
443	196249	86938307	21·0475652	7·6231519	443
444	197136	87528384	21·0713075	7·6288837	444
445	198025	88121125	21·0950231	7·6346067	445
446	198916	88716536	21·1187121	7·6403213	446
447	199809	89314623	21·1423745	7·6460272	447
448	200704	89915392	21·1660105	7·6517247	448
449	201601	90518849	21·1896201	7·6574138	449
450	202500	91125000	21·2132034	7·6630943	450
451	203401	91733851	21·2367606	7·6687665	451
452	204304	92345408	21·2602916	7·6744303	452
453	205209	92959677	21·2837967	7·6800857	453
454	206116	93576664	21·3072758	7·6857328	454
455	207025	94196375	21·3307290	7·6913717	455
456	207936	94818816	21·3541565	7·6970023	456
457	208849	95443993	21·3775583	7·7026246	457
458	209764	96071912	21·4009346	7·7082388	458
459	210681	96702579	21·4242853	7·7138448	459
460	211600	97336000	21·4476106	7·7194426	460
461	212521	97972181	21·4709106	7·7250325	461
462	213444	98611128	21·4941853	7·7306141	462
463	214369	99252847	21·5174348	7·7361877	463
464	215296	99897344	21·5406592	7·7417532	464
465	216225	100544625	21·5638587	7·7473109	465
466	217156	101194696	21·5870331	7·7528606	466
467	218089	101847563	21·6191828	7·7584023	467
468	219024	102503232	21·6333077	7·7639361	468
469	219961	103161709	21·6564078	7·7694620	469
470	220900	103823000	21·6794834	7·7749801	470
471	221841	104487111	21·7025344	7·7804904	471
472	222784	105154048	21·7255610	7·7859928	472
473	223729	105823817	21·7485632	7·7914875	473
474	224676	106496424	21·7715411	7·7969745	474
475	225625	107171875	21·7944947	7·8024538	475
476	226576	107850176	21·8174242	7·8079244	476
477	227529	108531333	21·8403297	7·8133892	477
478	228484	109215352	21·8632111	7·8188456	478
479	229441	109902239	21·8860686	7·8242942	479
480	230400	110592000	21·9089023	7·8297353	480

Number.	Square.	Cube.	Square Root.	Cube Root.	Number.
481	231361	111284641	21·9317122	7·8351688	481
482	232324	111980168	21·9544984	7·8405949	482
483	233289	112678587	21·9772610	7·8460134	483
484	234256	113379904	22·0	7·8514244	484
485	235225	114084125	22·0227155	7·8568281	485
486	236186	114791256	22·0454077	7·8622242	486
487	237169	115501303	22·0680765	7·8676130	487
488	238144	116214272	22·0907220	7·8729944	488
489	239131	116930169	22·1133444	7·8783684	489
490	240120	117649000	22·1359436	7·8837352	490
491	241081	118370771	22·1585198	7·8890946	491
492	242064	119095488	22·1810730	7·8944468	492
493	243049	119823157	22·2036033	7·8997917	493
494	244036	120553784	22·2261108	7·9051294	494
495	245025	121287375	22·2485955	7·9104599	495
496	246016	122023936	22·2710575	7·9157832	496
497	247009	122763473	22·2934968	7·9210994	497
498	248004	123505992	22·3159136	7·9264085	498
499	249001	124251499	22·3383079	7·9317104	499
500	250000	125000000	22·3606798	7·9370053	500
501	251001	125751501	22·3830293	7·9422932	501
502	252004	126406008	22·4053565	7·9475739	502
503	253009	127263527	22·4276615	7·9528477	503
504	254016	128024064	22·4499443	7·9581144	504
505	255025	128787625	22·4722051	7·9633743	505
506	256036	129554216	22·4944438	7·9686271	506
507	257049	130323843	22·5166605	7·9738731	507
508	258064	131096512	22·5388553	7·9791122	508
509	259081	131872229	22·5610283	7·9843444	509
510	260100	132651000	22·5831796	7·9895697	510
511	261121	133432831	22·6053091	7·9947883	511
512	262144	134217728	22·6274170	8·0	512
513	263169	135005697	22·6495033	8·0052049	513
514	264196	135796744	22·6715681	8·0104032	514
515	265225	136590875	22·6936114	8·0155946	515
516	266256	137388096	22·7156334	8·0207794	516
517	267289	138188413	22·7376340	8·0259574	517
518	268324	138991832	22·7596134	8·0311287	518
519	269361	139798359	22·7815715	8·0362935	519
520	270400	140608000	22·8035085	8·0414515	520

Number.	Square.	Cube.	Square Root.	Cube Root.	Number.
521	271441	141420761	22·8254244	8·0466030	521
522	272484	142236648	22·8473193	8·0517479	522
523	273529	143055667	22·8691933	8·0568862	523
524	274576	143877824	22·8910463	8·0620180	524
525	275625	144703125	22·9128785	8·0671432	525
526	276676	145531576	22·9346899	8·0722620	526
527	277729	146363183	22·9564806	8·0773743	527
528	278784	147197952	22·9782506	8·0824800	528
529	279841	148035889	23·0	8·0875794	529
530	280900	148877000	23·0217289	8·0926723	530
531	281961	149721291	23·0434372	8·0977589	531
532	283024	150568768	23·0651252	8·1028390	532
533	284089	151419437	23·0867928	8·1079128	533
534	285156	152273304	23·1084400	8·1129803	534
535	286225	153130375	23·1300670	8·1180414	535
536	287296	153990656	23·1516738	8·1230962	536
537	288369	154854153	23·1732605	8·1281447	537
538	289444	155720872	23·1948270	8·1331870	538
539	290521	156590819	23·2163735	8·1382230	539
540	291600	157464000	23·2379001	8·1432529	540
541	292681	158340421	23·2594067	8·1482765	541
542	293764	159220088	23·2808935	8·1532939	542
543	294849	160103007	23·3023604	8·1583051	543
544	295936	160989184	23·3238076	8·1633102	544
545	297025	161878625	23·3452351	8·1683092	545
546	298116	162771336	23·3666429	8·1733020	546
547	299209	163667323	23·3880311	8·1782888	547
548	300304	164566592	23·4093998	8·1832695	548
549	301401	165469149	23·4307490	8·1882441	549
550	302500	166375000	23·4520788	8·1932127	550
551	303601	167284151	23·4733892	8·1981753	551
552	304704	168196608	23·4946802	8·2031319	552
553	305809	169112377	23·5159520	8·2080825	553
554	306916	170031464	23·5372046	8·2130271	554
555	308025	170953875	23·5584380	8·2179657	555
556	309136	171879616	23·5796522	8·2228985	556
557	310249	172808693	23·6008474	8·2278254	557
558	311364	173741112	23·6220236	8·2327463	558
559	312481	174676879	23·6431808	8·2376614	559
560	313600	175616000	23·6643191	8·2425706	560

Number.	Square.	Cube.	Square Root.	Cube Root.	Number.
561	314721	176558481	23·6854386	8·2474740	561
562	315844	177504328	23·7065392	8·2523715	562
563	316969	178453547	23·7276210	8·2572633	563
564	318096	179406144	23·7486842	8·2621492	564
565	319225	180362125	23·7697286	8·2670294	565
566	320356	181321496	23·7907545	8·2719039	566
567	321489	182284263	23·8117618	8·2767726	567
568	322624	183250432	23·8327506	8·2816355	568
569	323761	184220009	23·8537209	8·2864928	569
570	324900	185193000	23·8746728	8·2913444	570
571	326041	186169411	23·8956063	8·2961903	571
572	327184	187149248	23·9165215	8·3010304	572
573	328329	188132517	23·9374184	8·3058651	573
574	329476	189119224	23·9582971	8·3106941	574
575	330625	190109375	23·9791576	8·3155175	575
576	331776	181102976	24·0	8·3203353	576
577	332929	182100033	24·0208243	8·3251475	577
578	334084	183100552	24·0416306	8·3299542	578
579	335241	184104539	24·0624188	8·3347553	579
580	336400	195112000	24·0831891	8·3395509	580
581	337561	196122941	24·1039416	8·3443410	581
582	338724	197137368	24·1246762	8·3491256	582
583	339889	198155287	24·1453929	8·3539047	583
584	341056	199176704	24·1660919	8·3586784	584
585	342225	200201625	24·1867732	8·3634466	585
586	343396	201230056	24·2074369	8·3682095	586
587	344569	202262003	24·2280829	8·3729668	587
588	345744	203297472	24·2487113	8·3777188	588
589	346921	204336469	24·2693222	8·3824653	589
590	348100	205379000	24·2899156	8·3872065	590
591	349281	206425071	24·3104916	8·3919423	591
592	350464	207474688	24·3310501	8·3966729	592
593	351649	208527857	24·3515913	8·4013981	593
594	352836	209584584	24·3721152	8·4061180	594
595	354025	210644875	24·3926218	8·4108326	595
596	355216	211708736	24·4131112	8·4155419	596
597	356409	212776173	24·4335834	8·4202460	597
598	357604	213847192	24·4540385	8·4249448	598
599	358801	214921799	24·4744765	8·4296383	599
600	360000	216000000	24·4948974	8·4343267	600

Number.	Square.	Cube.	Square Root.	Cube Root.	Number.
601	361201	217081801	24·5153013	8·4390098	601
602	362404	218167208	24·5356883	8·4436877	602
603	363609	219256227	24·5560583	8·4483605	603
604	364816	220348864	24·5764115	8·4530281	604
605	366025	221445125	24·5967478	8·4576906	605
606	367236	222545016	24·6170673	8·4623479	606
607	368449	223648543	24·6373700	8·4670000	607
608	369664	224755712	24·6576560	8·4716471	608
609	370881	225866529	24·6779254	8·4762892	609
610	372100	226981000	24·6981781	8·4809261	610
611	373321	228099131	24·7184142	8·4855579	611
612	374544	229220928	24·7386338	8·4901848	612
613	375769	230346397	24·7588368	8·4948065	613
614	376996	231475544	24·7790234	8·4994233	614
615	378225	232608375	24·7991935	8·5040350	615
616	379456	233744896	24·8193473	8·5086417	616
617	380689	234885113	24·8394847	8·5132435	617
618	381924	236029032	24·8596058	8·5178403	618
619	383161	237176659	24·8797106	8·5224321	619
620	384400	238328000	24·8997992	8·5270189	620
621	385641	239483061	24·9198716	8·5316009	621
622	386884	240641848	24·9399278	8·5361780	622
623	388129	241804367	24·9599679	8·5407501	623
624	389376	242970624	24·9799920	8·5453173	624
625	390625	244140625	25·0	8·5498797	625
626	391876	245314376	25·0199920	8·5544372	626
627	393129	246491883	25·0399681	8·5589899	627
628	394384	247673152	25·0599282	8·5635377	628
629	395641	248858189	25·0798724	8·5680807	629
630	396900	250047000	25·0998008	8·5726189	630
631	398161	251239591	25·1197134	8·5771523	631
632	399424	252435968	25·1396102	8·5816809	632
633	400689	253636137	25·1594913	8·5862047	633
634	401956	254840104	25·1793566	8·5907238	634
635	403225	256047875	25·1992063	8·5952380	635
636	404496	257259456	25·2190404	8·5997476	636
637	405769	258474853	25·2388589	8·6042525	637
638	407044	259694072	25·2586619	8·6087526	638
639	408321	260917119	25·2784493	8·6132480	639
640	409600	262144000	25·2982213	8·6177388	640

Number.	Square.	Cube.	Square Root.	Cube Root.	Number.
641	410881	263374721	25·3179778	8·6222248	641
642	412164	264609288	25·3377189	8·6267063	642
643	413449	265847707	25·3574447	8·6311830	643
644	414736	267089984	25·3771551	8·6356551	644
645	416025	268336125	25·3968502	8·6401226	645
646	417316	269586136	25·4165301	8·6445855	646
647	418609	270840023	25·4361947	8·6490437	647
648	419904	272097792	25·4558441	8·6534974	648
649	421201	273359449	25·4754784	8·6579465	649
650	422500	274625000	25·4950976	8·6623911	650
651	423801	275894451	25·5147016	8·6668310	651
652	425104	277167808	25·5342907	8·6712665	652
653	426400	278445077	25·5538647	8·6756974	653
654	427716	279726264	25·5734237	8·6801237	654
655	429025	281011375	25·5929678	8·6845456	655
656	430336	282300416	25·6124969	8·6889630	656
657	431649	283593393	25·6320112	8·6933759	657
658	432964	284890312	25·6515107	8·6977843	658
659	434281	286191179	25·6709953	8·7021882	659
660	435600	287496000	25·6904652	8·7065877	660
661	436921	288804781	25·7099203	8·7109827	661
662	438244	290117528	25·7293607	8·7153734	662
663	439569	291434247	25·7487864	8·7197596	663
664	440896	292754944	25·7681975	8·7241414	664
665	442225	294079625	25·7875939	8·7285187	665
666	443556	295408296	25·8069758	8·7328918	666
667	444889	296740963	25·8263431	8·7372604	667
668	446224	298077632	25·8456960	8·7416246	668
669	447561	299418309	25·8650343	8·7459846	669
670	448900	300763000	25·8843582	8·7503401	670
671	450241	302111711	25·9036677	8·7546913	671
672	451584	303464448	25·9229628	8·7590383	672
673	452929	304821217	25·9422435	8·7633809	673
674	454276	306182024	25·9615100	8·7677192	674
675	455625	307546875	25·9807621	8·7720532	675
676	456976	308915776	26·0	8·7763830	676
677	458329	310288733	26·0192237	8·7807084	677
678	459684	311665752	26·0384331	8·7850296	678
679	461041	313046839	26·0576284	8·7893466	679
680	462400	314432000	26·0768096	8·7936593	680

Number.	Square.	Cube.	Square Root.	Cube Root.	Number.
681	463761	315821241	26·0959767	8·7979679	681
682	465124	317214568	26·1151297	8·8022721	682
683	466489	318611987	26·1342687	8·8065722	683
684	467856	320013504	26·1533937	8·8108681	684
685	469225	321419125	26·1725047	8·8151598	685
686	470596	322828856	26·1916017	8·8194474	686
687	471969	324242703	26·2106848	8·8237307	687
688	473344	325660672	26·2297541	8·8280099	688
689	474721	327082769	26·2488095	8·8322850	689
690	476100	328509000	26·2678511	8·8365559	690
691	477481	329939371	26·2868789	8·8408227	691
692	478864	331373887	26·3058929	8·8450854	692
693	480249	332812557	26·3248932	8·8493440	693
694	481636	334255384	26·3438797	8·8535985	694
695	483025	335702375	26·3628527	8·8578489	695
696	484416	337153536	26·3818119	8·8620952	696
697	485809	338608873	26·4007576	8·8663375	697
698	487204	340068392	26·4196896	8·8705757	698
699	488601	341532099	26·4386081	8·8748099	699
700	490000	343000000	26·4575131	8·8790400	700
701	491401	344472101	26·4764046	8·8832661	701
702	492804	345948408	26·4952826	8·8874882	702
703	494209	347428927	26·5141472	8·8917063	703
704	495616	348913664	26·5329983	8·8959204	704
705	497025	350402625	26·5518361	8·9001304	705
706	498436	351895816	26·5706605	8·9043366	706
707	499849	353393243	26·5894716	8·9085387	707
708	501264	354894912	26·6082694	8·9127369	708
709	502681	356400829	26·6270539	8·9169311	709
710	504100	357911000	26·6458252	8·9211214	710
711	505521	359425431	26·6645833	8·9253078	711
712	506944	360944128	26·6833281	8·9294902	712
713	508369	362467097	26·7020598	8·9336687	713
714	509796	363994344	26·7207784	8·9378433	714
715	511225	365525875	26·7394839	8·9420140	715
716	512656	367061696	26·7581763	8·9461809	716
717	514089	368601813	26·7768557	8·9503438	717
718	515524	370146232	26·7955220	8·9545029	718
719	516961	371694959	26·8141754	8·9586581	719
720	518400	373248000	26·8328157	8·9628095	720

Number.	Square.	Cube.	Square Root.	Cube Root.	Number.
721	519841	374805361	26·8514432	8·9669570	721
722	521284	376367048	26·8700577	8·9711007	722
723	522729	377933067	26·8886593	8·9752406	723
724	524176	379503424	26·9072481	8·9793766	724
725	525625	381078125	26·9258240	8·9835089	725
726	527076	382657176	26·9443872	8·9876373	726
727	528529	384240583	26·9629375	8·9917620	727
728	529984	385828352	26·9814751	8·9958829	728
729	531441	387420489	27·0	9·0	729
730	532900	389017000	27·0185122	9·0041134	730
731	534361	390617891	27·0370117	9·0082229	731
732	535824	392223168	27·0554985	9·0123288	732
733	537289	393832837	27·0739727	9·0164309	733
734	538756	395446904	27·0924344	9·0205293	734
735	540225	397065375	27·1108834	9·0246239	735
736	541696	398688256	27·1293199	9·0287149	736
737	543169	400315553	27·1477439	9·0328021	737
738	544644	401947272	27·1661554	9·0368857	738
739	546121	403583419	27·1845544	9·0409655	739
740	547600	405224000	27·2029410	9·0450417	740
741	549081	406869021	27·2213152	9·0491142	741
742	550564	408518488	27·2396769	9·0531831	742
743	552049	410172407	27·2580263	9·0572482	743
744	553536	411830784	27·2763634	9·0613098	744
745	555025	413493625	27·2946881	9·0653677	745
746	556516	415160936	27·3130006	9·0694220	746
747	558009	416832723	27·3313007	9·0734726	747
748	559504	418508992	27·3495887	9·0775197	748
749	561001	420189749	27·3678644	9·0815631	749
750	562500	421875000	27·3861279	9·0856030	750
751	564001	423564751	27·4043792	9·0896392	751
752	565504	425259008	27·4226184	9·0936719	752
753	567009	426957777	27·4408455	9·0977010	753
754	568516	428661064	27·4590604	9·1017265	754
755	570025	430368875	27·4772633	9·1057485	755
756	571536	432081216	27·4954542	9·1097669	756
757	573049	433798093	27·5136330	9·1137818	757
758	574564	435519512	27·5317998	9·1177931	758
759	576081	437245479	27·5499546	9·1218010	759
760	577600	438976000	27·5680975	9·1258053	760

Number.	Square.	Cube.	Square Root.	Cube Root.	Number.
761	579121	440711081	27·5862284	9·1298061	761
762	580644	442450728	27·6043475	9·1338034	762
763	582169	444194947	27·6224546	9·1377971	763
764	583696	445943744	27·6405499	9·1417874	764
765	585225	447697125	27·6586334	9·1457742	765
766	586756	449455096	27·6767050	9·1497576	766
767	588289	451217663	27·6947648	9·1537375	767
768	589824	452984832	27·7128129	9·1577139	768
769	591361	454756609	27·7308492	9·1616869	769
770	592900	456533000	27·7488730	9·1656565	770
771	594441	458314011	27·7668868	9·1696225	771
772	595984	460099648	27·7848880	9·1735852	772
773	597529	461889917	27·8028775	9·1775445	773
774	599076	463684824	27·8208555	9·1815003	774
775	600625	465484375	27·8388218	9·1854527	775
776	602176	467288576	27·8567766	9·1894018	776
777	603729	469097433	27·8747197	9·1933474	777
778	605284	470910952	27·8926514	9·1972897	778
779	606841	472729139	27·9105715	9·2012286	779
780	608400	474552000	27·9284801	9·2051641	780
781	609961	476379541	27·9463772	9·2090962	781
782	611524	478211768	27·9642629	9·2130250	782
783	613089	480048687	27·9821372	9·2169505	783
784	614656	481890304	28·0	9·2208726	784
785	616225	483736625	28·0178515	9·2247914	785
786	617796	485587656	28·0356915	9·2287068	786
787	619369	487443403	28·0535203	9·2326189	787
788	620944	489303872	28·0713377	9·2365277	788
789	622521	491169069	28·0891438	9·2404333	789
790	624100	493039000	28·1069386	9·2443355	790
791	625681	494913671	28·1247222	9·2482344	791
792	627264	496793088	28·1424946	9·2521300	792
793	628849	498677257	28·1602557	9·2560224	793
794	630436	500566184	28·1780056	9·2599114	794
795	632025	502459875	28·1957444	9·2637973	795
796	633616	504358336	28·2134720	9·2676798	796
797	635209	506261573	28·2311884	9·2715592	797
798	636804	508169592	28·2488938	9·2754352	798
799	638401	510082399	28·2665881	9·2793081	799
800	640000	512000000	28·2842712	9·2831777	800

Number.	Square.	Cube.	Square Root.	Cube Root.	Number.
801	641601	513922401	28·3019434	9·2870440	801
802	643204	515849608	28·3196045	9·2909072	802
803	644809	517781627	28·3372546	9·2947671	803
804	646416	519718464	28·3548938	9·2986239	804
805	648025	521660125	28·3725219	9·3024775	805
806	649636	523606616	28·3901391	9·3063278	806
807	651249	525557943	28·4077454	9·3101750	807
808	652864	527514112	28·4253408	9·3140190	808
809	654481	529475129	28·4429253	9·3178599	809
810	656100	531441000	28·4604989	9·3216975	810
811	657721	533411731	28·4780617	9·3255320	811
812	659344	535387328	28·4956137	9·3293634	812
813	660969	537367797	28·5131549	9·3331916	813
814	662596	539353144	28·5306852	9·3370167	814
815	664225	541343375	28·5482048	9·3408386	815
816	665856	543338496	28·5657137	9·3446575	816
817	667489	545338513	28·5832119	9·3484731	817
818	669124	547343432	28·6006993	9·3522857	818
819	670761	549353259	28·6181760	9·3560952	819
820	672400	551368000	28·6356421	9·3599016	820
821	674041	553387661	28·6530976	9·3637049	821
822	675684	555412248	28·6705424	9·3675051	822
823	677329	557441767	28·6879766	9·3713022	823
824	678976	559476224	28·7054002	9·3750963	824
825	680625	561515625	28·7228132	9·3788873	825
826	682276	563559976	28·7402157	9·3826752	826
827	683929	565609283	28·7576077	9·3864600	827
828	685584	567663552	28·7749891	9·3902419	828
829	687241	569722789	28·7923601	9·3940206	829
830	688900	571787000	28·8097206	9·3977964	830
831	690561	573856191	28·8270706	9·4015691	831
832	692224	575930368	28·8444102	9·4053387	832
833	693889	578009537	28·8617394	9·4091054	833
834	695556	580093704	28·8790582	9·4128690	834
835	697225	582182875	28·8963666	9·4166297	835
836	698896	584277056	28·9136646	9·4203873	836
837	700569	586376253	28·9309523	9·4241420	837
838	702244	588480472	28·9482297	9·4278936	838
839	703921	590589719	28·9654967	9·4316423	839
840	705600	592704000	28·9827535	9·4353880	840

8*

Number.	Square.	Cube.	Square Root.	Cube Root.	Number.
841	707281	594823321	29·0	9·4391307	841
842	708964	596947688	29·0172363	9·4428704	842
843	710649	599077107	29·0344623	9·4466072	843
844	712336	601211584	29·0516781	9·4503410	844
845	714025	603351125	29·0688837	9·4540719	845
846	715716	605495736	29·0860791	9·4577999	846
847	717409	607645423	29·1032644	9·4615249	847
848	719104	609800192	29·1204396	9·4652470	848
849	720801	611960049	29·1376046	9·4689661	849
850	722500	614125000	29·1547595	9·4726824	850
851	724201	616295051	29·1719043	9·4763957	851
852	725904	618470208	29·1890390	9·4801061	852
853	727609	620650477	29·2061637	9·4838136	853
854	729316	622835864	29·2232784	9·4875182	854
855	731025	625026375	29·2403830	9·4912200	855
856	732736	627222016	29·2574777	9·4949188	856
857	734449	629422793	29·2745623	9·4986147	857
858	736164	631628712	29·2916370	9·5023078	858
859	737881	633839779	29·3087018	9·5059980	859
860	739600	636056000	29·3257566	9·5096854	860
861	741321	638277381	29·3428015	9·5133699	861
862	743044	640503928	29·3598365	9·5170515	862
863	744769	642735647	29·3768616	9·5207303	863
864	746496	644972544	29·3938769	9·5244063	864
865	748225	647214625	29·4108823	9·5280794	865
866	749956	649461896	29·4278779	9·5317497	866
867	751689	651714363	29·4448637	9·5354172	867
868	753424	653972032	29·4618397	9·5390818	868
869	755161	656234909	29·4788059	9·5427437	869
870	756900	658503000	29·4957624	9·5464027	870
871	758641	660776311	29·5127091	9·5500589	871
872	760384	663054848	29·5296461	9·5537123	872
873	762129	665338617	29·5465734	9·5573630	873
874	763876	667627624	29·5634910	9·5610108	874
875	765625	669921875	29·5803989	9·5646559	875
876	767376	672221376	29·5972972	9·5682982	876
877	769129	674526133	29·6141858	9·5719377	877
878	770884	676836152	29·6310648	9·5755745	878
879	772641	679151439	29·6479342	9·5792085	879
880	774400	681472000	29·6647939	9·5828397	880

Number.	Square.	Cube.	Square Root.	Cube Root.	Number.
881	776161	683797841	29·6816442	9·5864682	881
882	777924	686128968	29·6984848	9·5900939	882
883	779689	688465387	29·7153159	9·5937169	883
884	781456	690807104	29·7321375	9·5973373	884
885	783225	693154125	29·7489498	9·6009548	885
886	784996	695506456	29·7657521	9·6045696	886
887	786769	697864103	29·7825452	9·6081817	887
888	788544	700227072	29·7993289	9·6117911	888
889	790321	702595369	29·8161030	9·6153977	889
890	792100	704969000	29·8328676	9·6190017	890
891	793881	707347971	29·8496231	9·6226030	891
892	795664	709732288	29·8663690	9·6262016	892
893	797449	712121957	29·8831056	9·6297975	893
894	799236	714516984	29·8998328	9·6333907	894
895	801025	716917375	29·9165506	9·6369812	895
896	802816	719323136	29·9332591	9·6405690	896
897	804609	721734273	29·9499583	9·6441542	897
898	806404	724150792	29·9666481	9·6477367	898
899	808201	726572699	29·9833287	9·6513166	899
900	810000	729000000	30·0	9·6548938	900
901	811801	731432701	30·0166620	9·6584684	901
902	813604	733870808	30·0333148	9·6620403	902
903	815409	736314327	30·0499584	9·6656096	903
904	817216	738763264	30·0665928	9·6691762	904
905	819025	741217625	30·0832179	9·6727403	905
906	820836	743677416	30·0998339	9·6763017	906
907	822649	746142643	30·1164407	9·6798604	907
908	824464	748613312	30·1330383	9·6834166	908
909	826281	751089429	30·1496269	9·6869701	909
910	828100	753571000	30·1662063	9·6905211	910
911	829921	756058031	30·1827765	9·6940694	911
912	831744	758550528	30·1993377	9·6976151	912
913	833569	761048497	30·2158899	9·7011583	913
914	835396	763551944	30·2324329	9·7046989	914
915	837225	766060875	30·2489669	9·7082369	915
916	839056	768575296	30·2654919	9·7117723	916
917	840889	771095213	30·2820079	9·7153051	917
918	842724	773620632	30·2985148	9·7188354	918
919	844561	776151559	30·3150128	9·7223631	919
920	846400	778688000	30·3315018	9·7258883	920

Number.	Square.	Cube.	Square Root.	Cube Root.	Number.
921	848241	781229961	30·3479818	9·7294109	921
922	850084	783777448	30·3644529	9·7329309	922
923	851929	786330467	30·3809151	9·7364484	923
924	853776	788889024	30·3973683	9·7399634	924
925	855625	791453125	30·4138127	9·7434758	925
926	857476	794022776	30·4302481	9·7469857	926
927	859329	796597983	30·4466747	9·7504930	927
928	861184	799178752	30·4630924	9·7539979	928
929	863041	801765089	30·4795013	9·7575002	929
930	864900	804357000	30·4959014	9·7610001	930
931	866761	806954491	30·5122926	9·7644974	931
932	868624	809557568	30·5286750	9·7679922	932
933	870489	812166237	30·5450487	9·7714845	933
934	872356	814780504	30·5614136	9·7749743	934
935	874225	817400375	30·5777697	9·7784616	935
936	876096	820025856	30·5941171	9·7819466	936
937	877969	822656953	30·6104557	9·7854288	937
938	879844	825293672	30·6267857	9·7889087	938
939	881721	827936019	30·6431069	9·7923861	939
940	883600	830584000	30·6594194	9·7958611	940
941	885481	833237621	30·6757233	9·7993336	941
942	887364	835896888	30·6920185	9·8028036	942
943	889249	838561807	30·7083051	9·8062711	943
944	891136	841232384	30·7245830	9·8097362	944
945	893025	843908625	30·7408523	9·8131989	945
946	894916	846590536	30·7571130	9·8166591	946
947	896809	849278123	30·7733651	9·8201169	947
948	898704	851971392	30·7896086	9·8235723	948
949	900601	854670349	30·8058436	9·8270252	949
950	902500	857375000	30·8220700	9·8304757	950
951	904401	860085351	30·8382879	9·8339238	951
952	906304	862801408	30·8544972	9·8373695	952
953	908209	865523177	30·8706981	9·8408127	953
954	910116	868250664	30·8868904	9·8442536	954
955	912025	870983875	30·9030743	9·8476920	955
956	913936	873722816	30·9192497	9·8511280	956
957	915849	876467493	30·9354166	9·8545617	957
958	917764	879217912	30·9515751	9·8579929	958
959	919681	881974079	30·9677251	9·8614218	959
960	921600	884736000	30·9838668	9·8648483	960

Number.	Square.	Cube.	Square Root.	Cube Root.	Number.
961	923521	887503681	31·0	9·8682724	961
962	925444	890277128	31·0161248	9·8716941	962
963	927369	893056347	31·0322413	9·8751135	963
964	929296	895841344	31·0483494	9·8785305	964
965	931225	898632125	31·0644491	9·8819451	965
966	933156	901428696	31·0805405	9·8853574	966
967	935089	904231063	31·0966236	9·8887673	967
968	937024	907039232	31·1126984	9·8921749	968
969	938961	909853209	31·1287648	9·8955801	969
970	940900	912673000	31·1448230	9·8989830	970
971	942841	915498611	31·1608729	9·9023835	971
972	944784	918330048	31·1769145	9·9057817	972
973	946729	921167317	31·1929479	9·9091776	973
974	948676	924010424	31·2089731	9·9125712	974
975	950625	926859375	31·2249900	9·9159624	975
976	952576	929714176	31·2409987	9·9193513	976
977	954529	932574833	31·2569992	9·9227379	977
978	956484	935441352	31·2729915	9·9261222	978
979	958441	938313739	31·2889757	9·9295042	979
980	960400	941192000	31·3049517	9·9328839	980
981	962361	944076141	31·3209195	9·9362613	981
982	964324	946966168	31·3368792	9·9396363	982
983	966289	949862087	31·3528308	9·9430092	983
984	968256	952763904	31·3687743	9·9463797	984
985	970225	955671625	31·3847097	9·9497479	985
986	972196	958585256	31·4006369	9·9531138	986
987	974169	961504803	31·4165561	9·9564775	987
988	976144	964430272	31·4324673	9·9598389	988
989	978121	967361669	31·4483704	9·9631981	989
990	980100	970299000	31·4642654	9·9665549	990
991	982081	973242271	31·4801525	9·9699095	991
992	984064	976191488	31·4960315	9·9732619	992
993	986049	979146657	31·5119025	9·9766130	993
994	988036	982107784	31·5277655	9·9799599	994
995	990025	985074875	31·5436206	9·9833055	995
996	992016	988047936	31·5594677	9·9866488	996
997	994009	991026973	31·5753068	9·9899900	997
998	996004	994011992	31·5911380	9·9933289	998
999	998001	997002999	31·6069613	9·9966656	999
1000	1000000	1000000000	31·6227766	10·0	1000

Number.	Square.	Cube.	Square Root.	Cube Root.	Number.
1001	1002001	1003003001	31·6385840	10·0033322	1001
1002	1004004	1006012008	31·6543836	10·0066622	1002
1003	1006009	1009027027	31·6701752	10·0099899	1003
1004	1008016	1012048064	31·6859590	10·0133155	1004
1005	1010025	1015075125	31·7017349	10·0166389	1005
1006	1012036	1018108216	31·7175030	10·0199601	1006
1007	1014049	1021147343	31·7332633	10·0232791	1007
1008	1016064	1024192512	31·7490157	10·0265958	1008
1009	1018081	1027243729	31·7647603	10·0299104	1009
1010	1020100	1030301000	31·7804972	10·0332228	1010
1011	1022121	1033364331	31·7962262	10·0365330	1011
1012	1024144	1036433728	31·8119474	10·0398410	1012
1013	1026169	1039509197	31·8276609	10·0431469	1013
1014	1028196	1042590744	31·8433666	10·0464506	1014
1015	1030225	1045678375	31·8590646	10·0497521	1015
1016	1032256	1048772096	31·8747549	10·0530514	1016
1017	1034289	1051871913	31·8904374	10·0563485	1017
1018	1036324	1054977832	31·9061123	10·0596435	1018
1019	1038361	1058089859	31·9217794	10·0629364	1019
1020	1040400	1061208000	31·9374388	10·0662271	1020
1021	1042441	1064332261	31·9530906	10·0695156	1021
1022	1044484	1067462648	31·9687347	10·0728030	1022
1023	1046529	1070599167	31·9843712	10·0760863	1023
1024	1048576	1073741824	32·0000000	10·0793684	1024
1025	1050625	1076890625	32·0156212	10·0826484	1025
1026	1052676	1080045576	32·0312348	10·0859262	1026
1027	1054729	1083206683	32·0468407	10·0892019	1027
1028	1056784	1086373952	32·0624391	10·0924755	1028
1029	1058841	1089547389	32·0780298	10·0957469	1029
1030	1060900	1092727000	32·0936131	10·0990163	1030
1031	1062961	1095912791	32·1091887	10·1022835	1031
1032	1065024	1099104768	32·1247568	10·1055487	1032
1033	1067089	1102302937	32·1403173	10·1088117	1033
1034	1069156	1105507304	32·1558704	10·1120726	1034
1035	1071225	1108717575	32·1714159	10·1153314	1035
1036	1073296	1111934656	32·1869539	10·1185882	1036
1037	1075369	1115157653	32·2024844	10·1218428	1037
1038	1077444	1118386872	32·2180074	10·1250953	1038
1039	1079521	1121622319	32·2335229	10·1283457	1039
1040	1081600	1124864000	32·2490310	10·1315941	1040

Number.	Square.	Cube.	Square Root.	Cube Root.	Number.
1041	1083681	1128111921	32·2645316	10·1348403	1041
1042	1085764	1131366088	32·2800248	10·1380845	1042
1043	1087849	1134626507	32·2955105	10·1413266	1043
1044	1089936	1137893184	32·3109888	10·1445667	1044
1045	1092025	1141166125	32·3264598	10·1478047	1045
1046	1094116	1144445336	32·3419233	10·1510406	1046
1047	1096209	1147730823	32·3573794	10·1542744	1047
1048	1098304	1151022592	32·3728281	10·1575062	1048
1049	1100401	1154320649	32·3882695	10·1607359	1049
1050	1102500	1157625000	32·4037035	10·1639636	1050
1051	1104601	1160935651	32·4191301	10·1671893	1051
1052	1106704	1164252608	32·4345495	10·1704129	1052
1053	1108809	1167575877	32·4499615	10·1736344	1053
1054	1110916	1170905464	32·4653662	10·1768539	1054
1055	1113025	1174241375	32·4807635	10·1800714	1055
1056	1115136	1177583616	32·4961536	10·1832868	1056
1057	1117249	1180932193	32·5115364	10·1865002	1057
1058	1119364	1184287112	32·5269119	10·1897116	1058
1059	1121481	1187648379	32·5422802	10·1929209	1059
1060	1123600	1191016000	32·5576412	10·1961283	1060
1061	1125721	1194389981	32·2729949	10·1993336	1061
1062	1127844	1197770328	32·5883415	10·2025369	1062
1063	1129969	1201159047	32·6036807	10·2057382	1063
1064	1132096	1204550144	32·6190129	10·2089375	1064
1065	1134225	1207949625	32·6343377	10·2121347	1065
1066	1136356	1211355496	32·6496554	10·2153300	1066
1067	1138489	1214767763	32·6649659	10·2185233	1067
1068	1140624	1218186432	32·6803693	10·2217146	1068
1069	1142761	1221611509	32·6955654	10·2249039	1069
1070	1144900	1225043000	32·7108544	10·2280912	1070
1071	1147041	1228480911	32·7261363	10·2312766	1071
1072	1149184	1231925248	32·7414111	10·2344599	1072
1073	1151329	1235376017	32·7566787	10·2376413	1073
1074	1153476	1238833224	32·7719392	10·2408207	1074
1075	1155625	1242296875	32·7871926	10·2439981	1075
1076	1157776	1245766976	32·8024389	10·2471735	1076
1077	1159929	1249243533	32·8176782	10·2503470	1077
1078	1162084	1252726552	32·8329103	10·2535186	1078
1079	1164241	1256216039	32·8481354	10·2566881	1079
1080	1166400	1259712000	32·8633535	10·2598557	1080

Number.	Square.	Cube.	Square Root.	Cube Root.	Number.
1081	1168561	1263214441	32·8785644	10·2630213	1081
1082	1170724	1266723368	32·8937684	10·2661850	1082
1083	1172889	1270238787	32·9089653	10·2693467	1083
1084	1175056	1273760704	32·9241553	10·2725065	1084
1085	1177225	1277289125	32·9393382	10·2756644	1085
1086	1179396	1280824056	32·9545141	10·2788203	1086
1087	1181569	1284365503	32·9696830	10·2819743	1087
1088	1183744	1287913472	32·9848450	10·2851264	1088
1089	1185921	1291467969	33·0000000	10·2882765	1089
1090	1188100	1295029000	33·0151480	10·2914247	1090
1091	1190281	1298596571	33·0302891	10·2945709	1091
1092	1192464	1302170688	33·0454233	10·2977153	1092
1093	1194649	1305751357	33·0605505	10·3008577	1093
1094	1196836	1309338584	33·0756708	10·3039982	1094
1095	1199025	1312932375	33·0907842	10·3071368	1095
1096	1201216	1316532736	33·1058907	10·3102735	1096
1097	1203409	1320139673	33·1209903	10·3134083	1097
1098	1205604	1323753192	33·1360830	10·3165411	1098
1099	1207801	1327373299	33·1511689	10·3196721	1099
1100	1210000	1331000000	33·1662479	10·3228012	1100
1101	1212201	1334633301	33·1813200	10·3259284	1101
1102	1214404	1338273208	33·1963853	10·3290537	1102
1103	1216609	1341919727	33·2114438	10·3321770	1103
1104	1218816	1345572864	33·2264955	10·3352985	1104
1105	1221025	1349232625	33·2415403	10·3384181	1105
1106	1223236	1352899016	33·2565783	10·3415358	1106
1107	1225449	1356572043	33·2716095	10·3446517	1107
1108	1227664	1360251712	33·2866339	10·3477657	1108
1109	1229881	1363938029	33·3016516	10·3508778	1109
1110	1232100	1367631000	33·3166625	10·3539890	1110
1111	1234321	1371330631	33·3316666	10·3570964	1111
1112	1236544	1375036928	33·3466640	10·3602029	1112
1113	1238769	1378749897	33·3616546	10·3633076	1113
1114	1240996	1382469544	33·3766385	10·3664103	1114
1115	1243225	1386195875	33·3916157	10·3695113	1115
1116	1245456	1389928896	33·4065862	10·3726103	1116
1117	1247689	1393668613	33·4215499	10·3757076	1117
1118	1249924	1397415032	33·4365070	10·3788030	1118
1119	1252161	1401168159	33·4514573	10·3818965	1119
1120	1254400	1404928000	33·4664011	10·3849882	1120

Number.	Square.	Cube.	Square Root.	Cube Root.	Number.
1121	1256641	1408694561	33·4813381	10·3880781	1121
1122	1258884	1412467848	33·4962684	10·3911661	1122
1123	1261129	1416247867	33·5111921	10·3942523	1123
1124	1263376	1420034624	33·5261092	10·3973366	1124
1125	1265625	1423828125	33·5410196	10·4004192	1125
1126	1267876	1427628376	33·5559234	10·4034999	1126
1127	1270129	1431435383	33·5708206	10·4065787	1127
1128	1272384	1435249152	33·5857112	10·4096557	1128
1129	1274641	1439069689	33·6005952	10·4127310	1129
1130	1276900	1442897000	33·6154626	10·4158044	1130
1131	1279161	1446731091	33·6303434	10·4188760	1131
1132	1281424	1450571968	33·6452077	10·4219458	1132
1133	1283689	1454419637	33·6600653	10·4250138	1133
1134	1285956	1458274104	33·6749165	10·4280800	1134
1135	1288225	1462135375	33·6897610	10·4311448	1135
1136	1290496	1466003456	33·7045991	10·4342069	1136
1137	1292769	1469878353	33·7194306	10·4372677	1137
1138	1295044	1473760072	33·7342556	10·4403267	1138
1139	1297321	1477648619	33·7490741	10·4433839	1139
1140	1299600	1481544000	33·7638860	10·4464393	1140
1141	1301881	1485446221	33·7786915	10·4494929	1141
1142	1304164	1489355288	33·7934905	10·4525448	1142
1143	1306449	1493271207	33·8082830	10·4555948	1143
1144	1308736	1497193984	33·8230691	10·4586431	1144
1145	1311025	1501123625	33·8378486	10·4616896	1145
1146	1313316	1505060136	33·8526218	10·4647343	1146
1147	1315609	1509003523	33·8673884	10·4677773	1147
1148	1317904	1512953792	33·8821487	10·4708185	1148
1149	1320201	1516910949	33·8969025	10·4738579	1149
1150	1322500	1520875000	33·9116499	10·4768955	1150
1151	1324801	1524845951	33·9263909	10·4799314	1151
1152	1327104	1528823808	33·9411255	10·4829656	1152
1153	1329409	1532808577	33·9558537	10·4859980	1153
1154	1331716	1536800264	33·9705755	10·4890286	1154
1155	1334025	1540798875	33·9852910	10·4920575	1155
1156	1336336	1544804416	34·0000000	10·4950847	1156
1157	1338649	1548816893	34·0147027	10·4981101	1157
1158	1340964	1552836312	34·0293990	10·5011331	1158
1159	1343281	1556862679	34·0440890	10·5041556	1159
1160	1345600	1560896000	34·0587727	10·5071757	1160

Number.	Square.	Cube.	Square Root.	Cube Root.	Number.
1161	1347921	1564936281	34·0734501	10·5101942	1161
1162	1350244	1568983528	34·0881211	10·5132109	1162
1163	1352569	1573037747	34·1027858	10·5162259	1163
1164	1354896	1577098944	34·1174442	10·5192391	1164
1165	1357225	1581167125	34·1320963	10·5222506	1165
1166	1359556	1585242296	34·1467422	10·5252604	1166
1167	1361889	1589324463	34·1613817	10·5282685	1167
1168	1364224	1593413632	34·1760150	10·5312749	1168
1169	1366561	1597509809	34·1906420	10·5342795	1169
1170	1368900	1601613000	34·2052627	10·5372825	1170
1171	1371241	1605723211	34·2198773	10·5402837	1171
1172	1373584	1609840448	34·2344855	10·5432832	1172
1173	1375929	1613964717	34·2490875	10·5462810	1173
1174	1378276	1618096024	34·2636834	10·5492771	1174
1175	1380625	1622234375	34·2782730	10·5522715	1175
1176	1382976	1626379776	34·2928564	10·5552642	1176
1177	1385329	1630532233	34·3074336	10·5582552	1177
1178	1387684	1634691752	34·3220046	10·5612445	1178
1179	1390041	1638858339	34·3365694	10·5642322	1179
1180	1392400	1643032000	34·3511281	10·5672181	1180
1181	1394761	1647212741	34·3656805	10·5702024	1181
1182	1397124	1651400568	34·3802268	10·5731849	1182
1183	1399489	1655595487	34·3947670	10·5761658	1183
1184	1401856	1659797504	34·4093011	10·5791449	1184
1185	1404225	1664006625	34·4238289	10·5821225	1185
1186	1406596	1668222856	34·4383507	10·5850983	1186
1187	1408969	1672446203	34·4528663	10·5880725	1187
1188	1411344	1676676672	34·4673759	10·5910450	1188
1189	1413721	1680914269	34·4818793	10·5940158	1189
1190	1416100	1685159000	34·4963766	10·5999850	1190
1191	1418481	1689410871	34·5108678	10·5999525	1191
1192	1420864	1693669888	34·5253530	10·6029184	1192
1193	1423249	1697936057	34·5398321	10·6058826	1193
1194	1425636	1702209384	34·5543051	10·6088451	1194
1195	1428025	1706489875	34·5687720	10·6118060	1195
1196	1430416	1710777536	34·5832329	10·6147952	1196
1197	1432809	1715072373	34·5976879	10·6177228	1197
1198	1435204	1717374392	34·6121366	10·6206788	1198
1199	1437601	1723683599	34·6265794	10·6236331	1199
1200	1440000	1728000000	34·6410162	10·6265857	1200

To find the square of a greater number than is contained in the table.

RULE 1.—If the number required to be squared exceed, by 2, 3, 4, or any other number of times, any number contained in the table, let the square affixed to the number in the table be multiplied by the square of 2, 3, or 4, &c., and the product will be the answer sought.

EXAMPLE.—Required the square of 2595.

2595 is three times greater than 865; and the square of 865, as per table, is 748225.

Then, $748225 \times 3^2 = 6734025$, Ans.

RULE 2.—If the number required to be squared be an odd number, and do not exceed twice the amount of any number contained in the table, find the two numbers nearest to each other, which, added together, make that sum; then, the sum of the squares of these two numbers, as per table, multiplied by 2, will exceed the square required by 1.

EXAMPLE.—Required the square of 1865.

The two nearest numbers $(932 + 933) = 1865$.

Then, per table $(932^2 = 868624) + (933^2 = 870489) = 1739113 \times 2 = 3478226 - 1 = 3478225$, Ans.

To find the cube of a greater number than is contained in the table.

RULE.—Proceed, as in squares, to find how many times the number required to be cubed exceeds the number contained in the table. Multiply the cube of that nnmber by the cube of as many times as the number sought exceeds the number in the table, and the product will be the answer required.

EXAMPLE.—Required the cube of 3984.

3984 is 4 times greater than 996; and the cube of 996, as per table, is 988047936.

Then $988047936 \times 4^3 = 63235067904$, Ans.

To find the square or cube root of a higher number than is in the table.

RULE.—Refer to the table, and seek in the column of squares or cubes, the number nearest to that number whose root is sought, and the number from which that square or cube is derived will be the answer required, when decimals are not of importance.

EXAMPLE.—Required the square root of 542869.

In the table of squares, the nearest number is 543169; and the number from which that square has been obtained is 737.

Therefore, $\sqrt{542869} = 737$ nearly, Ans.

To find more nearly the cube root of a higher number than is in the table.

RULE.—Ascertain, by the table, the nearest cube number to the number given, and call it the assumed cube.

Multiply the assumed cube and the given number,

respectively, by 2; to the product of the assumed cube add the given number, and to the product of the given number add the assumed cube.

Then, by proportion, as the sum of the assumed cube is to the sum of the given number, so is the root of the assumed cube to the root of the given number.

EXAMPLE.—Required the cube root of 412568555.

Per table, the nearest number is 411830784; and its cube root is 744.

Therefore, 411830784 × 2 + 412568555 = 1236230123.

And, 412568555 ×2+ 411830784 = 1236967894.

Hence, as 1236230123 : 1236967894 :: 744 : 744·369, very nearly, Ans.

To find the square or cube root of a number containing decimals.

Subtract the square root or cube root of the *integer* of the given number from the root of the next higher number, and multiply the difference by the decimal part. The product, added to the root of the integer of the given number, will be the answer required.

EXAMPLE.—Required the square root of 321·62.

$\sqrt{}$ 321 = 17·9164729, and $\sqrt{}$ 322 = 17·9443584; the difference (·0278855) × ·62 + 17·9164729 = 17·9337619, Ans.

THE CONIC SECTIONS.

The plane figures formed by the cutting of a cone by a plane, are five in number, viz: The Triangle, the Circle, the Ellipse, the Hyperbola, and the Parabola. The methods of finding their linear and superficial admeasurement have been already described; the several directions in which the section of the cone is to be made, in order to produce them, are as follows:—

The *Triangle* is formed by cutting the cone through the vertex and any part of the base.

The *Circle*, by cutting the cone through the sides, parallel to the base.

The *Ellipse*, by a cut passing obliquely, or at an angle with the base, through both sides of the cone.

The *Hyperbola*, by cutting through one side and the base parallel to the axis, or at a *greater* angle with the base than that made by the opposite side.

The *opposite Hyperbola* is formed by continuing the cutting plane through an opposite and equal cone, produced by continuing the sides of the first cone through its vertex.

The *Parabola*, by cutting through one side and the base of the cone in a direction *parallel* to the opposite side, or making an *equal* angle with the base.

The Ellipse has two vertices, being the points in the curve at the extremities of the longest diameter; the Hyperbola has one vertex, or, rather, the opposite Hyperbolas one each; the Parabola has one only.

The Transverse Axis is the line uniting the two vertices.

The Conjugate Axis is a line drawn through the *centre* of the transverse axis, and at right angles to it.

A Diameter is a right line drawn through the centre, in any direction, and terminated at each end by the curve.

A Conjugate Diameter is a line drawn through the centre of any diameter, parallel to the tangent of the curve at the extremity of such diameter.

An Ordinate to a Diameter is a line between the diameter and the curve, parallel to its conjugate.

The part of the diameter cut off by an ordinate and terminated by its vertex, is called the Abscissa.

The Parameter, or *latus rectum*, is a line drawn through the focus, at right angles to the transverse axis, and terminated by the curve. The parameter of a diameter, in the ellipse and hyperbola, is a third proportional to the diameter and its conjugate; in the parabola, it is a third proportional to one abscissa and its ordinate.

The Focus is that point in the transverse axis where the ordinate is equal to half the parameter.

By the foregoing proportions, therefore, the focus of either curve may be found.

The Ellipse has two foci; as have likewise the opposite Hyperbolas; but the Parabola has one only. The Ellipse has its several parts lying within the circumference of the curve; the axis and centre of the Hyperbola lie on the outside, in consequence of the axis being drawn between the vertices of the two opposite Hyperbolas. The axis of the Parabola is of infinite length, because the axis can only touch one point or vertex in the curve.

MENSURATION OF SURFACES.

OF FOUR-SIDED FIGURES.

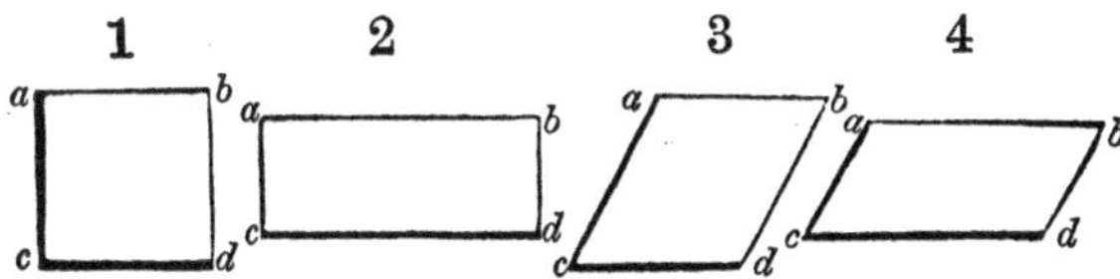

To find the area of a four-sided figure, whether it be a square, fig. 1, *a parallelogram, fig.* 2, *a rhombus, fig.* 3, *or a rhomboid, fig.* 4.

RULE.—Multiply the length, *a b*, or *c d*, by the breadth or *perpendicular* height; the product will be the area.

OF TRIANGLES.

Fig. 5. Fig. 6. Fig. 7.

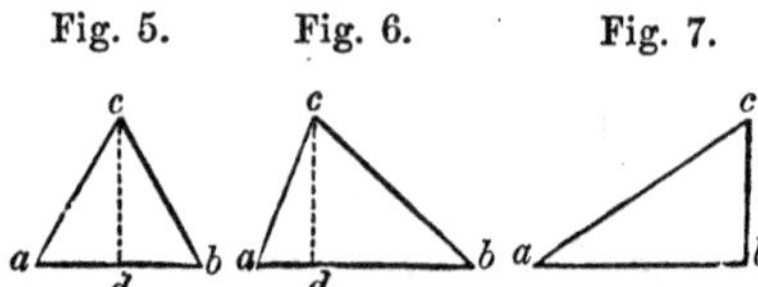

To find the area of a triangle, whether it be isosceles, fig. 5, *scalene, fig.* 6, *or right-angled, fig.* 7.

RULE.—Multiply the length, *a b*, of one of the sides, by the perpendicular, *c d*, falling upon it; half the product will be the area.

To find the length of one side of a right-angled triangle, when the lengths of the other two sides are given.

RULE 1.—*To find the hypothenuse, a c, fig.* 7, add together the squares of the two legs, *a b* and *b c*, and extract the square root of that sum.

RULE 2.—*To find one of the legs,* subtract the square of the leg, of which the length is known, from the square of the hypothenuse, and the square root of the difference will be the answer.

OF REGULAR POLYGONS.

To find the Area of a regular Polygon.

RULE.—Multiply the length of a perpendicular, drawn from the centre to one of the sides (or the radius of its inscribed circle) by the length of one side, and this product again by the number of sides; and half the product will be the area of the polygon.

[For a table of the areas of regular polygons, see pages 67, 68.]

OF TRAPEZIUMS AND TRAPEZOIDS.

Fig. 8. Fig. 9.

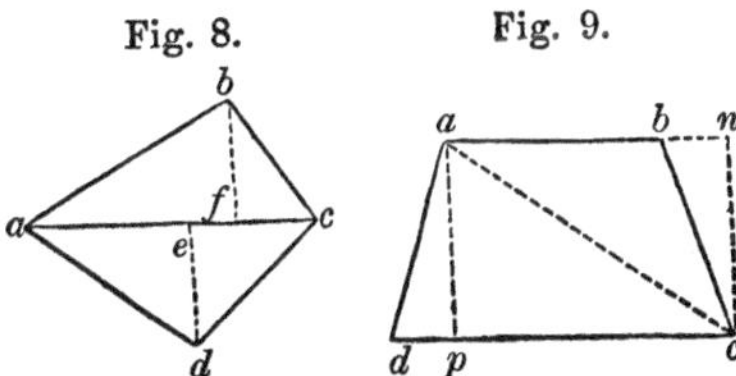

To find the Area of a Trapezium, fig. 8.

RULE 1.—Draw a diagonal line, *a c*, to divide the trapezium into two triangles; find the areas of these triangles separately, and add them together.

RULE 2.—Divide the trapezium into two triangles, by the diagonal *a c*, and let two perpendiculars, *b f*, and *d e*, fall on the diagonal from the opposite angles; then, the sum of these perpendiculars multiplied by the diagonal, and divided by 2, will be the area of the trapezium.

To find the Area of a Trapezoid, fig. 9.

RULE 1.—Multiply the sum of the two parallel sides, *a h*, *d c*, by *a p*, the perpendicular distance between them, and half the product will be the area.

RULE 2.—Draw a diagonal, *a c*, to divide the trapezoid into two triangles; find the areas of those triangles separately, and add them together.

OF IRREGULAR FIGURES.

Fig. 10. Fig. 11.

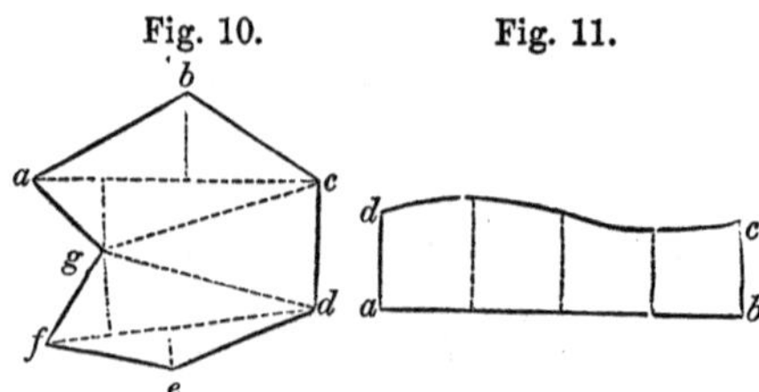

To find the Area of an Irregular Polygon, a b c d e f g, fig. 10.

RULE.—Draw diagonals to divide the figure into trapeziums and triangles; find the area of each separately, by either of the rules before given for that purpose; and the sum of the whole will be the area of the figure.

To find the Area of a Long Irregular Figure, d c a b, fig. 11.

RULE.—Take the breadth in several places, and at equal distances from each other; add all the breadths together, and divide the sum by this number, for the mean breadth; then multiply the mean breadth by the length of the figure, and the product will be the area.

OF CIRCLES.

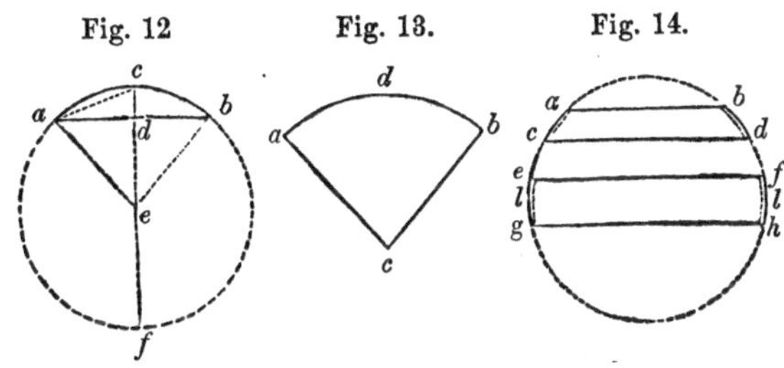

To find the Circumference of a Circle when the Diameter is given; or the Diameter when the Circumference is given.

RULE 1.—Multiply the diameter by 3·1416, and the product will be the circumference; or divide the circumference by 3·1416, and the quotient will be the diameter.

RULE 2.—As 7 is to 22, so is the diameter to the circumference. As 22 is to 7, so is the circumference to the diameter.

RULE 3 —As 113 is to 355, so is the diameter to the circumference. As 355 is to 113, so is the circumference to the diameter.

To find the Area of a Circle.

RULE 1.—Multiply the square of the diameter by ·7854; or the square of the circumference by

·07958; the product, in either case, will be the area.

Rule 2.—Multiply the circumference by the diameter, and divide the product by 4.

Rule 3.—As 14 is to 11, so is the square of the diameter to the area. Or, as 88 is to 7, so is the square of the circumference to the area.

To find the length of any Arc of a Circle.

Rule 1.—From 8 times the chord of half the arc, *a c*, *fig.* 12, subtract the chord, *a b*, of the whole arc; one-third of the remainder will be the length of the arc, nearly.

Rule 2.—

As 180 is to the number of degrees in the arc;
So is 3·1416 times the radius to its length.
Or, as 3 is to the number of degrees in the arc;
So is ·05236 times the radius its length.

To find the Area of a Sector of a Circle, fig. 13.

Rule 1.—Multiply the length of the arc, *a d b*, by half the length of the radius, *a c*; the product will be the area.

Rule 2.—As 360 degrees is to the number of degrees in the arc of the sector; so is the area of the circle to the area of the sector.

To find the Area of a Segment of a Circle, fig. 12.

Rule 1.—To the chord, *a b*, of the whole arc

add the chord, *a c*, of half the arc and one-third of it more. Then multiply the sum by the versed sine, or height of the segment *c d*, and four-tenths of the product will be the area of the segment.

Rule 2.—Divide the height, or versed sine, by the diameter of the circle, and find the quotient in the column of versed sines, at the end of Mensuration of Solids.

Then take out the corresponding area in the next column on the right-hand, and multiply it by the square of the diameter, for the answer.

To find the Area of a Circular Zone, fig. 14.

Rule 1.—*When the Zone is less than a Semicircle*, to the area of the trapezoid, *a b c d*, add the area of the circular segments, *a c* and *b d*; the sum is the area of the zone.

Rule 2.—*When the Zone is greater than a Semicircle*, to the area of the parallelogram, *e f g h*, add the area of the circular segments, *e k g* and *f l h*; the sum is the area of the zone.

To find the Area of a Circular Ring, or Space, included between two Concentric Circles.

Rule.—Find the areas of the two circles separately; then the difference between them will be the area of the ring.

OF ELLIPSES.

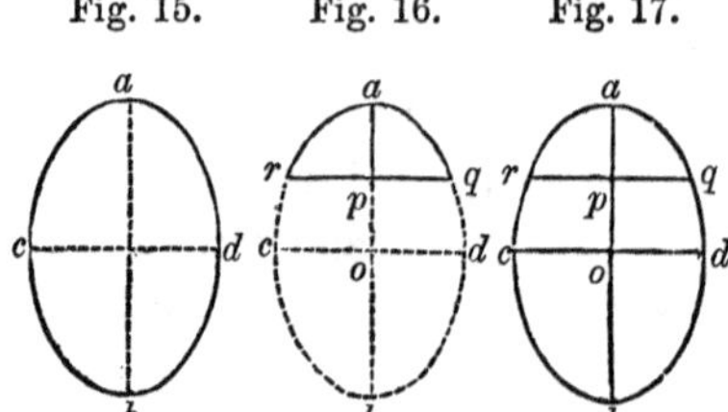

Fig. 15. Fig. 16. Fig. 17.

To find the Circumference of an Ellipse, fig. 15.

RULE.—Square the two axes, *a b* and *c d*, and multiply the square root of half that sum by 3·1416; the product will be the circumference nearly.

To find the Area of an Ellipse, fig. 15.

RULE.—Multiply the transverse diameter, *a b*, by the conjugate *c d*, and the product by ·7854.

To find the Area of an Elliptic Segment, fig. 16.

RULE.—Divide the height of the segment, *a p*, by the axis *a b*, of which it is a part, and find, in the table of circular segments at the end of Mensuration of Solids, a circular segment having the same versed sine as this quotient. Then, multiply the segment thus found and the two axes of the ellipse continually together, and the product will give the area required.

When the transverse, a b, *the conjugate,* c d, *and the abscissæ,* a p *and* p b, *are given, to find the ordinate,* p q, *fig.* 17.

RULE.—Multiply the abscissæ into each other, and extract the square root of the product; this will give the mean between them. Then, as the transverse diameter is to the conjugate diameter, so is the mean to the ordinate required.

When the transverse, a b, *the conjugate,* c d, *and the ordinate,* p q, *are given, to find the abscissa, fig.* 17.

RULE.—From the square of half the conjugate, take the square of the ordinate, and extract the square root of the remainder.

Then, as the conjugate diameter is to the transverse, so is that square root to half the difference of the two abscissæ.

Add this half difference to half the transverse, for the greater abscissa; and subtract it for the less.

When the transverse, a b, *the ordinate,* p q, *and the two abscissæ,* a p *and* p b, *are given, to find the conjugate,* c d.

RULE.—As the square root of the product of the two abscissæ is to the ordinate, so is the transverse diameter to the conjugate.

Note.—In the same manner the transverse diameter may be found from the conjugate, using the two abscissæ of the conjugate, and their ordinate perpendicular to the conjugate.

When the conjugate, c d, *ordinate,* p q, *and abscissæ,* a p *and* b p, *are given, to find the transverse diameter.*

Rule.—From the square of half the conjugate subtract the square of the ordinate, and extract the root of the remainder. Add this root to the half conjugate if the less abscissa be given; but subtract it when the greater abscissa is given.

Then, as the square of the ordinate is to the rectangle of the abscissa and conjugate, so is the reserved sum, or difference, to the transverse diameter.

OF PARABOLAS.

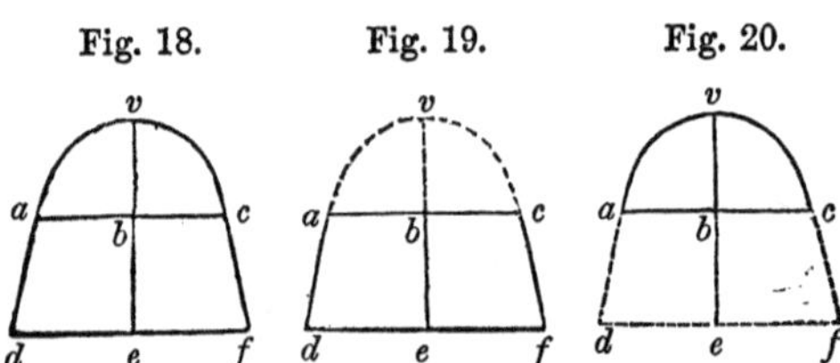

To find the Area of a Parabola.

Rule.—Multiply the base by the height, and two-thirds of the product will be the area.

To find the Area of a Frustum of a Parabola, fig. 19.

Rule.—Multiply the difference of the cubes of the two ends of the frustum, *a c d f*, by twice its altitude, *b e*, and divide the product by thrice the difference of their squares.

To find the Abscissa or Ordinate of a Parabola, fig. 18.

Rule.—The abscissæ, *v b* and *b e*, are to each other as the squares of their ordinates, *a b* and *d e*, that is, as any abscissa is to the square of its ordinate, so is any other abscissa to the square of its ordinate.

Or, as the square root of any abscissa is to its ordinate, so is the square root of another abscissa to its ordinate.

To find the Length of a Parabolic Curve, cut off by a Double Ordinate, fig. 20.

Rule.—To the square root of the ordinate, *a b*, add $\frac{4}{3}$ of the square of the abscissa, *v b*; the square root of that sum, multiplied by 2, will give the length of the curve nearly.

OF HYPERBOLAS.

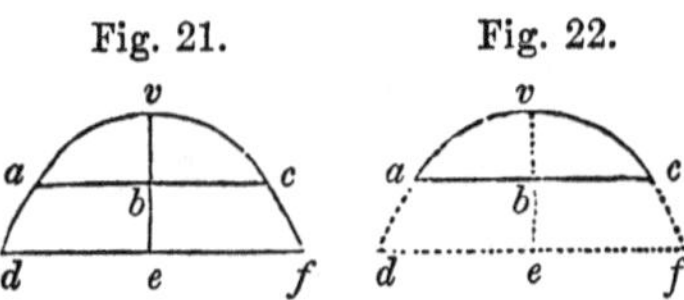

To find the Area of a Hyperbola, fig. 21.

RULE.—To five-sevenths of the abscissa, *v b*, add the transverse diameter, *v e*; multiply the sum by the abscissa, and extract the square root of the product. Then multiply the transverse diameter by the abscissa, and extract the square root of that product.

Then, to 21 times the first root add 4 times the second root; multiply the sum by double the product of the conjugate and abscissa, and divide by 75 times the transverse; this will give the area nearly.

To find the Length of a Hyperbolic Curve, fig. 22.

RULE.—To 21 times the square of the conjugate, *a b*, add 9 times the square of the transverse; also, to 21 times the square of the conjugate add 19 times the square of the transverse, and multiply each of these sums by the abscissa, *v b*.

To each of the two products add 15 times the product of the transverse and square of the conjugate.

Then, as the less sum is to the greater, so is the ordinate to the length of the curve nearly.

When the transverse, v e, *the conjugate,* d f, *and the abscissæ,* v b *and* b e, *are given, to find the ordinate,* a b, *fig.* 21.

RULE.—As the transverse diameter is to the conjugate, so is the square root of the product of the two abscissæ to the ordinate required.

Note.—In the hyperbola, the less abscissæ added to the axis gives the greater; and the greater abscissa subtracted from the axis gives the less.

When the transverse and conjugate diameters, and the ordinate, are given, to find the abscissæ.

RULE.—To the square of half the conjugate add the square of the ordinate, and extract the square root of that sum.

Then, as the conjugate diameter is to the transverse, so is the square root to half the sum of the abscissæ.

To this half sum add half the transverse diameter for the greater abscissa, and subtract it for the less.

When the transverse diameter, ordinate, and abscissa, are given, to find the conjugate.

RULE.—As the square root of the product of the two abscissæ is to the ordinate, so is the transverse diameter to the conjugate.

When the conjugate diameter, the ordinate, and the two abscissæ, are given, to find the transverse diameter.

Rule.—To the square of half the conjugate add the square of the ordinate, and extract the square root of that sum.

To this root add the half conjugate when the less abscissa is used; and subtract it when the greater abscissa is used; reserving the sum or difference.

Then, as the square of the ordinate is to the product of the abscissa and conjugate, so is the reserved sum or difference to the transverse.

MENSURATION OF SOLIDS.

OF CUBES AND PARALLELOPIPEDONS.

Fig. 23. Fig. 24.

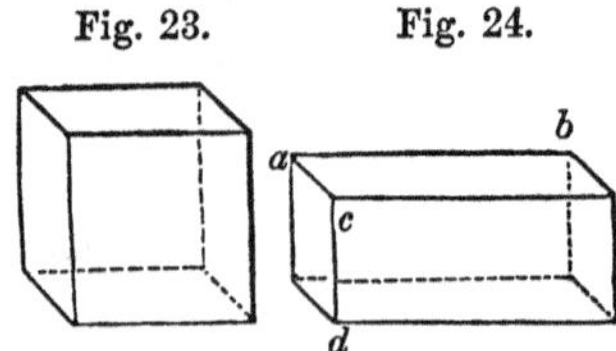

To find the Solidity of a Cube, fig. 23.

Rule.—Multiply the side of the cube by itself, and that product again by the side; the last product will be the solidity of the given cube.

To find the Solidity of a Parallelopipedon, fig. 24.

Rule.—Multiply the length, breadth, and depth or altitude, continually together, or, in other words, multiply the length, *a b*, by the breadth, *a c*, and that product by the depth or altitude, *c d*; this will give the required solidity.

OF CYLINDERS AND PRISMS.

Fig. 25. Fig. 26.

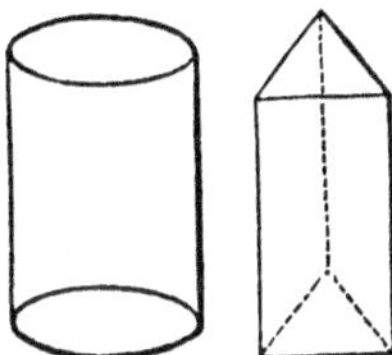

To find the Solidity of Cylinders and Prisms.

Rule.—Multiply the area of the base by the height of the cylinder or prism, and the product will give the solid content.

To find the Convex Surface of a Cylinder.

Rule.—Multiply the circumference by the length of the cylinder; the product will be the convex surface required.

OF CONES AND PYRAMIDS.

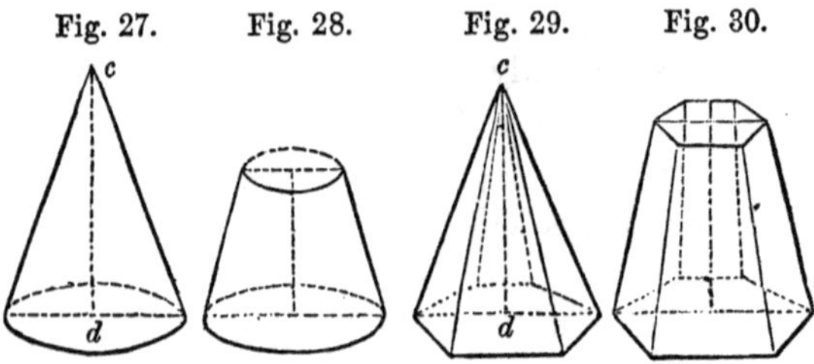

To find the Convex Surface of a Right Cone, or Pyramid, fig. 27.

Rule.—Multiply the perimeter, or circumference of the base, by the slant height, or length of the side of the cone, and half the product will be the surface.

To find the Convex Surface of a Frustum of a Right Cone, or Pyramid, fig. 28.

Rule.—Multiply the sum of the perimenters of the two ends by the slant height or side of the frustum, and half the product will be the surface required.

To find the solidity of a Cone, or Pyramid, figs. 27 *and* 29.

Rule.—Multiply the area of the base by the height, *c d*, and one-third of the product will be the content.

To find the Solidity of the Frustum of a Cone, fig. 28.

RULE.—Divide the difference of the cubes of the diameters of the two ends by the difference of the diameters; this quotient, multiplied by ·7854 and again by one-third for the height, will give the solidity.

To find the Solidity of the Frustum of a Pyramid, fig. 30.

RULE.—Add to the areas of the two ends of the frustum the square root of their product, and this sum, multiplied by one-third of the height, will give the solidity.

OF WEDGES AND PRISMOIDS.

Fig. 31. Fig. 32.

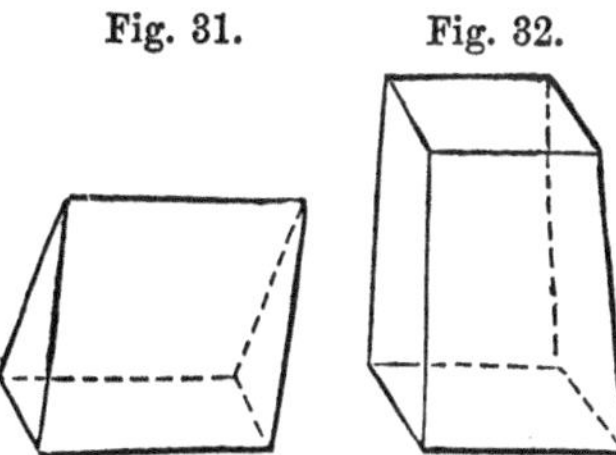

To find the Solidity of a Wedge, fig. 31.

RULE.—To the length of the edge of the wedge add twice the length of the back; multiply this sum by the height of the wedge, and then by the breadth of the back; one-sixth of the product will be the solid content.

To find the Solidity of a Prismoid, fig. 32.

Rule.—Add into one sum the areas of the two ends and four times the middle section, parallel to them; then, this sum multiplied by one-sixth of the height, will give the content.

Note.—The length of the middle section is equal to half the sum of the lengths of the two ends; and its breadth is equal to half the sum of the breadths of the two ends.

OF SPHERES.

Fig. 33. Fig. 34. Fig. 35.

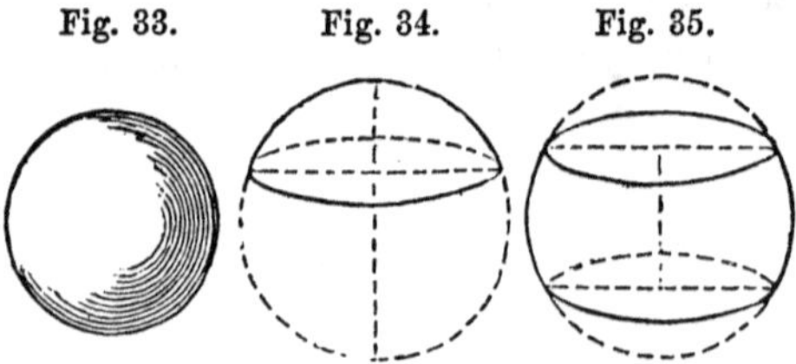

To find the Convex Surface of a Sphere, or Globe, fig. 33.

Rule.—Multiply the diameter of the sphere by its circumference.

Or, multiply 3·1416 by the square of the diameter; the product will be the convex surface required.

Note.—The convex surface of any zone or segment may be found, in like manner, by multiplying its height by the whole circumference of the sphere.

To find the Solidity of a Sphere, or Globe, fig. 33.

RULE.—Multiply the cube of the axis by ·5236; the product will be the solidity.

To find the Solidity of a Spherical Segment, fig. 34.

RULE.—To three times the square of the radius of its base add the square of its height; then, multiply the sum by the height, and the product by ·5236.

To find the Solidity of a Spherical Zone or Frustum, fig. 35.

RULE.—To the sum of the squares of the radius of each end add one-third of the square of the height of the zone; this sum, multiplied by the said height, and the product by 1·5708, will give the solidity.

OF SPHEROIDS.

To find the Solidity of a Spheroid, fig. 36.

RULE.—Multiply the square of the revolving axis, *c d*, by the fixed axis, *a b*; the product, multiplied by ·5236, will give the content.

To find the Solidity of the Segment of a Spheroid, figs. 37 *and* 38.

RULE.—*When the base,* e f, *is circular or parallel to the revolving axis,* c d, *fig.* 37, multiply the

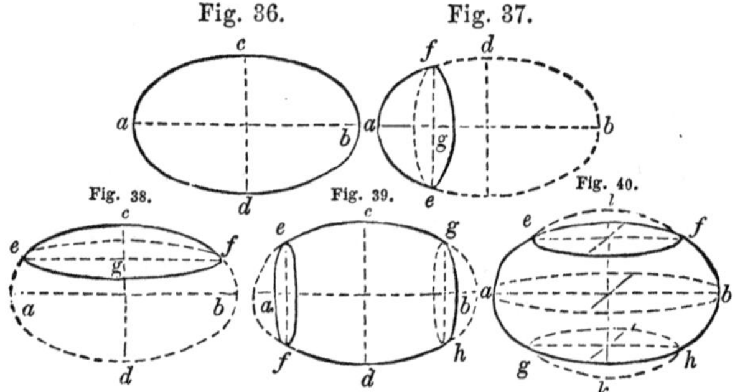

fixed axis, *a b*, by 3, the height of the segment, *a g*, by 2, and subtract the one product from the other; then multiply the remainder by the square of the height of the segment, and the product by ·5236.

Then, as the square of the fixed axis is to the square of the revolving axis, so is the last product to the content of the segment.

RULE.—*When the base,* e f, *is perpendicular to the revolving axis,* c d, *fig.* 38, multiply the revolving axis by 3, and the height of the segment, *c g*, by 2, and subtract the one from the other; then, multiply the remainder by the square of the height of the segment, and the product by ·5236.

Then, as the revolving axis is to the fixed axis, so is the last product to the content.

To find the Solidity of the Middle Frustum of a Spheroid, figs. 39 *and* 40.

RULE.—*When the ends,* e f *and* g h, *are circu-*

lar, or parallel to the revolving axis, c d, *fig.* 39, to twice the square of the revolving axis, *c d*, add the square of the diameter of either end, *e f*, or *g h*; then multiply this sum by the length, *a b*, of the frustum, and the product again by ·2618; this will give the solidity.

RULE.—*When the ends,* e f *and* g h, *are elliptical, or perpendicular to the revolving axis,* l k, *fig.* 40, to twice the product of the transverse and conjugate diameters of the middle section, *a b*, add the product of the transverse and conjugate of either end; multiply this sum by the length, *l k*, of the frustum, and the product by ·2618; this will give the solidity.

OF CIRCULAR SPINDLES.

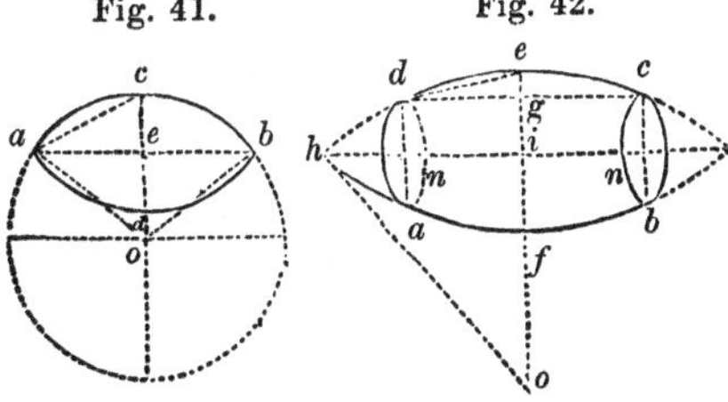

To find the Surface of a Circular Spindle, fig. 41.

RULE.—Multiply the length, *a b*, of the spindle by the radius, *o c*, of the revolving arc. Multiply also the said arc, *a c b*, by the central distance, *o e*, or distance between the centre of the spindle and centre of the revolving arc. Subtract this last product from the former; double the remainder; multiply it by 3·1416, and the product will give the surface of the spindle.

Note.—The same rule will serve for any segment, or zone, cut off perpendicularly to the chord of the revolving arc; but, in this case, the particular length of the part, and the part of the arc which describes it, must be used, instead of the whole length and whole arc.

To find the Solidity of a Circular Spindle, fig. 41.

Rule.—Multiply the central distance, *o e*, by half the area of the revolving segment, *a c b e a*. Subtract the product from one-third of the cube, *a e*, of half the length of the spindle. Then, multiply the remainder by 12·5664, or 4 times 3·1416, and the product will be the solidity required.

To find the Solidity of the Frustum, or Zone, of a Circular Spindle, fig. 42.

Rule.—From the square of half the length, *h i*, of the whole spindle, take one-third of the square of half the length, *n i*, of the frustum, and multiply the remainder by the said half-length of the frustum. Multiply the central distance, *o i*, by the revolving area, which generates the frustum. Subtract the last product from the former; and the remainder, multiplied by 6·2832, or twice 3·1416, will give the content.

OF ELLIPTIC SPINDLES.

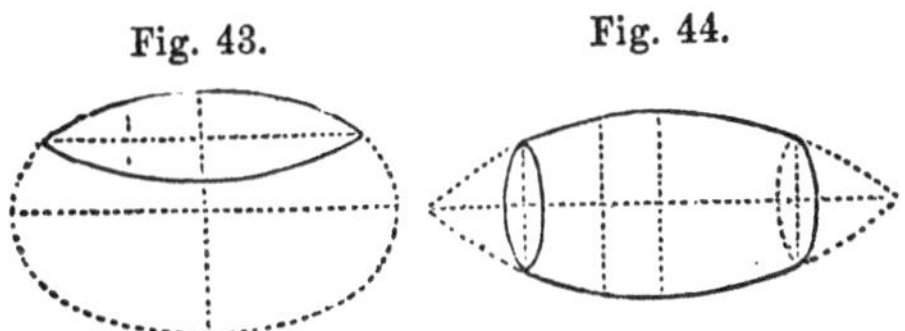

Fig. 43. Fig. 44.

To find the Solidity of an Elliptic Spindle, fig. 43.

RULE.—To the square of the greatest diameter add the square of twice the diameter at one-fourth of its length; multiply the sum by the length, and the product by ·1309, and it will give the solidity very nearly.

To find the Solidity of a Frustum or Segment of an Elliptic Spindle, fig. 44.

RULE.—Proceed, as in the last rule, for this, or any other solid, formed by the revolution of a conic section about an axis; namely,

Add together the squares of the greatest and least diameters, and the square of double the diameter in the middle between the two; multiply the sum by the length, and the product by ·1309, and it will give the solidity.

Note.—For all such solids, this rule is exact when the body is formed by the conic section, or a part of it revolving about the axis of the section; and will always be very near the truth when the figure revolves about another line.

OF PARABOLIC CONOIDS AND SPINDLES.

Fig. 45. Fig. 46. Fig. 47.

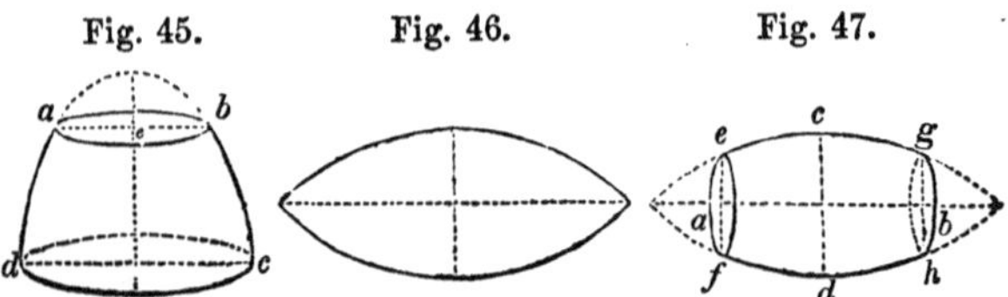

To find the Solidity of a Parabolic Conoid.

RULE.—Multiply the square of the diameter of the base by the altitude, and the product by ·3927.

To find the Solidity of a Frustum of a Paroboloid, fig. 45.

RULE.—Multiply the sum of the squares of the diameters of the two ends, *a b* and *d c*, by the height of the frustum, *e f*, and the product by ·3927.

To find the Solidity of a Parabolic Spindle, fig. 46.

RULE.—Multiply the square of the middle diameter by the length of the spindle, and the product by ·41888, (which is eight-fifteenths of ·7854,) and it will give the content.

To find the Solidity of the Middle Frustum of a Parabolic Spindle, fig. 47.

RULE.—Add together 8 times the square of the greatest diameter, *c d*, 3 times the square of the least diameter, *g h*, and 4 times the product of these two diameters; multiply the sum by the length, *a b*, and the product by ·05236, (which is $\frac{1}{60}$ of 3·1416;) this will give the solidity.

OF CYLINDRICAL RINGS.

Fig. 48.

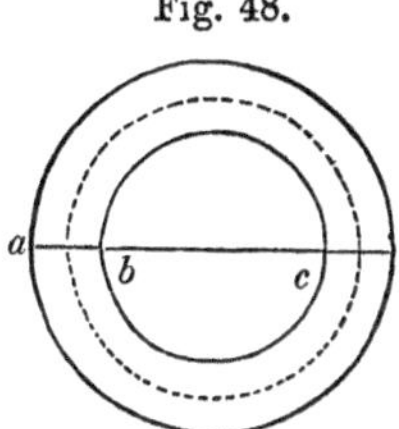

To find the Convex Surface of a Cylindrical Ring.

RULE.—To the thickness of the ring, *a b*, add the inner diameter, *b c*; multiply this sum by the thickness, and the product by 9·8696, (which is the square of 3·14159,) and it will give the superficies required.

To find the Solidity of a Cylindrical Ring.

RULE.—To the thickness of the ring add the inner diameter; then multiply the sum by the square of the thickness, and the product by 2·4674, (which is one-fourth of the square of 3·1416,) and it will give the solidity.

To find the superficies or solidity of any regular body.

RULE 1.—Multiply the tabular area by the square of the linear edge, and the product will be the superficies.

RULE 2.—Multiply the tabular solidity by the cube of the linear edge, and the product will be the solidity.

Surfaces and Solidities of the Regular Bodies, when the linear edge is 1.

No. of Sides.	Names.	Surfaces.	Solidities.
4	Tetrahedron	1·73205	0·11785
6	Hexahedron	6·00000	1·00000
8	Octahedron	3·46410	0·47140
12	Dodecahedron	20·64573	7·66312
20	Icosahedron	8·66025	2·18169

TABLE *of the Weight of Flat and Rolled Iron per foot, in length.*

Thickness in Inches and parts.	Breadth in Inches and Parts of an Inch.															
	4	3¾	3½	3¼	3	2¾	2½	2¼	2	1¾	1½	1⅜	1¼	1	¾	½
⅛	1·68	1·57	1·47	1·36	1·26	1·15	1·05	0·94	0·84	0·73	0·63	0·57	0·52	0·42	0·31	0·21
3/16	2·52	2·36	2·20	2·04	1·89	1·73	1·57	1·41	1·26	1·10	0·94	0·86	0·78	0·63	0·47	0·31
¼	3·36	3·15	2·94	2·73	2·52	2·31	2·10	1·89	1·68	1·47	1·26	1·18	1·05	0·84	0·63	0·42
⅜	5·04	4·72	4·41	4·09	3·78	3·46	3·15	2·83	2·52	2·20	1·89	1·73	1·57	1·26	0·94	0·63
½	6·72	6·30	5·88	5·46	5·04	4·62	4·20	3·78	3·36	2·94	2·52	2·31	2·10	1·68	1·26	
⅝	8·40	7·87	7·35	6·82	6·30	5·77	5·25	4·72	4·20	3·67	3·15	2·88	2·62	2·10	1·57	
¾	10·08	9·45	8·82	8·19	7·56	6·93	6·30	5·66	5·04	4·41	3·78	3·46	3·15	2·52		
⅞	11·76	11·02	10·29	9·55	8·82	8·08	7·35	6·61	5·88	5·14	4·41	4·04	3·67	2·94		
1	13·44	12·60	11·76	10·92	10·08	9·24	8·40	7·56	6·72	5·87	5·04	4·62	4·20			
1⅛	15·12	14·16	13·20	12·28	11·34	10·39	9·55	8·50	7·56	6·60	5·67	5·19	4·72			
1¼	16·80	15·75	14·70	13·65	12·60	11·55	10·50	9·45	8·40	7·35	6·30	5·77				
1⅜	18·46	17·32	16·16	15·01	13·86	12·70	11·55	10·39	9·24	8·07						
1½	20·18	18·90	17·64	16·38	15·12	13·86	12·60	11·34	10·08	8·80						
1¾	23·54	22·05	20·58	19·11	17·64	16·17	14·70	13·22								
2	26·88	25·20	23·52	21·84	20·16	18·48	16·80	15·12								
2½	33·65	31·50	29·40	27·39	25·20	23·10										
3	40·32	37·80	35·28	32·76												
3½	47·04															

TABLE *of the Weight of Cast-Iron Pipes, in Lengths.*

Bore.	Thick.	Long.	Weight.	Bore.	Thick.	Long.	Weight.	Bore.	Thick.	Long.	Weight.
In.	In.	Ft.	C. qr. lb.	In.	In.	Ft.	C. qr. lb.	Inch.	In.	Ft.	C. qr. lb.
1	¼	3½	12	6½	⅜	9	2 0 16	11½	½	9	5 0 7
	⅜	3½	21		½	9	2 3 20		⅝	9	6 1 12
1½	¼	4½	21		⅝	9	3 2 21		¾	9	7 2 8
	⅜	4½	1 4		¾	9	4 1 21		1	9	10 1 2
2	¼	6	1 8		1	9	6 0 14	12	½	9	5 0 24
	⅜	6	2 0	7	½	9	3 0 7		⅝	9	6 2 8
2½	¼	6	1 16		⅝	9	3 3 20		¾	9	7 3 20
	⅜	6	2 10		¾	9	4 3 5		1	9	10 3 0
	½	6	3 10		1	9	6 2 4	12½	½	9	5 1 16
3	¼	9	2 20	7½	½	9	3 1 6		⅝	9	6 3 9
	⅜	9	1 0 6		⅝	9	4 0 22		¾	9	8 1 0
	½	9	1 1 12		¾	9	5 0 10		1	9	11 0 21
	⅝	9	1 3 6		1	9	7 0 0	13	½	9	5 2 20
	¾	9	2 1 0	8	½	9	3 2 4		⅝	9	7 0 14
3½	¼	9	3 0		⅝	9	4 1 25		¾	9	8 2 7
	⅜	9	1 0 21		¾	9	5 1 18		1	9	11 2 12
	½	9	1 2 14		1	9	7 1 16	13½	½	9	5 3 7
	⅝	9	2 0 8	8½	½	9	3 3 2		⅝	9	7 1 12
	¾	9	2 2 0		⅝	9	4 2 26		¾	9	8 3 16
4	⅜	9	1 1 10		¾	9	5 2 22		1	9	11 3 24
	½	9	1 3 12		1	9	7 3 8	14	½	9	6 0 4
	⅝	9	2 1 12	9	½	9	4 0 0		⅝	9	7 2 16
	¾	9	2 3 21		⅝	9	5 0 4		¾	9	9 1 0
4½	⅜	9	1 2 2		¾	9	6 0 2		1	9	12 1 14
	½	9	2 0 4		1	9	8 0 26	14½	½	9	6 0 24
	⅝	9	2 2 14	9½	½	9	4 0 18		⅝	9	7 3 14
	¾	9	3 0 21		⅝	9	5 1 0		¾	9	9 2 2
5	⅜	9	1 2 22		¾	9	6 1 6		1	9	12 3 6
	½	9	2 1 10		1	9	8 2 20	15	½	9	6 1 21
	⅝	9	2 3 17	10	½	9	4 1 10		¾	9	9 3 7
	¾	9	3 1 24		⅝	9	5 1 26		1	9	13 0 26
5½	⅜	9	1 3 10		¾	9	6 2 14		1¼	9	16 3 5
	½	9	2 2 0		1	9	9 0 8	15½	½	9	6 2 14
	⅝	9.	3 0 18	10½	½	9	4 2 14		¾	9	10 0 10
	¾	9	3 3 7		⅝	9	5 3 7		1	9	13 2 17
	1	9	5 0 12		¾	9	7 0 0		1¼	9	17 1 6
6	⅜	9	2 0 0		1	9	9 2 0	16	½	9	7 0 22
	½	9	2 2 21	11	½	9	4 3 14		¾	9	10 1 20
	⅝	9	3 1 17		⅝	9	6 0 11		1	9	14 0 8
	¾	9	4 0 16		¾	9	7 1 7		1¼	9	17 3 14
	1	9	5 2 20		1	9	9 3 20		1½	9	21 3 4

Table of the Weight of one foot length of Malleable Iron.

Square Iron.		Round Iron.			
Scantling.	Weight.	Diameter.	Weight.	Circum.	Weight.
Inches.	Pounds.	Inches.	Pounds.	Inches.	Pounds.
¼	0·21	¼	0·16	1	0·26
⅜	0·47	⅜	0·37	1¼	0·41
½	0·84	½	0·66	1½	0·59
⅝	1·34	⅝	1·03	1¾	0·82
¾	1·89	¾	1·48	2	1·05
⅞	2·57	⅞	2·02	2¼	1·34
1	3·36	1	2·63	2½	1·65
1⅛	4·25	1⅛	3·33	2¾	2·01
1¼	5·25	1¼	4·12	3	2·37
1⅜	6·35	1⅜	4·98	3¼	2·79
1½	7·56	1½	5·93	3½	3·24
1⅝	8·87	1⅝	6·96	3¾	3·69
1¾	10·29	1¾	8·08	4	4·23
1⅞	11·81	1⅞	9·27	4½	5·35
2	13·44	2	10·55	5	6·61
2¼	17·01	2¼	13·35	5½	7·99
2½	21·00	2½	16·48	6	9·51
2¾	25·41	2¾	19·95	6½	11·18
3	30·24	3	23·73	7	12·96
3½	41·16	3¼	27·85	7½	14·78
4	53·76	3½	32·32	8	16·92
4½	68·04	3¾	37·09	8½	19·21
5	84 00	4	42·21	9	21·53
6	120·96	4½	53·41	10	26·43
7	164·64	5	65·93	12	31·99

Weight of Cast-Iron Plates, per superficial foot, from one-eighth of an inch to one inch thick.

⅛ inch.	¼ inch.	⅜ inch.	½ inch.	⅝ inch.	¾ inch.	⅞ inch.	1 inch.
lbs. oz.	lbs. oz.	lbs. oz.	lbs. oz.	lbs. oz.	lbs. oz.	lbs. oz.	lbs. oz.
4 13¼	9 10⅝	14 8	19 5⅜	24 2¾	29 0	33 13⅜	38 10¾

Table of the Bore and Weight of Cocks.

Content of Copper.	Bore of Cock.	Weight of Cock.	Content of Copper.	Bore of Cock.	Weight of Cock.
Gallons.	Inches.	Pounds.	Gallons.	Inches.	Pounds.
30	1½	7	200	2¾	30
50	1¾	8	260	3	34
80	2	12	340	3¼	44
120	2¼	19	420	3½	56
150	2½	26	430 and upwards.	3¾	70

Three-fourths of the diameter of the bore, taken at the hinder part, will give the diameter of the cock at the mouth.

Table of the Dimensions and Weight of Coppers, from 1 *to* 208 *galls. The Dimensions taken from lag to brim.*

Inches, lag to brim.	Gallons.	Weight in lbs.	Inches, lag to brim.	Gallons.	Weight in lbs.	Inches, lag to brim.	Gallons.	Weight in lbs.
9¾	1	1½	24	15	22½	29½	29	43½
12¼	2	3	24½	16	24	30	30	45
14	3	4½	25	17	25½	32	36	54
15½	4	6	25½	18	27	34	43	64½
16½	5	7½	26	19	28½	35	48	72
17½	6	9	26½	20	30	36	53	79½
18½	7	10½	26¾	21	31½	37	58	87
19½	8	12	27	22	33	38	63	94½
20¼	9	13½	27¼	23	34½	39	67	100½
21	10	15	27½	24	36	40	71	106½
21½	11	16½	27¾	25	37½	45	104	156
22	12	18	28	26	39	50	146	219
22½	13	19½	28½	27	40½	55	208	312
23¼	14	21	29	28	42			

Table of the Weight of Lead, per superficial foot, from one-sixteenth of an inch to one inch thick.

Thickness.	Weight.	Thickness.	Weight.	Thickness.	Weight.	Thickness.	Weight.
inch.	lbs.	inch.	lbs.	inch.	lbs.	inch.	lbs.
1-16th	3¾	1-8th	7½	1-4th	14¾	3-4ths	44¼
1-12th	5	1-6th	10	1-3d	19¾	1 inch	59
1-10th	6	1-5th	12	1-half	29½		

Weight of Lead Pipe of the usual thicknesses, per foot in length.

½-inch bore ..... 1 lb. 1 oz.
¾ " ..... 1 lb. 8 oz. — 1 lb. 12 oz. — 2 lbs.
1 " ..... 2 lbs. — 2 lbs. 11 oz. — 2 lbs. 14 oz.
1¼ " ..... 3 lbs. — 3 lbs. 11 oz. — 4 lbs. 7 oz.
1½ " ..... 4 lbs. — 4 lbs. 11 oz. — 5 lbs. 9 oz.
2 " ..... 5 lbs. 9 oz. — 7 lbs. — 8 lbs. 5 oz.
2½ " ..... 7 lbs. — 8 lbs. 9 oz. — 10 lbs.

Weight of Copper Tubing of the usual thickness.

When the inside diameter is ¼ of an inch, 3 ounces; ⅜ of an inch, 5 ounces; ½ of an inch, 6 ounces; ⅝ of an inch, 8 ounces; and ¾ of an inch, 10 ounces per foot.

TABLE *of the Weight of Metals, Woods, Stones, Earths, etc.*

METALS.	Weight of a cubic foot, in Ounces.	Weight of a cubic foot, in Pounds.	Weight of a cubic inch, in Pounds.
Antimony in a metallic state, fused	6,624	414·0	0·238
" glass of	4,946	309·1	0·182
" sulphur of	4,064	254·0	0·147
" ore, gray and foliated	4,368	273·0	0·159
" " radiated	4,440	277·5	0·161
Bismuth, cast	9,823	614·0	0·355
" native	9,822	614·0	0·355
" ore, in plumes	4,371	273·2	0·159
Brass, common cast	7,824	489·0	0·283
" cast, not hammered	8,396	524·8	0·303
" wire-drawn	8,544	534·0	0·308
Copper, cast	8,788	549·2	0·317
" wire-drawn	8,878	554·9	0·320
" pyrites	4,080	255·5	0·148
" ore, Cornish	5,452	340·8	0·202
" " white	4,500	281·2	0·163
" " gray	4,500	281·2	0·163
" " yellow	4,300	266·8	0·156
" " blue	3,400	212·5	0·123
" " prismatic	4,200	262·5	0·152
" " foliated, florid-red	3,950	247·0	0·143
" " radiated, azure	3,231	202·0	0·117
" " emerald	3,300	206·2	0·120
Gold, pure, cast	19,258	1203·6	0·697
" the same, hammered	19,362	1210·1	0·701
" 22 carats, fine, standard	17,486	1093·0	0·633
" the same, hammered	15,589	974·4	0·564
" 20 carats, fine, trinket	15,709	982·0	0·568
" the same, hammered	15,775	986·0	0·570
Iron, cast	7,207	450·5	0·260
" bars	7,788	486·8	0·281
" pyrites, cubic	4,702	294·0	0·170
" " radiated	4,775	298·5	0·173
" " dodecahedral	4,830	302·0	0·175
" " from Freyburg	4,682	292·6	0·170
" " from Cornwall	4,789	299·4	0·173
" ore, specular	5,218	326·1	0·189
" " micaceous	5,070	317·0	0·184
" " prismatic	7,355	459·8	0·266

METALS.	Weight of a cubic foot, in Ounces.	Weight of a cubic foot, in Pounds.	Weight of a cubic inch, in Pounds.
Lead, cast	11,352	709·5	0·410
" litharge	6,300	393·8	0·228
" ore, cubic	7,587	474·2	0·274
" " horned	6,072	379·5	0·220
" " corneous	6,065	379·1	0·220
" " reniform	3,920	345·0	0·142
" " blue	5,461	341·4	0·198
" " black	5,670	360·6	0·210
" " brown	6,974	436·0	0·252
" " white	7,236	452·2	0·261
" " red or red-lead spar	6,027	376·8	0·219
" " yellow, molybdenated	11,352	709·5	0·410
Mercury, solid, 40 deg. below 0° Fahr.	15,632	977·0	0·566
" at 32 deg. of heat	13,619	851·2	0·493
" at 60 deg.	13,580	848·8	0·491
" at 212 deg.	13,375	836·8	0·484
Nickel, cast	7,807	488·0	0·282
" ore, called Kupper-nickel, of Saxe	6,648	415·5	0·240
" " " of Bohemia	6,207	388·0	0·225
Platina, crude, in grains	15,602	975·1	0·570
" purified	19,500	1218·8	0·706
" the same, hammered	20,337	1271·1	0·736
" " rolled	22,069	1379·4	0·799
" " wire-drawn	21,042	1315·1	0·773
Silver, cast, pure	10,474	654·6	0·379
" cast, pure, hammered	10,511	657·6	0·381
" Parisian standard	10,175	636·0	0·368
" the same, hammered	10,376	648·5	0·375
" French coin	10,048	628·0	0·364
" the same, hammered	10,408	650·5	0·376
" shilling, George III.	10,534	658·4	0·380
Steel, soft	7,833	489·6	0·283
" hardened, not tempered	7,840	490·0	0·283
" tempered, not hardened	7,816	488·5	0·283
" tempered and hardened.	7,818	488·6	0·283
Tin, pure Cornish	7,291	455·6	0·263
" the same, hardened	7,299	456·0	0·263
" Molacca, fused	7,296	456·0	0·263
" " hardened	7,307	456·8	0·263

Metals and Woods.	Weight of a cubic foot, in Ounces.	Weight of a cubic foot, in Pounds.	Weight of a cubic inch, in Pounds.
Tin ore, red	6,935	433·5	0·250
" black	6,901	431·4	0·250
" white	6,008	375·5	0·221
Tungsten	6,066	379·1	0·220
Uranium	6,440	402·5	0·232
Wolfram	7,119	445·0	0·257
Zinc, in its usual state	6,862	429·0	0·248
" pure and compressed	7,191	449·5	0·259
" formed by sublimation, and full of cavities	5,918	269·9	0·156
" sulphate of	1,900	118·8	0·069
" saturated solution, the temp. 42 deg.	1,386	86·6	0·050
Woods.			
Alder	800	50·0	0·029
Apple-tree	793	49·6	0·029
Ash	845	52·9	0·031
Bay-tree	822	51·4	0·029
Beech	852	53·2	0·031
Box, Dutch	912	57·0	0·033
" French	1,328	83·0	0·048
" Brazilian, red	1,031	64·5	0·037
Campechy	913	57·1	0·033
Cedar, American	561	35·1	0·020
" Indian	1,315	82·2	0·047
" Palestine	613	38·4	0·022
" Wild	596	37·2	0·021
Cherry-tree	715	44·8	0·026
Citron	726	45·4	0·026
Cocoa	1,040	65·0	0·037
Cork	240	15·0	0·009
Cypress	644	40·2	0·023
Ebony, Indian	1,209	75·6	0·044
" American	1,331	83·2	0·048
Elder	695	43·5	0·025
Elm	671	42·0	0·024
Filbert	600	37·5	0·021
Fir, yellow	657	41·1	0·023
" white	569	35·6	0·021
" male	550	34·4	0·019

Woods, Stones, Earths, etc.	Weight of a cubic foot, in Ounces.	Weight of a cubic foot, in Pounds.	Weight of a cubic inch, in Pounds.
Fir, female	498	31·1	0·018
Hazel	600	37·5	0·021
Jasmin, Spanish	770	48·1	0·028
Juniper	556	34·8	0·020
Lemon-tree	703	44·0	0·025
Lignum-vitæ	1,333	83·4	0·048
Lime-tree	604	37·8	0·022
Logwood	913	57·1	0·033
Mahogany	1,063	66·5	0·038
Maple	750	47·0	0·027
Mastic-tree	849	53·1	0·031
Medlar	941	59·0	0·034
Mulberry	897	56·1	0·032
Oak, heart of, 60 years old	1,170	73·1	0·043
" dry	932	58·2	0·033
Olive-tree	927	58·0	0·033
Orange-tree	705	44·1	0·025
Pear-tree	661	41·4	0·024
Pomegranate-tree	1,354	84·6	0·049
Poplar	383	24·0	0·014
" white, Spanish	529	33·1	0·019
Plum-tree	755	47·2	0·027
Quince-tree	705	44·1	0·025
Sassafras	482	30·1	0·017
Vine	1,327	83·0	0·048
Walnut	671	42·0	0·024
Willow	585	36·6	0·021
Yew, Spanish	807	50·5	0·029
" Dutch	788	49·2	0·028
Stones, Earths, etc.			
Alabaster, yellow	2,699	168·8	0·098
" stained brown	2,744	171·5	0·099
" veined	2,691	168·2	0·098
" Dallias	2,611	163·2	0·095
" Malaga	2,876	179·8	0·104
" Malta	2,699	168·8	0·098
" Oriental, white	2,730	170·6	0·099
" " semi-transparent	2,762	172·6	0·100
" Piedmont	2,693	168·4	0·098

Stones, Earths, etc.	Weight of a cubic foot, in Ounces.	Weight of a cubic foot, in Pounds.	Weight of a cubic inch, in Pounds.
Alabaster, Spanish Saline	2,713	169·6	0·099
" Valencia	2,638	164·9	0·096
Ambergris	926	58·0	0·033
Amianthus, long	909	57·0	0·033
" short	2,313	144·6	0·084
Asbestos, ripe	2,578	161·1	0·094
" starry	3,073	192·1	0·111
Borax	1,714	107·1	0·062
Brick, earth	2,000	125·0	0·073
Chalk, British	2,784	174·0	0·100
" Bianҫon, coarse	2,727	170·5	0·098
" Spanish	2,790	174·4	0·100
Coal, Cannel	1,270	79·4	0·046
" Newcastle	1,270	79·4	0·046
" Staffordshire	1,240	77·5	0·045
" Scotch	1,300	81·2	0·047
Cutler's-stone	2,111	132·0	0·076
Emery	4,000	250·0	0·144
Flint, black	2,582	162·0	0·094
" veined	2,612	163·2	0·095
" white	2,594	162·1	0·094
" Egyptian	2,565	160·4	0·093
Glass, flint	2,933	170·9	0·099
" white	2,892	168·2	0·098
" bottle	2,732	170·8	0·099
" green	2,642	165·1	0·096
" St. Gobin	2,488	155·5	0·090
" Leith, crystal	3,189	199·4	0·116
" fluid	3,329	208·1	0·120
Granite, Aberdeen, blue kind ..	2,625	164·1	0·095
" Cornish	2,662	166·4	0·096
" Egyptian, red	2,654	165·9	0·096
" " gray	2,728	170·5	0·099
" beautiful red	2,761	172·6	0·100
" Girardmor	2,716	169·8	0·098
" violet, of Gyromagny	2,685	168·0	0·098
" Dauphiny, red	2,643	165·2	0·096
" " green	2,684	167·8	0·098
" " radiated ...	2,668	166·8	0·097
" Semur, red	2,638	164·9	0·096
" Bretagne, gray	2,738	171·1	0·098
" " yellowish ...	2,619	162·8	0·095

STONES, EARTHS, ETC.	Weight of a cubic foot, in Ounces.	Weight of a cubic foot, in Pounds.	Weight of a cubic inch, in Pounds.
Granite, Carinthia, blue	2,956	184·8	0·107
Grindstone	2,143	134·0	0·077
Gypsum, opaque	2,168	135·5	0·077
" semi-transparent	2,306	144·1	0·083
" fine ditto	2,274	142·1	0·082
" cuneiform, cryst.	2,306	144·1	0·083
" rhomboidal	2,311	144·5	0·083
" ditto, ten faces	2,312	144·5	0·083
Hone, white, razor	2,876	179·8	0·104
Jet, a bituminous substance	1,259	78·8	0·046
Lime-stone, green	3,182	199·0	0·116
" arenaceous	2,742	171·4	0·098
" white fluor	3,156	197·2	1·014
" compact	2,720	170·0	0·098
" foliated	2,837	177·4	0·102
" granular	2,800	175·0	0·101
Manganese	7,000	437·5	0·252
" gray ore, striated	4,756	297·2	0·172
" gray, foliated	3,742	234·0	0·135
" red, from Kapnick	3,233	202·1	0·117
" black	3,000	187·5	0·108
" scaly	4,116	257·2	0·149
" sulphuret of	3,950	246·9	0·142
" phosphate of	2,600	162·5	0·094
Marble, African	2,708	169·2	0·098
" Biscayan, black	2,695	168·5	0·098
" Brocatelle	2,650	165·6	0·097
" Campanian, green	2,742	171·4	0·099
" Carrara, white	2,717	169·9	0·098
" Castilian	2,700	168·8	0·098
" Egyptian, green	2,668	166·8	0·097
" French	2,649	165·6	0·099
" Grenada, white	2,705	169·1	0·098
" Italian, violet	2,858	166·1	0·097
" Norwegian	2,728	170·5	0·099
" Parian, white	2,838	164·9	0·096
" Pyrenean	2,726	170·4	0·098
" Red	2,724	170·2	0·098
" Roman violet	2,755	172·2	0·099
" Siberian	2,718	169·9	0·098
" Siennian	2,678	167·4	0·097
" Switzerland	2,714	169·6	0·098

STONES, EARTHS, ETC.	Weight of a cubic foot, in Ounces.	Weight of a cubic foot, in Pounds.	Weight of a cubic inch, in Pounds.
Marble, Valencia	2,710	169·4	0·098
Mill-stone	2,484	155·2	0·090
" phosphoric	1,714	107·1	0·062
Porcelain, China	2,385	149·1	0·086
" Limoges	2,341	146·4	0·084
" Sevres	2,146	134·1	0·077
" British			
Portland-stone	2,570	160·6	0·094
Pumice-stone	915	57·2	0·033
Paving-stone	2,416	151·0	0·088
Purbeck-stone	2,601	162·6	0·094
Porphyry, red	2,765	172·9	0·099
" green	2,676	167·2	0·097
" red, from Cordone	2,754	172·1	0·099
" green, from ditto	3,728	233·0	0·135
" red, from Dauphiny	2,793	174·6	0·101
Pyrites, copper	4,954	309·6	0·180
" ferruginous, cubic	3,900	241·2	0·140
" " round	4,101	256·4	0·149
" " of St. Domingo	3,440	215·0	0·125
Rotten-stone	1,981	124·0	0·071
Salt	2,130	133·1	0·077
Serpentine, opaque, green, Italian	2,430	152·0	0·088
" " veined, black & olive	2,594	162·1	0·094
" " red and black	2,627	164·2	0·095
" semi-transparent, grained.	2,586	161·6	0·094
" fibrous	3,000	187·5	0·108
" from Dauphiny	2,669	167·0	0·097
Slate, common	2,672	167·0	0·097
" new	2,854	178·4	0·104
" black stone	2,186	136·6	0·079
" fresh polished	2,766	173·0	0·099
Stalactite, opaque	2,478	154·9	0·090
" transparent	2,324	145·2	0·084
Stone, Bristol	2,510	157·0	0·091
" Burford	2,049	128·1	0·075
" common	2,520	157·5	0·091

Stones, Earths, etc.	Weight of a cubic foot, in Ounces.	Weight of a cubic foot, in Pounds.	Weight of a cubic inch, in Pounds.
Stone, Clicard, from Brachet..	2,357	147·4	0·085
" " from Ouchain..	2,274	142·1	0·082
" Notre-Dame	2,378	148·6	0·085
" Oriental blue	2,771	173·2	0·099
" paving	2,416	151·0	0·088
" Portland	2,570	160·6	0·094
" pumice	915	57·2	0·033
" Purbeck	2,601	162·6	0·094
" prismatic basaltes	2,722	170·1	0·099
" rag	2,470	155·4	0·090
" rotten	1,981	124·0	0·071
" rock of Chatillon	2,122	132·6	0·076
" Siberian blue	2,945	184·1	0·107
" St. Cloud	2,201	137·6	0·079
" St. Maur	2,034	127·1	0·075
" touch	2,415	151·0	0·088
Sulphur, native	2,033	127·1	0·075
" melted	1,991	124·5	0·071
Talc, black	2,900	181·2	0·105
" crayon	2,089	130·6	0·075
" German	2,246	140·4	0·081
" Muscovy	2,792	174·5	0·101
" yellow	2,653	166·0	0·097

APPLICATION.

Rule.—Find, by the rules in the "Mensuration of Solids," the solidity of the material of which the weight is required, and multiply that solidity by the factor, in the foregoing table.

Example 1.—Required the weight of a bar of iron 12 feet long and 1 inch square?

Weight of 1 inch bar-iron, as per table, page 135, is 0·281.

12 feet = 144 inches.

Then ·281 × 144 inches = 40·464, or $40\frac{5}{10}$, or $40\frac{1}{2}$ lbs. nearly.

Example 2.—Required the weight of a plank of yellow fir, 11 inches wide, 3 inches thick, and 20 feet long?

20 feet = 240 inches.

One cubic inch yellow fir, as per table, = 0·023; therefore ·023 × 240 × 11 × 3 = 182·160, or $182\frac{2}{10}$, or $182\frac{1}{5}$ lbs. nearly.

THE STEAM-ENGINE.

THE power of the steam-engine is estimated by that exerted by the horse. A horse-power, as fixed by Watt, is equal to 33,000 lbs. avoirdupois, raised one foot high per minute; and one day's work of a horse, is this power, acting through eight hours. The pressure of steam is calculated in pounds avoirdupois on the square inch, in perpendicular inches of mercury, and in atmospheres; each atmosphere is estimated as equal to the average pressure of our atmosphere at the surface of the earth. The pressure of the atmosphere is reckoned as equal to that of 30 perpendicular inches of mercury; or 14·7 lbs. per square inch, or 11·55 lbs. per circular inch.

To find the Horses' power of an Engine, according to Mr. Watt's rule.

From the diameter of the cylinder in inches, subtract 1, square the remainder, multiply the square by the velocity of the piston in feet per minute, and divide the product by 5640. The quotient will be the number required.

GENERAL PROPORTIONS OF CONDENSING ENGINES.

Cylinder.—The best proportion is when the length is twice the diameter; because the cooling surface is then least, in proportion to the content of steam.

Air-Pump and Condenser.—In double condensing engines, these are made, by Boulton and Watt's rule, each to measure one-eighth the content of the cylinder.

Velocity of the Piston to produce the best effect.—In engines working the steam expansively, 100 times the square root of the length of the stroke in feet, is the best velocity in feet per minute.

In engines not working expansively, 103 times the square root of the length of the stroke in feet, is the best velocity in feet per minute.

To find the quantity of Water required for Steam and Injection.—Multiply the area of the cylinder in feet, by half the velocity in feet for *single*, and by the whole velocity in feet for *double* engines. Add $\frac{1}{10}$ for cooling and wasting; and this, divided by 1497, (at the common pressure on the valve of 2 lbs. per circular inch,) will give the quantity of water required for steam per minute.

The quantity of water for injection should be 24 times that required for steam.

The diameter of the injection-pipe should be $\frac{1}{36}$th part of that of the cylinder.

The valves should be as large as practicable.

The boiler should be capable of evaporating about 12 gallons per hour for each horse-power.

NON-CONDENSING, OR HIGH PRESSURE ENGINES.

The length of the cylinder should be at least twice its diameter.

The velocity of the piston, in feet per minute, should be 103 times the square root of the length of the stroke in feet; or 100 times, if the steam is worked expansively.

The area of the cylinder should be, to the area of the steam-passages, as 4800 is to the velocity of the piston, found as above.

Form and Direction of Steam-pipes.—Enlargements in steam-pipes succeeded by contractions, always retard the velocity of the steam—more or less according to the nature of the contraction—and the like effect is produced by bends and angles in the pipes. These should, therefore, be made as straight, and their internal surface as uniform and free from inequalities as may be practicable. The following proportions of velocity, from Mr. Tredgold, will exemplify this:—

The velocity of motion that would result from the direct unretarded action of the column of fluid which produces it, being unity.............	1000 or 8
The velocity through an aperture in a thin plate by the same pressure is	·625 or 5
Through a tube from two to three diameters in length, projecting outwards.........................	·813 or 6·5
Through a tube of the same length, projecting inwards...	·681 or 5·45
Through a conical tube, or mouth-piece, of the form of the contracted vein.........................	·983 or 7·9

Friction of the parts of Engines.—The amount of pressure upon the piston, expended in overcoming friction, appears, on an average, to be not more than 1 lb. to the square inch, in well-constructed engines. The difference in loss of power from this cause, between beam and direct action engines, is found by experiment to be inconsiderable.

Mr. Tredgold's Estimate of the Distribution and Expenditure of the Steam in an Engine.

IN A NON-CONDENSING ENGINE.

Let the pressure on the boiler be..................		10·000
Force required to produce motion of the steam in the cylinder will be..............................	0·069	
Loss by cooling in the cylinder and pipes........	0·160	
Loss by friction of piston and waste........	2·000	
Force required to expel the steam into the atmosphere..	0·069	
Force expended in opening the valves, and friction of the various parts........................	0·622	
Loss by the steam being cut off before the end of the stroke..	1·000	
Amount of deductions	———	3·920
Effective pressure................		6·080

IN A CONDENSING ENGINE.

Let the pressure on the boiler be..................		10·000
Force required to produce motion of the steam in the cylinder..	0·070	
Loss by cooling in the cylinder and pipes........	0·160	
Loss by friction of the piston and waste..........	1·250	

Force required to expel the steam through the passages	0·070	
Force required to open and close the valves, raise the injection water, and overcome the friction of the axes	0·630	
Loss by the steam being cut off before the end of the stroke	1·000	
Power required to work the air-pump	0·500	
Amount of deductions		3·680
Effective pressure		6·320

Steam-power required to drive various kinds of Machinery.

A series of experiments instituted by Mr. Davison, at Messrs. Truman and Co.'s Brewery, gave the following results:

1st. That an engine which indicated 50 horses' power when fully loaded, showed, after the load and the whole of the machinery were thrown off, 5 horses', or one-tenth of the whole power.

2d. 190 feet of horizontal, and 180 feet of upright shafting, with 34 bearings, whose superficial area was 3300 square inches, together with 11 pair of spur and bevel wheels, varying from 2 feet to 9 feet in diameter, required a power equal to 7·65 horses.

3d. A set of three-throw pumps, 6 inches in diameter, pumping 120 barrels per hour, to a height of 165 feet, = 4·7 horses.

4th. A similar set of three-throw pumps, 6 inches

in diameter, pumping 160 barrels per hour, to a height of 140 feet, = 6·2 horses.

5th. A set of three-throw pumps, 5 inches in diameter, raising 80 barrels per hour, to a height of 54 feet, = 1 horse.

6th. A set of three-throw "starting" pumps, pumping 250 barrels of beer per hour, to a height of 48 feet, = 4·87 horses.

7th. Two pair of iron rollers and an elevator, grinding and raising 40 quarters of malt per hour, = 8·5 horses.

8th. An ale-mashing machine, mashing at the time 100 quarters of malt, = 5·68 horses.

9th. Two porter-mashing machines, mashing at the time, 250 quarters of malt, = 10·8 horses.

10th. 95 feet of horizontal Archimedes screw, 15 inches diameter, and an elevator, conveying 40 quarters of malt per hour, to a height of 65 feet, = 3·13 horses.

Steam-engines for Cotton-mills.—With a mean pressure on the piston, with low pressure steam, of 5 lbs. per circular inch, each circular inch will drive three spindles of cotton yarn twist with the machinery. For mule yarn, add 15 to the number of the yarn, and multiply the sum by ·26, for the number of spindles for each circular inch of piston.

Or, one-horse power will drive 100 spindles with *cotton yarn*, and machinery. For *mule yarn*, add

15 to the number of the yarn, and multiply by 8, for the number of spindles for each horse-power.

Economy of Steam-jackets.—The following Table presents the results of three experiments made in France to ascertain the economy of steam-jackets to the cylinders of engines, in the consumption of fuel. In the 1st, the steam first entered the jacket round the cylinder, and passed from thence into the cylinder. In the 2d, the steam entered the cylinder directly, without passing into the jacket. In the 3d, the steam entered both the cylinder and jacket directly, by means of separate communications between them and the boiler. The result shows an increase in the consumption of fuel of nearly five-sevenths, in the 2d experiment, over that in the 1st.

Experiments.	Duration of Experiments.	Total Consumption in pounds avoirdupois.		Mean Pressure in Atmospheres.			Consumption per hour in lbs.		Water evaporated by 1 lb. of Coal.
		Coals.	Water.	Boil'r.	Cylinder.	Condens'r.	Coals.	Water.	
	h. m.								
1	43 15	1482·7	8387·1	3·82	2·57	0·26	34·28	193·9	5·66
2	33 30	1982·12	11111·59	3·5	2·55	0·28	58·16	331·7	5·61
3	32 30	1469·5	7822·23	3·5	2·73	0·24	45·22	240·7	5·32

MARINE ENGINES.

The following Dimensions are given by Mr. Russell, for the Cylinders of Marine Engines of various power :—

Horse Power.	Inches Diameter.	Stroke.	Horse Power.	Inches Diameter.	Stroke.
10	20	2 ft. 0 in.	125	59	6 ft. 0 in.
20	27	2 ft. 6 in.	150	62	6 ft. 3 in.
30	32	3 ft. 2 in.	175	66	6 ft. 6 in.
40	36	3 ft. 6 in.	200	70	7 ft. 0 in.
50	40	4 ft. 0 in.	250	76	7 ft. 6 in.
60	48	4 ft. 3 in.	300	82	8 ft. 0 in.
70	46	4 ft. 6 in.	350	87	8 ft. 6 in.
80	49	4 ft. 9 in.	400	92	9 ft. 2 in.
90	52	5 ft. 0 in.	500	100	10 ft. 0 in.
100	55	5 ft. 6 in.			

The improvements in Marine Engines have of late years been various and extensive. Those in oscillating and direct action engines have far exceeded previous calculation. In recently constructed war-steamers with screw-propellers, the whole machinery is placed seven or eight feet below the water-line, and the screw is driven by direct action at the rate of 45 revolutions per minute.

RAILWAYS.

Summary of the average Items of the Construction of a Mile of Railway. By Mr. DEMPSEY.

"The average quantities, per mile, of the several items which are involved in the formation of a double line of railway, of the 4 ft. 8½ in. gauge, up to the completion of the permanent way, and exclusive of the stations and buildings, and locomotive and carrying stock, may be computed as follows:

"The quantity of excavations in 342 miles of double line of railway, (comprised in ten railways,) amounted to 35,338,000 cubic yards, giving an average of about 103,330 yards per mile, or 58·71 cubic yards of earth-work for each yard forward of the line. Assuming the width of the formation level to be 10 yards, or 30 feet, (which is about the average,) with an additional width of 5 yards on each side, for ditches, hedges, &c., the slopes at 1½ base to 1 of height,—and also assuming the whole line to be, either in cutting or embankment, of an average depth of height of 11 feet,—we shall require 56·73 cubic yards of earth-work per yard forward of the line. This is sufficiently near to the actual average of 58·71 yards to answer the pur pose of this general calculation. The average width of land required will thus be,

Central width.		Base of Slopes.				Ditches, &c.	
30	+	16·5 + 16·5	+	15 + 15	= 93 ft. or 31 yds.,		

which will give about $11\frac{1}{4}$ acres of land per mile. Allowing for severance, &c., this may be assumed at 12 acres.

"The quantity of ballasting, 30 feet wide, and 18 inches thick, will equal 5 cubic yards per yard forward, or 8800 cubic yards per mile.

"The sleepers, transverse, 8 feet long, and 10 by 5 inches, placed 2 feet 6 inches apart, will require 11·733 cubic feet, or 235 loads of timber; or 4224 sleepers per mile.

"The chairs required, supposing the rails to be rolled in lengths of 15 feet each, will be 1408 joint chairs, and 7040 intermediate; and their weight, reckoning each joint chair at 20 lbs., and each intermediate chair at 15 lbs., will be 12 tons 11 cwt. 1 qr. 20 lbs., and 47 tons 2 cwt. 3 qrs. 12 lb., respectively, or 59 tons 14 cwt. 1 qr. 4 lbs. altogether.

"The rails, assuming the weight at 56 lbs. per yard, will weigh 176 tons,—1408 lengths being required.

"If two oak trenails and two iron spikes be required for each chair, 16,896 of each will be wanted per mile, with 8448 wooden keys for fixing the rails in the chairs.

"If felt be interposed between the chairs and sleepers, and the former be assumed at 10 × 5 inches bearing surface, 2933 square feet of felt will be required per mile.

"The timber in the side fences, formed of posts 8 feet long, 6 × 4 inches, 9 feet apart, with four rails 5 × 2½ inches, and intermediate upright stay 3 × 2 inches, will consume as follows: 1174 posts = 1565 cubic feet; 4696 rails = 3666 cubic feet; 1174 stays = 269 cubic feet; or a total of 110 loads.

"Of the masonry, timber, iron, &c., &c., in bridges, viaducts, culverts, drains, retaining walls, &c., scarcely any estimate can be formed. Taking the average of a few cases, the masonry would appear to amount to about 110,000 cubic feet per mile; but in some cases from 30 to 50 per cent. of this quantity is substituted by timber and iron."

Weight of Rails.

On railways with much heavy traffic, the weight of the rails should be, to insure firmness and durability, as on the London and North-western Railway, about 75 lbs. per yard, and their bearing-surface about 2½ inches broad. The best distances for the bearings being about 2 feet 9 inches to 3 feet asunder.

Atmospheric Railway.

An experimental line of Atmospheric Railway on Hallette's principle, about 100 yards long, has been laid down, to exhibit its peculiar valve, and its working power, on a small scale. The valve is closed by longitudinal caoutchouc pipes, covered with cotton and leather, and filled with compressed air, at about 5 lbs. to the inch pressure. The wear and tear of these elastic lips, by the continual rubbing of the wedge which opens them as the train passes, can be satisfactorily ascertained only by experiments on a large practical scale.

Menai Tubular Bridge.

The tubular bridge designed by Mr. Stephenson for crossing the Menai Straits, or the line of the Chester and Holyhead Railway, is proposed to be rectangular, and of the following dimensions, viz. length 450 feet, width 15 feet, height 30 feet; made of iron plates one inch in thickness. Numerous experiments have been made on the strength of iron tubes, by Messrs. Hodgkinson and Fairbairn, to determine the requisite strength, and the weight it would support. The estimated strength of this tube would be equal to 1100 tons applied in the centre, including its own weight; or 747 tons, deducting its own weight. But this being the full strain that the tube would bear without breaking, a much less weight must be fixed upon as within the point of safety. The addition of chains is proposed to add to the support of the tube, and experiments are still in progress to determine a form that would sustain a more considerable weight. Its *practicability* has been established, in the opinion of the engineers, by the results of experiments on a tube 75 feet long, 2½ feet wide, and 4½ feet deep, weighing about 5 tons; which broke with a weight on the middle of 35 tons.

Resistance to Railway Trains.

The resistance of the air to railway trains is estimated, by Mr. Barlow, at not more than ten pounds on each ton weight, on the average. The loss of velocity estimated by comparison of the actual with the theoretical velocity, is caused by the consumption of power in overcoming the inertia of the train, and not from defect or loss of power in the action of the engine.

A paper was read at the meeting of the British Association in September, by Mr. Scott Russell, on "The law which governs the resistance to the motion of railway trains at high velocities." His experiments have been undertaken "on a large scale, with railway trains of a great variety of size and weight, and at velocities as high as sixty-one miles an hour," and were combined with those formerly made by the Association, and by Mr. W. Harding; and he presents the results in the following Table.

Mr. Russell remarks that the experiments show not only a great amount of resistance at high velocities, but likewise a great variation and anomaly in the results. He describes the resistance as consisting of three elements. Firstly, the friction of the axles and wheels, as an ascertained quantity, equal in the best carriages to 6 lbs. per ton of the train. Secondly, the resistance of the air; which, acting on a solid body such as a railway train, he regards as much less in amount than that inferred by Smeaton, from experiments on thin plates. And, thirdly, a large amount of resistance, increasing with the velocity of the train, and amounting, at ten miles an hour, to about 3 lbs. per ton, at thirty miles to 10 lbs., and at sixty miles an hour to 20 lbs. per ton; and which Mr. Russell ascribes to the concussions, oscillations, frictions of various kinds, &c., which are produced at high velocities.

Mr. Russell has constructed a formula compounded of these resistances, the comparison of the results of which, with those of the actual experiments, is shown in the Table; but the great anomalies observable at the various velocities remain yet unexplained, and appear incapable of being accounted for on any theory. Much is probably due to the combined action of inaccuracy in construction, and variation in the quality of the materials employed. A doubt may likewise be suggested whether, in practice with heavy trains, the quantity of the first-named element of resistance, the friction of the axles, &c., is constant at all velocities.

TABLE *referred to above.*

No. of Experiment.	Uniform velocity maintained in miles, per hour.	Resistance in lbs., per ton, by Experiment.	Resistance in lbs., per ton, by Formula.
1	10	8·40	9·30
2	14	12·60	13·90
3	14	12·60	13·90
4	29	16·50	15·70
5	31	23·30	25·40
6	31	18·20	16·30
7	32	22·50	27·20
8	33	22·50	22·70
9	33	15·68	16·90
10	33	15·96	17·00
11	34	16·60	17·30
12	34	16·95	17·30
13	34	17·70	17·30
14	34	23·30	27·20
15	34	25·00	23·10
16	35	22·50	26·10
17	36	22·50	22·40
18	36	22·40	21·50
19	37	17·50	18·20
20	37	25·00	28·40
21	39	30·00	31·00
22	41	22·99	19·60
23	41	26·78	19·60
24	45	21·70	21·00
25	46	23·10	21·30
26	46	30·31	31·00
27	47	33·70	33·10
28	50	32·90	36·30
29	51	26·40	23·00
30	53	41·70	42·10
31	61	52·60	54·80

New Sand Cement.

A metallic sand cement, of great hardness and tenacity, has been lately used on the London and South-western Railway and elsewhere, in forming mortar and concrete. The sand is brought from Swansea, and the proportions of the cement are,—for mortar, the metallic sand, ordinary sand, and lime, in equal quantities; for concrete, metallic sand 1 part, lime 1 part, gravel 6 parts. The iron contained in the metallic sand becomes disseminated through the mass, and acts as a firm bond to the whole composition.

GAUGE OF RAILWAYS.

The experiments instituted by the advocates of the broad and narrow gauge, respectively, with the object of testing their respective merits as to speed and power, have not led to any satisfactory conclusion. The direction of the wind, the state of the rails, and the inclination of the road operated so variously during the trials, as to destroy all uniformity in the conditions of the several experiments.

Mr. Bidder, in his report on the recent gauge experiments, gives the following results:—

NARROW GAUGE.

Date of experiment................	Dec. 30.	Dec. 31.	Dec. 31.
Draft in tons	50	50	80

Date of experiment	Dec. 30.	Dec. 31.	Dec. 31.
Distance travelled in miles	42	85	42
Time in minutes and seconds	72 6	106 12	56 52
Water evaporated, lb	12215	19708	9900
Ditto do. per mile, lb.	291	232	235·7
Ditto do. per hour, lb.	10160	11150	10430
Cubic feet per hour	162½	178	167
Coke consumed, lb.	1381		1176
Water evaporated per lb. of coke, lb	9·3	9·6	8·8
Coke consumed per mile, lb.	31·2	24	26·6
Pressure		71	60
Engine		A	
Surface of fire-box, feet square		58	
Areas of blast pipes in circular inches		3364¼	
Contents of cylinders, do.		4725	

BROAD GAUGE.

Date of experiment	Dec. 17.	Dec. 16.	Dec. 16.
Draft in tons	60	80	80
Distance travelled in miles	101½	100½	101½
Time in minutes and seconds	112 42	117 4	121 3
Water evaporated, lb	22596	23489	24838
Ditto do. per mile, lb.	232	233¾	245
Ditto do. per hour, lb.	11820	12020	12300
Cubic feet per hour	198	192½	196¾
Coke consumed, lb.			
Water evaporated per lb. of coke, lb	7·8	7·12	7·12
Coke consumed per mile, lb.	29·6	33·6	33·6
Pressure.			
Engine	Ixion		
Surface of fire-box, feet square	97		
Areas of blast pipes in circular inches	3721¼		
Contents of cylinders, do.	4961		

The friction of air through tubes, Mr. Bidder observes, is tolerably well ascertained: it appears that, with a pressure of ·04 lbs. per inch, the velocity of the air through the long tubes of the A engine used in the narrow gauge experiments was 16 miles per hour; and through the shorter tubes of the Ixion 18 miles per hour.

Opinion of Mr. W. Cubitt *on Uniformity of Gauge, (Evidence before Select Committee of the House of Lords.)*

Proposes a 6-feet gauge, the alteration to which would cost between £500 to £1000 per mile.

Says that the bridges and tunnels on the existing narrow gauge railways are wide enough to admit of rails 6 feet apart, the only alteration necessary in the carriages being that of bringing out the wheels 6 or 8 inches each side, as the carriages themselves are already wide enough, and the wheels would still be under the body of the carriage.

The enlarging this gauge to 6 feet would make a better gauge, and enable them to bring the centre of gravity of the engine lower, and allow larger engines than can now be used with safety upon the narrow gauge.

Long engines (as long as 20 feet) may be made to run with very large driving wheels, and go safely round curves, by using what is called in America a "Bogy Carriage," viz. supporting the engine on two trucks with four low wheels each, which trucks could turn independently at each end, while large driving wheels without flanges may be placed between the trucks.

Estimates the altering of carriages to the 6 feet gauge at less than £30 each, and the engine and tender at £350 to £400 each.

Extract from a Return to the House of Lords, of the WORKING STOCK *of Existing Railways.*

	Locomotive Engines.	Passenger Carriages.	Luggage Vans, &c.
Arbroath and Forfar	5	12	110
Birmingham and Gloucester	40	46	586
Bristol and Gloucester	11	20	213
Chester and Birkenhead	10	60	36
Dublin and Drogheda	15	69	105
Dundee and Newtyle	7	9	138
(Also 3 stationary engines.)			
Durham and Sunderland	—	23	28
(13 stationary engines.)			
Dunfermline and Charlestown	—	2	189
(Horses used on this line.)			
Eastern Counties	66	204	1142
Edinburgh and Dalkeith	—	28	104
(Horses used on this line.)			
Edinburgh, Leith and Granton	—	8	—
(Horses used on this line.)			
Glasgow, Paisley, Kilmarnock, &c.	31	133	1334
Grand Junction—including Liverpool and Manchester and Bolton and Leigh	128	343	1978
Gravesend and Rochester	4	16	6
Great North of England	37	46	717
Great Western	127	232	919
Hartlepool	5	8	6

	Locomotive Engines.	Passenger Carriages.	Luggage Vans, &c.
Hayle and Redruth	7	6	119
(Also 2 stationary engines.)			
Hull and Selby	17	45	238
Lancaster and Preston Junction	6	37	36
Leicester and Swannington	8	4	13
Llanelly and Llandillo	4	2	454
London and Blackwall	—	47	7
(Eight stationary engines.)			
London and Brighton	44	163	423
London and Croydon	8	56	89
London and Southwestern	47	212	508
Manchester and Birmingham	27	100	961
Manchester, Bolton, and Bury	12	52	228
Maryport and Carlisle	8	16	135
Midland	109	251	1842
Newcastle and Darlington	37	81	2515
Newcastle and North Shields	5	28	124
Newcastle and Carlisle	26	67	653
(Also hire 470 coal-wagons.)			
Newtyle and Coupar	1	2	48
Norfolk	18	50	497
North Union	19	49	54
Pontop and South Shields	13	—	2649
(Newcastle and Darlington passenger-carriages.)			
Preston and Wyre	8	40	108
St. Helen's	9	—	20
Sheffield, Ashton, and Manchester	25	105	469
Stockton and Hartlepool, and Clarence	19	23	67
South-eastern	90	409	881
Taff Vale	12	23	328
Ulster	11	34	102
Wishaw and Coltness	11	10	1016
York and North Midland	48	109	1050

Cost of European Railways per Mile, *extracted from a Report published by order of the House of Commons.*

Belgian Lines.

Ghent to Courtray	£6.620
Ghent to Bruges	7,675
Landen to St. Trond	8,990
Louvain to Tirlemont	19,957
Liege to Prussian Frontiers	40,797
Ans to Liege	62,325
Average of State Lines	17,132

French Lines.

Paris and Orleans	24,390
Paris and Rouen	23,754
Strasbourg and Basle	18,485
Amiens and Boulogne	20,000
Rouen and Havre	28,300
Avignon and Marseilles	28,600
Orleans and Bordeaux	20,830
The Centre	18,050
The North with Calais Branch	19,900
Paris and Lyons	24,840
Lyons and Avignon, with Branch to Grenoble	25,800

Austrian Lines.

Olmütz to Prague	11,657
Brünn to Bohmisch Trübau	16,360

Prussian Lines.

Berlin and Potsdam	12,323
Magdeburg and Leipsic	10,179
Cologne to Belgian Frontiers	28,334

English Lines, with Scotch and Irish.

Arbroath and Forfar	9,214
Chester and Birkenhead	34,198

Dublin and Drogheda	£15,652
Dublin and Kingstown	59,122
Dundee and Arbroath	8,570
Durham and Sunderland	14,281
Edinburgh and Glasgow	35,024
Eastern Counties and North-eastern	46,355
Glasgow, Kilmarnock, and Air	20,607
Glasgow and Greenock	35,451
Gravesend and Rochester	13,333
Great Western	43,885
Hartlepool	26,660
London and Birmingham	38,440
London and Blackwall	287,678
London and Brighton	56,981
London and Croydon	80,400
London and South-western	28,004
Manchester, Bolton, and Bury	70,000
Manchester and Birmingham	61,624
Manchester and Leeds	64,582
Midland	30,949
Newcastle, Darlington, and Brandling	22,992
Newcastle and Carlisle	17,837
Newcastle and North Shields	44,233
Norfolk	13,150
North Union, and Bolton and Preston	27,799
Preston and Wyre	22,261
Sheffield and Manchester	48,543
South-eastern	44,412
Taff Vale	21,610
Ulster	14,334
York and North Midland, &c.	25,924

Problems, and one which is most generally used.

For example, supposing we wish to find out the variation from a straight line on a curve of 400 feet radius with a locomotive whose extreme centre of wheels are 20 feet. We wish to know this to find the width of tire to be put on the forward driving wheels to prevent falling off the rails. We are supposing now an 8-wheel engine, 4 drivers, and 4 wheels in a truck.

Fig. 49.

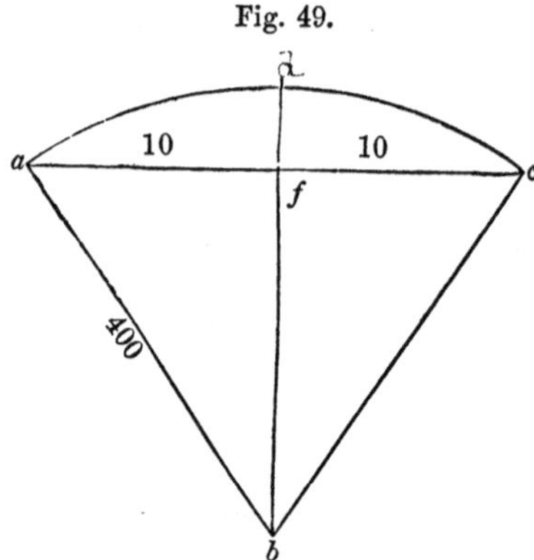

Now we have the radius, *a b*, 400 feet, and the chord, *a c*, 20 feet, which is the distance the wheel centres are apart; from *b*, as a centre, we describe the arc, *a d c*, with *b a*, as radius. Bisect the chord, *a c*, at *f*; then *a f* will equal 10 feet, and *f c* equal

10 feet. Now to find the distance, *f d*, which is the versed sine:

RULE.—Find the square of *a b*, and from it subtract the square of *a f*; the remainder find the square root of, then the product; subtract from *a b*, and the remainder will give the distance, *d f*.

```
      400      100
        400
      ------
      160000
         100
      ------
   3)159900(399·87      400
        9               399·87
      ----             -------
  69)  699               0·13 Feet, Answer.
       621
      -----
   789)7800
       7101
       ------
  7988)69900
        63904
        -------
 79967)599600
        559769
        -------
         39831
```

A TABLE *of the Fractional Parts of an Inch, when divided into thirty-two parts; likewise a foot of twelve inches, reduced to decimals.*

Parts.	Decimals.	Parts.	Decimals.	Parts of a Foot.	Decimals.
$\frac{1}{32}$	·03125	$\frac{1}{2}$ and $\frac{1}{32}$	·53125	11	·9166
$\frac{1}{16}$	·0625	$\frac{1}{2}$ and $\frac{1}{16}$	·5625	10	·8333
$\frac{3}{32}$	·09375	$\frac{1}{2}$ and $\frac{3}{32}$	·59375	9	·75
$\frac{1}{8}$	·125	$\frac{5}{8}$	·625	8	·6666
$\frac{1}{8}$ and $\frac{1}{32}$	·15625	$\frac{5}{8}$ and $\frac{1}{32}$	·65625	7	·5833
$\frac{1}{8}$ and $\frac{1}{16}$	·1875	$\frac{5}{8}$ and $\frac{1}{16}$	·6875	6	·5
$\frac{1}{8}$ and $\frac{3}{32}$	·21875	$\frac{5}{8}$ and $\frac{3}{32}$	·71875	5	·4166
$\frac{1}{4}$	·25	$\frac{3}{4}$	·75	4	·3333
$\frac{1}{4}$ and $\frac{1}{32}$	·28125	$\frac{3}{4}$ and $\frac{1}{32}$	·78125	3	·25
$\frac{5}{16}$	·3125	$\frac{3}{4}$ and $\frac{1}{16}$	·8125	2	·1666
$\frac{3}{8}$	·375	$\frac{3}{4}$ and $\frac{3}{32}$	·84375	1	·0833
$\frac{3}{8}$ and $\frac{1}{32}$	·40625	$\frac{7}{8}$	·875	$\frac{7}{8}$	·07291
$\frac{3}{8}$ and $\frac{1}{16}$	·4375	$\frac{7}{8}$ and $\frac{1}{32}$	·90625	$\frac{3}{4}$	·0625
$\frac{3}{8}$ and $\frac{3}{32}$	·46875	$\frac{7}{8}$ and $\frac{1}{16}$	·9375	$\frac{5}{8}$	·0528
$\frac{1}{2}$	·5	$\frac{7}{8}$ and $\frac{3}{32}$	·96875	$\frac{1}{2}$	·04166
				$\frac{3}{8}$	·03125
				$\frac{1}{4}$	·02083
				$\frac{1}{8}$	·01031

The great utility of the above table is to facilitate the multiplication and division of parts of an inch; also in calculations. For example, suppose a sheet of iron to be $20\frac{5}{8}$ inches long, $12\frac{3}{4}$ and $\frac{1}{32}$ inches broad, and $\frac{3}{4}$ and $\frac{3}{32}$ of an inch in thickness, what number of cubic inches does it contain?

```
    20·625          263·58
     12·78             ·84
    ------          ------
    165000          105432
   144375          210864
   41250          --------
  20625           221·4072 cubic inches of iron.
 ---------        --------
 263·58750
```

THE LEVER.

1. A LEVER is an inflexible bar, either straight or bent, supposed capable of turning round a fixed point, called the fulcrum.

According to the relative positions of the weight, power, and fulcrum, on the lever, it is said to be of three kinds, viz. when the fulcrum is somewhere betwixt the weight and power, it is of the first kind; when the weight is between the power and the fulcrum, it is of the second kind; and when the power is between the weight and the fulcrum, it is of the third kind, thus:

```
                                        P.
1st. ___________________________________
     W.                 F

                                        P.
2d.  ___________________________________
     F.                 W.

                        P.              W
3d.  ___________________________________
     F.
```

2. In the first and second kinds there is an advantage of power, but a proportionate loss of velocity; and in the third kind there is an advantage in velocity, but a loss of power.

3. When the weight × its distance from the fulcrum = the power × its distance from the fulcrum, then the lever will be at rest, or in equilibrio; but if one of these products be greater than the other, the lever will turn round the fulcrum in the direction of that side whose product is the greater.

4. In all the three kinds of levers, any of these quantities, the weight, or its distance from the fulcrum, or the power or its distance from the fulcrum, may be found from the rest, such, that when applied to the lever, it will remain at rest, or the weight and power will balance each other.

5. $$\frac{\text{Weight} \times \text{its distance from fulc.}}{\text{Dist. of power from fulc.}} = \text{power.}$$

6. $$\frac{\text{Power} \times \text{its distance from fulc.}}{\text{Dist. of weight from fulc.}} = \text{weight.}$$

7. $$\frac{\text{Weight} \times \text{dist. weight from fulc.}}{\text{Power.}} = \text{dist. power from fulc.}$$

8. $$\frac{\text{Power} \times \text{dist. power from fulc.}}{\text{Weight.}} = \text{dist. weight from fulc.}$$

9. In the first kind of lever, the pressure upon the fulcrum = sum of weight and power: in the second and third = their difference.

10. If there be several weights on both sides of the fulcrum, they may be reckoned powers on the one side of the fulcrum, and weights on the other.

Then, if the sum of the product of all the weights × their distances from the fulcrum be = to the sum of the products of all the powers × their distances from the fulcrum, the lever will be at rest; if not, it will turn round the fulcrum in the direction of that side whose products are greatest.

11. In these calculations the weight of the lever is not taken into account; but if it is, it is just reckoned like any other weight or power acting at the centre of gravity.

12. When two, three, or more levers act upon each other in succession, then the entire mechanical advantage which they give, is found by taking the product of their separate advantages.

13. It is to be observed in general, before applying these observations to practice, that if a lever be bent, the distances from the fulcrum must be taken, as perpendiculars drawn from the lines of direction of the weight and power of the fulcrum.

Example.—In a lever of the first kind, the weight is 16, its distance from the fulcrum 12, and the power is 8; therefore by No. 7 of this chapter, $\frac{16 \times 12}{8} = 24$ the distance of power from the fulcrum.

In a lever of the second kind, a power of 3 acts at a distance of 12; what weight can be balanced at a distance of 4 from the fulcrum? Here, by No. 6, $\frac{3 \times 12}{4} = 9$ weight.

In a lever of the third kind the weight is 60, and its distance 12, and the power acts at a distance of 9 from the fulcrum; therefore, by No. 5, $\frac{60 \times 12}{9} =$ 80 the power required.

If there be a lever of the first kind, having three weights, 7, 8, and 9, at the respective distances of 6, 15, and 29, from the fulcrum on one side, and a power of 17 at the distance of 9 on the other side of the fulcrum, then a power is to be applied at the distance of 12 from the fulcrum, in the last-mentioned side; what must that power be to keep the lever in balance?

Here $(6 \times 7) + (15 \times 8) + (29 \times 9) = 423 =$ the effect of the three weights on the one side of the fulcrum, and $17 \times 9 = 153 =$ the effect of the power on the other side. Now, it is clear that the effect of the weight is far greater than the effect of the power; and the difference, $423 - 153 = 273$, requires to be balanced by a power applied at the distance of 12, which will evidently be found by dividing 270 by 12, which gives 22·5, the weight required.

14. The Roman steel-yard is a lever of the first kind, so contrived that only one movable weight is employed.

TABLE *showing the Effects of a Force of Traction of* 100 *pounds, at different Velocities, on Canals, Railroads, and Turnpike Roads.**

VELOCITY OF MOTION.		LOAD MOVED BY A POWER OF 100 LBS.					
Miles per Hour.	Feet per Second.	On a Canal.		On a level Railway.		On a level Turnpike Road.	
		Tot. Mass moved.	Useful effect.	Tot. Mass moved.	Useful effect.	Tot. Mass moved.	Useful effect.
		lbs.	lbs.	lbs.	lbs.	lbs.	lbs.
2½	3·66	55,500	39,400	14,400	10,800	1,800	1,350
3	4·40	38,542	27,361	14,400	10,800	1,800	1,350
3½	5·13	28,316	20,100	14,400	10,800	1,800	1,350
4	5·86	21,680	15,390	14,400	10,800	1,800	1,350
5	7·33	13,875	9,850	14,400	10,800	1,800	1,350
6	8·80	9,635	6,840	14,400	10,800	1,800	1,350
7	10·26	7,080	5,026	14,400	10,800	1,800	1,350
8	11·73	5,420	3,848	14,400	10,800	1,800	1,350
9	13·20	4,282	3,040	14,400	10,800	1,800	1,350
10	14·66	3,468	2,462	14,400	10,800	1,800	1,350
13·5	19·9	1,900	1,350	14,400	10,800	1,800	1,350

* The force of traction on a canal varies as the square of the velocity; but the mechanical power necessary to move the boat, is usually reckoned to increase as the cube of the velocity. On a railroad or turnpike, the force of traction is constant, but the mechanical power necessary to move the carriage increases as the velocity.

TABLE *of the Tractive Power of the Locomotive Engine, when the adhesion is from one-fifth to one-fifteenth that of the insistent weight of the Driving Wheels,*

Insistent weight on driv. wheels, in tons.	TRACTION IN LBS. WHEN THE ADHESION IS IN THE FOLLOWING RATIOS.										
	$\frac{1}{5}$	$\frac{1}{6}$	$\frac{1}{7}$	$\frac{1}{8}$	$\frac{1}{9}$	$\frac{1}{10}$	$\frac{1}{11}$	$\frac{1}{12}$	$\frac{1}{13}$	$\frac{1}{14}$	$\frac{1}{15}$
5	2240	1866·6	1600	1400	1244·4	1120	1018·1	933·3	861·5	800	746·6
6	2688	2440	1920	1680	1493·3	1344	1221·8	1120	1033·8	960	896
7	3136	2613·3	2240	1960	1792	1568	1425·5	1306·6	1206·1	1120	1045·3
8	3584	2986·6	2560	2240	1991·1	1792	1629	1493·4	1378·4	1280	1194·6
9	4032	3360	2880	2520	2240	2016	1832·7	1680	1550·7	1440	1344
10	4480	3733·3	3200	2800	2489	2240	2036·3	1866·6	1723	1600	1493·3
11	4928	4106·6	3520	3080	2737·7	2464	2240	2053·3	1895·4	1760	1642·6
12	5376	4480	3840	3360	2986·6	2688	2443·6	2240	2067·7	1920	1792
13	5824	4853·3	4160	3640	3235·5	2912	2647·2	2426·6	2240	2080	1941·3
14	6272	5226·6	4480	3920	3484·4	3136	2851	2613·3	2412·3	2240	2090·6
15	6720	5600	4800	4200	3733·3	3360	3054·5	2800	2584·6	2400	2240
16	7168	5973·3	5120	4480	3982·2	3584	3280	2986·6	2757	2560	2389·3
17	7610	6346·7	5440	4760	4231·1	3808	3483·7	3173·3	2929·3	2720	2538·6
18	8064	6720	5760	5040	4480	4032	3687·5	3360·0	3101·6	2880	2688
19	8512	7093·3	6080	5320	4729	4256	3891	3546·7	3274·0	3040	2837·3
20	8960	7466·7	6400	5600	4977·7	4480	4094·8	3733·3	3446·3	3200	2986·7
21	9408	7840	6720	5880	5226·6	4704	4298·3	3920	3618·6	3360	3136
22	9856	8213·3	7040	6160	5475·5	4928	4502·2	4106·7	3791·0	3520	3285·3
23	10304	8586·7	73[illegible]	6440	5724·4	5152	4705·7	4293·3	3963·3	3680	3334·6
24	10725	8960	7680	6720	5973·3	5376	4909·5	4480	4135·6	3840	3484
25	11200	9333·3	8000	7000	6222·2	5600	5091	4666·7	4307·6	4000	3633·3

TO CONSTRUCT AN ECCENTRIC WHEEL.

From the centre of the shaft O take O P equal to half the length of the stroke which you intend the wheel to work; and from P as a centre, with any radius greater than P D, describe a circle, and this circle will represent the required wheel. For every circle, drawn from the centre P, will work the same length of stroke, whatever may be its radius; as, whatever you increase the distance of the circumference of the circle from the centre of motion on the one side, you will have a corresponding increase on the opposite side equal to it.

Thus, suppose an eccentric wheel to work a stroke of 18 inches is required, the diameter of the shaft being 6 inches; and if 2 inches be the thickness of metal necessary for keying it on to the shaft, then set off, from O to P, 9 inches; and $9 + 5 = 14$ inches, the radius of the wheel required.

Fig. 50.

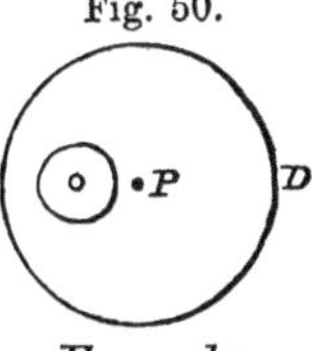

Formulæ.

Let S represent the space the end A is moved through by the eccentric wheel, and *s* the space the slide moves.

Then, $A\,B \times s = B\,C \times S$; and this equation,

solved for A B, B C, S, and s, gives the following:

$$A\,B = \frac{B\,C \times S}{s} \quad (1.) \qquad S = \frac{A\,B \times s}{B\,C} \quad (3.)$$

$$B\,C = \frac{A\,B \times s}{S} \quad (2.) \qquad s = \frac{B\,C \times S}{A\,B} \quad (4.)$$

Mode of Setting the Eccentrics on the Main Shaft of Driving Wheels of Locomotives.

We suppose the use of an additional eccentric for working the valves half stroke.

Fig. 51.

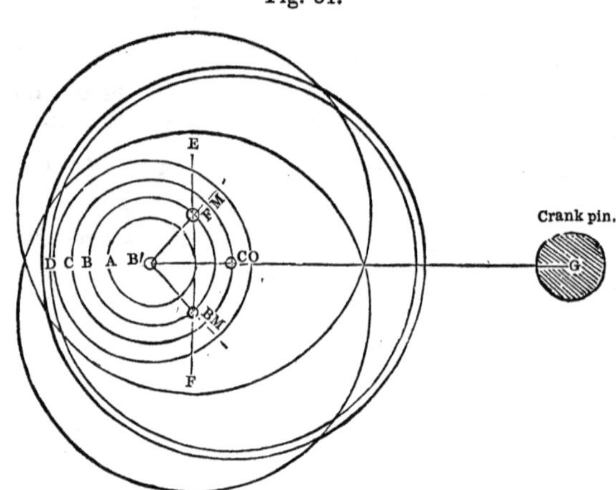

Fig. 50 represents the true position of eccentrics on right-hand side of engine when the rock arm is used. Cylinders and eccentric rod supposed to be horizontal, the crank being on its forward centre, g.

B′ G is the length of crank.

B′ D is half radius of axle.

B′ B equal half the throw of valve.

B′ C equal half the throw of cut-off eccentric.

B′ A equal lap and lead.

Draw the line, E F, perpendicular to the line of eccentric rod, and tangent to the lap and lead circle, and when it intersects the throw of valve at the points, F M and B M, is the centre of the eccentrics; the cut-off eccentric, *c o*, is set on the line of crank when the throw of eccentric intersects tha line.

Crank Drawn on the Centre.

Fig. 52.

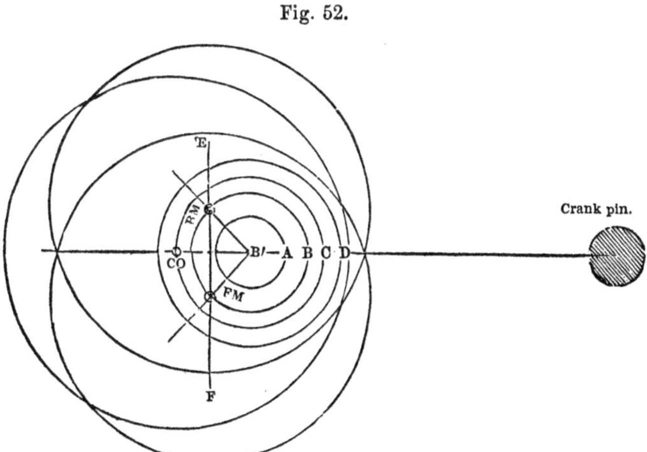

Fig. 52 is the same construction as fig. 51, working direct to the valve, without the intervention of rock arm, only the centres of eccentrics are on the left side instead of right, and the forward motion eccentric is below, and the backward motion eccentric above.

E F line drawn at right angle with eccentric rod.

A B′ lap and lead.

B B′ ½ throw of valve.

B′ C ½ throw of cut-off eccentric.

B′ D radius of axle.

For any other angle of cylinder or eccentric rod, the construction is precisely similar. The angle of connecting rod, being so trifling, is not taken into consideration in practice.

Tire-Bars, Lengths required to make Inside Diameter.

Thickness when finished.	Inside Diameter.	Outside Diameter.	Length of Bar required.	
Inches.	Inches.	Inches.	Feet.	Inches.
1½	33	36	9	
1⅝	38⅝	42	10	8
2½	39	44	10	9
1⅝	42⅝	46	11	7
2	44⅛	48	12	2
2	51	55	13	8¾
2	56	60	15	2½
2	68	72	18	3
2	80	84	21	3
2	92	96	24	2

The alloy of 2 zinc and 1 copper may be crumbled in a mortar when cold. The ordinary range of good yellow brass, that files and turns well, is from about 4½ to 9 oz. to the pound. Brazing solders—3 copper and 1 part zinc, (very hard;) 8 parts of brass and 1 zinc, (hard;) 6 parts brass and 1 tin, 1 zinc, (soft.) Solder for iron, copper, and brass, consists of nearly equal parts copper and zinc. Muntz's metal—40 parts zinc, 60 copper. Any proportions between the extremes of 50 zinc and 50 copper, and 37 zinc and 63 copper, will roll and break at the red-heat; but 40 zinc to 60 copper are the proportions preferred. Large bells—4½ oz. to 5 oz. of tin to 1 lb. of copper. Tough brass for engine work—1½ lb. tin, 1½ zinc, and 10 lbs. copper. Brass for heavy bearings—2½ oz. tin, ½ oz. zinc, and 1 lb. copper. Babbit's metal—1 lb. copper, 5 lbs. regulus of antimony, and 50 lbs. tin. Melt copper first, add the antimony with a small portion of the tin, charcoal being strewed over the metal in the crucible to prevent oxidation.

ON THE SAFETY VALVE AND LEVER.

The apertures for safety valves require no nice calculations. It is only necessary to have the aperture sufficient to let the steam off from the boiler as fast as it is generated, when the engine is not at work.

The safety valve is loaded sometimes by putting a heavy weight upon it, and sometimes by means of a lever with a weight to move along to suit the required pressure.

When the whole weight is put on the valve, to find the pressure to each square inch:—

Multiply the square of the diameter of the valve by ·7854, and this product will give the area, or number of square inches in the valve.

And if the whole weight upon the valve, in pounds, be divided by the number of square inches in the valves, the quotient will give the number of pounds pressure to each square inch in the valve.

Ex.—If a weight of 40 lbs. be placed upon a valve, the diameter of which is 3 inches, what will be the pressure to each square inch?

$3^2 \times \cdot7854 = 7$ square inches; then, $40 \div 7 = 5\frac{5}{7}$ lbs. per square inch.

ON THE SAFETY VALVE LEVER.

This being a lever of the third order, it may be calculated as follows; and also the weight of the lever will be considered; for when the lever is large and the valve is small, the weight of the lever is such as to produce a very sensible pressure upon the valve to each square inch. But previous to the calculation, it will be necessary to make the following remarks.

Since the fulcrum is at one end, and the power or the action of the steam between that end and the movable weight, (see fig. 2, where F is the fulcrum, A is the point where the steam acts, and W the movable weight,) some have taken A for the fulcrum, and thereby have committed very great errors; for, according to this rule, a weight put on at twice the distance from A that A is from F, would, if the weight of the lever were not considered, be twice its own weight upon the valve; whereas, if it had been reckoned from F, its real fulcrum, it would be three times its own weight upon the valve.

It has been shown, and indeed it is almost self-evident, that if we have two, three, or four times, &c. the leverage, we will have two, three, or four times &c. the effect produced respectively, the weight remaining the same. Therefore divide the length of the lever by the distance between the fulcrum and valve, and the quotient gives the leverage; and the leverage, multiplied by the weight, gives the whole weight upon the valve; and this product, divided by the number of square inches in the valve, gives the weight per square inch. Or, if the weight per inch be known, multiply the number of pounds per square inch by the number of square inches, and this product gives the whole weight upon the valve, which, divided by the leverage, gives the weight. Or, if the weight be given, divide by it, and the quotient will give the leverage; and the leverage, multiplied by the distance between the fulcrum and the valve, gives the length of the lever.

Ex.—Given the whole length of the lever 24 inches, the distance between the fulcrum and valve 3 inches, the diameter of the valve $2\frac{1}{2}$ inches; required the weight put on at the end of the lever, so as to have 50 lbs. per square inch upon the valve; also to divide the lever so as to have 40, 30, 20 lbs. &c. upon the valve with the same weight.

$(2{\cdot}5)^2 \times {\cdot}7854 = 4{\cdot}9$ = area of the valve.

$4{\cdot}9 \times 50 = 245$ lbs. whole weight on the valve.

$\frac{245}{8} = 30{\cdot}625$ lbs. = the weight which must be put on at the end of the lever to give 50 lbs. per square inch.

And $\frac{4{\cdot}9 \times 40}{30{\cdot}625} = 6{\cdot}4$; then, $6{\cdot}4 \times 3 = 19{\cdot}2$ inches, the distance from the fulcrum the weight must be placed to have 40 lbs.

$24 - 19{\cdot}2 = 4{\cdot}8$; that is, the weight must be shifted in towards the fulcrum 4·8 inches to have 40 lbs. per inch; and for 30 lbs. per square inch, move it in 4·8 inches more, &c.

To find what weight must be put on at the end of a Lever to give any number of pounds pressure per square inch upon the Valve, the weight of the Lever being taken into consideration.

RULE.—Find the area of the valve by multiplying the square of the diameter by ·7854; then multiply this area by the number of pounds per square inch which you want upon the valve, and this product will give the whole weight upon the valve.

Next divide the whole length of the lever by the distance between the fulcrum and valve,* and the quotient will give the leverage which any weight will have when put on at the end of the lever.

Multiply this leverage by half the weight of the lever, and the product will give the pressure on the whole valve from the action of the lever alone: add to this product the weight of the valve, &c. and subtract the sum from the whole weight on the valve above mentioned; the remainder will give the weight which will be pressing on the valve from the action of the weight alone; and this, divided by the leverage, gives the weight itself.

Note.—If, instead of considering half the weight of the lever to act at the end, we conceive the whole weight to act at the centre of gravity, the result will be the same, the lever being uniform.

* What is here meant by the distance between the fulcrum and valve, is that part of the lever between the fulcrum and the point where the lever acts upon the valve.

Ex. 1.—Given the length of the lever 24 inches, the distance between the fulcrum and valve 3 inches, the weight of the valve 3 lbs. the weight of the lever 3 lbs.; it is required to determine what weight must be put upon the end of the lever that it may press 30 lbs. per square inch, the diameter of the valve being 3 inches.

Now, $3 \times 3 = 9$, and $9 \times \cdot 7854 = 7 \cdot 0686$ = area, or number of square inches in the valve; and $7 \times 30 = 210$ lbs. = whole weight upon the valve; and if we conceive the whole weight of the lever to be concentrated in its centre of gravity, and acting with the leverage of the centre of gravity, the lever being uniform throughout its length, we have, since 12 = the distance between the fulcrum and centre of gravity, $12 \div 3 = 4$, the leverage of the centre of gravity; and 3 lbs. the weight of the lever, multiplied by 4, gives 12 lbs. the weight that the lever will give upon the whole valve. 12 lbs. added to 3 lbs. the weight of the valve, gives 15 lbs. the weight from both lever and valve; and this, subtracted from 210 lbs. gives 195 lbs., the weight upon the valve from the action of the weight alone, independent of the weight of the lever; and this, divided by the leverage, gives the weight. Thus, $24 \div 3 = 8$ = leverage of the end of the lever; and $195 \div 8$ gives $24\frac{3}{8} = 24 \cdot 375$ lbs. the weight put on at the end of the lever to give 30 lbs. per inch, when the weight of the lever is taken into consideration.

Now, this being determined, we must mark the lever in those points, where the above found weight will give 20 lbs. per inch, and also 10 lbs. per inch. This is found by inverting the above operation; for you have the weight given, the valve, &c. to find the leverage; and the leverage, multiplied by the distance between the fulcrum and valve, gives the distance from the fulcrum the given weight must be put. Thus 7 × 20 = 140 = whole weight upon the valve; from this subtract 15 lbs., the weight from the valve and lever, and the remainder gives what the weight must put on = 125 lbs.; and this weight, divided by the given weight, 24·375 lbs., gives 5·128 = the leverage; and 5·128 × 3 = 15·384 inches from the fulcrum, for 20 lbs. per inch.

Now, to determine the distance from the fulcrum when there are 10 lbs. per inch, proceed as above. Thus, 7 × 10 = 70 lbs. upon the whole valve; subtract from this again 15 lbs., the weight of the lever and valve, and 55 remains; and 55 ÷ 24·375 = 2·256 = leverage; and 2·256 × 3 = 6·768 inches from the fulcrum.

Ex. 2.—Given the length of the lever 16 inches, and its weight 2 lbs.; the distance between the fulcrum and valve 2 inches, and the weight of the valve and spindle 1½ lb.; to find what weight must be put on at the end of the lever to press 40 lbs.

per square inch upon the valve, the diameter of which is 2 inches.

The square of 2 is 4; hence,

·7854
4

3·1416 = area of the valve, or number of square inches in it.
40 lbs.

125·6640 lbs. = weight on the whole valve.

16 ÷ 2 = 8 = leverage which the weight will have at the end.

Now, to consider half the weight of the lever to act at the end, is the same as to consider the whole weight of the lever to act at its centre of gravity, the lever being uniform.

1 lb. = half the weight of the lever.
8 = leverage at the end of the lever.

8 lbs. = weight on the whole valve from the action of the lever.
1·5 lbs. = weight of valve, &c.

9·5 lbs. = weight on the valve from the action of both lever and valve.

125·664
9·5

116·164

That is, the weight put on at the end of the lever must be such as to press 116·164 lbs. on the whole valve; but the leverage of the weight is 8, therefore one-eighth part of this weight will do. Thus, 116·164 ÷ 8 = 14·52 lbs. = weight which must be put on at the end to press 40 lbs. per inch upon the valve. Now, to mark the lever where we will have 35 lbs., 30 lbs., 25 lbs., 20 lbs., &c. per square inch, we must proceed thus:—

3·1416 = number of square inches in the area of the valve.
35

157080
94248

109·956
9·5

100·456 = weight on the valve from the action of the weight.

And 100·456 ÷ 14·52 = 6·918 = the leverage which the weight must have; and if this leverage be multiplied by the distance between the fulcrum and valve, thus:—

6·918 = leverage.
2 = distance between the fulcrum and valve.

13·836 = the distance along the lever from the fulcrum.

16 — 13·836 = 2·164 inches = the distance which the weight must be moved in towards the valve.

And if you want 30 lbs. per square inch, move it in 2·164 inches farther, and so on, as far as you please, making the division always 2·164 inches.

TABLES OF SAFETY VALVE LEVERS.

1. Diameter of the valve 4 inches, weight of the valve, &c. 3 lbs., length of the lever 24 inches, the distance between the fulcrum and valve 4 inches, and the weight of the lever 8 lbs.; then the weight put on at the end of the lever, to give 30 lbs. per square inch upon the valve, will be 58·332 lbs., or 58 lbs. 5⅓ oz. nearly.

For 10 lbs. pressure, dist. from fulcrum 6·765 inches.
20 lbs..................................15·382 inches.
30 lbs..................................24 inches.

2. Length of the lever 16 inches, distance between the fulcrum and valve 2 inches, diameter of valve 2 inches, the weight of the lever 4 lbs., and weight of valve ½ lb.; it will require a weight of 9·7185 lbs. to be put on at the end of the lever to give 30 lbs. per square inch upon the valve; and the distances in inches which the weight must be from the fulcrum to give 10, 15, 20, 25, and 30 lbs. are respectively as follow:—

10 lbs.	15 lbs.	20 lbs.	25 lbs.	30 lbs.
3·068	6·301	9·534	12·767	16

If the weight be taken off from the lever, then the weight on the valve from the action of the lever alone will give 5¼ lbs. per square inch.

Note.—9·7185 lbs. is 9 lbs. 11½ oz.

3. Weight of lever 4 lbs., and weight of valve, &c. 1 lb.; whole length of the lever 24 inches, distance between the fulcrum and valve 3 inches, diameter of valve 3 inches, weight put on at the end 42·05375 lbs. Distances from the fulcrum in inches:—

10 lbs.	20 lbs.	30 lbs.	40 lbs.	50 lbs.
3·8292	8·8719	13·9146	18·9573	24

SHRINKAGE OF TIRE BARS.

The general allowance for shrinkage is ⅛ of an inch to the foot of diameter of wheel centre.

Example.—Suppose we wish to turn a centre of driving wheel to fit a tire which is 5 feet the inside diameter, equal to 188½ inches circumference; then we must turn the centre ⅝ larger in circumference, which is 189⅛ inches.

Shrinkage of Castings.

In making all patterns of work, we make an allowance of $\frac{1}{8}$ inch larger per foot in cast iron; for brass allow $\frac{1}{8}$ full.

SPRING STEEL.

I give the following result of experiment made by me with spring steel. The bar made use of was supported on both extremities, and the weight suspended in the middle. The following are the results:—Length between the fulcrum 2 feet; width of bar 1 inch.

Number of Experiments.	Bending Weight.	Deflection.	Thickness of Bar.
1	82 lbs.	$\frac{5}{16}$	$\frac{5}{16}$
2	118 lbs.	$\frac{5}{16}$	$\frac{5}{16}$

The table shows that the deflection was equal in both cases. At the same time it appears that the squares of the thickness are to each other as the bending weights, $\frac{82}{118} = \frac{25}{36}$ very near, thus conforming to the general theory.

For calculating the Radius of a Curve when the Angle of Deflection and Chord are given.

Railroad curves are always laid off with chords of 100 feet, and we often find, when speaking of curves, the angle of deflection is merely given. Now to find the radius:

5730 feet are a common radius, which is equal to a deflection of 1°.

Rule.—Divide the number of degrees deflected into 5730; the product will be the radius of the curve.

Example.—We have a curve with a deflection of 6°, and the chord 100 feet.

6)5730

955 feet radius of curve, Ans.

TABLE *of Revolutions, per Mile, of Driving Wheels, and consumption of Steam, Water, and Fuel, for each sized Wheel; taking the Steam admitted to each Cylinder as exactly one cubic foot at a gross pressure of* 114·7 *lbs., or* 100 *lbs. on the spring balance.*

DRIVING WHEELS.			CONSUMPTION PER MILE.				
Diameter.	Circumference.	Revolutions per Mile.	Steam.	Water.	Wood.	Anthracite Coal.	Coke.
Feet.	Feet.	Number.	Cubic feet.	Pounds.	Pounds.	Pounds.	Pounds.
3	9·4248	560·2	2240	478	119·5	76·33	59·75
3½	11·0	480·1	1920·8	409·74	102·41	68·3	51·22
4	12·566	420·3	1680·4	358·45	89·61	59·76	44·8
4½	14·137	373·4	1493·6	318·6	79·65	53·1	39·8
5	15·708	336·3	1345·2	286·94	71·73	47·82	35·87
5½	17·278	305·6	1222·4	261·35	65·34	43·56	32·67
6	18·849	280·5	1122	239·33	59·83	39·89	29·92
6½	20·420	258·6	1034·4	220·65	55·14	36·78	27·58
7	22·0	240·0	960	204·78	51·2	34·13	25·6
7½	23·562	224·0	906	193·26	48·31	32·21	24·16
8	25·132	210·1	840·4	179·27	44·82	29·88	22·41
8½	26·703	197·4	789·6	168·43	42·11	28·07	21·05
9	28·274	186·7	745·8	159·1	39·8	26·5	19·9
9½	29·845	176·9	707·6	150·9	37·82	25·15	18·9
10	31·416	168·0	672	143·35	35·84	23·89	18·

WEIGHTS REQUIRED TO CRUSH SOME OF THE MORE IMPORTANT MATERIALS.

	On the square inch.
1. Metals.	
Cast iron	115813—177776 lbs.
Brass, fine	164864
Copper, molten	117088
Copper, hammered	103040
Tin, molten	15456
Lead, molten	7728
2. Woods.	
Oak	3860—5147
Pine	1928
Pinus sylvestris	1606
Elm	1284
3. Stones.	
Gneiss	4970
Sandstone, Rothenburg	2556
Brick, well baked	1092

THE MECHANICAL POWERS.

Power is compounded of the weight or expansive force of a moving body multiplied into its velocity.

THE power of a body which weighs 40 lbs., and moves with the velocity of 50 feet in a second, is the same as that of another body which weighs 80 lbs., and moves with the velocity of 25 feet in a second; for the products of the respective weights and velocities are the same.

$$40 \times 50 = 2000; \text{ and } 80 \times 25 = 2000.$$

Power cannot be increased by mechanical means.

Power is applied to mechanical purposes by the lever, wheel and axle, pulley, inclined plane, wedge, and screw, which are the simple elements of all machines.

The whole theory of these elements consists simply in causing the weight which is to be raised, to pass through a greater or a less space than the power which raises it; for, as power is compounded of the weight or mass of a moving body multiplied into its velocity, a weight passing through a certain space may be made to raise, through a less space, a weight heavier than itself.

Power is gained at the expense of space, by the lever, the wheel and axle, the pulley, the inclined plane, the wedge, and the screw.

LEVER.

Case 1.—*When the fulcrum of the lever is between the power and the weight.*

Rule.—Divide the weight to be raised by the power to be applied; the quotient will give the difference of leverage necessary to support the weight in equilibrio. Hence, a small addition either of leverage or weight will cause the power to preponderate.

EXAMPLE 1.—A ball weighing 3 tons, is to be raised by 4 men, who can exert a force of 12 cwt.: required the proportionate length of lever?

$$3 \text{ tons} = 60 \text{ cwt.; and } \frac{60}{12} = 5.$$

In this example, the proportionate lengths of the lever to maintain the weight in equilibrio, are as 5 to 1. If, therefore, an additional pound be added to the power, the power side of the lever will preponderate, and the weight will be raised. But, although the ball is raised by a force of only one-fifth of its weight, no power is gained, for the weight passes through only one-fifth of the space. The products, therefore, arising from the multiplication of the respective weights and velocities are the same.

EXAMPLE 2.—A weight of 1 ton is to be raised with a lever 8 feet in length, by a man who can exert, for a short time, a force of rather more than 4 cwt.: required at what part of the lever the fulcrum must be placed?

$\frac{20 \text{ cwt.}}{4 \text{ cwt.}} = 5$; that is, the weight is to the power as 5 to 1; therefore, $\frac{8}{5 \times 1} = 1$ foot and a third from the weight.

EXAMPLE 3.—A weight of 40 lbs. is placed one

foot from the fulcrum of a lever; required the power to raise the same when the length of the lever on the other side of the fulcrum is five feet?

$$\frac{40 \times 1}{5} = 8 \text{ lbs., Ans.}$$

CASE 2.—*When the fulcrum is at one extremity of the lever and the power at the other.*

RULE.—As the distance between the power and the fulcrum is to the distance between the weight and the fulcrum, so is the effect to the power.

EXAMPLE 1.—Required the power necessary to raise 120 lbs., when the weight is placed six feet from the power, and two feet from the fulcrum?

As 8 : 2 :: 120 : 30 lbs., Ans.

EXAMPLE 2.—A beam, 20 feet in length, and supported at both ends, bears a weight of two tons at the distance of eight feet from one end; required the weight on each support?

$\frac{40 \text{ cwt.} \times 8 \text{ feet}}{20 \text{ feet}} = 16$ cwt. on the support that is furthest from the weight; and $\frac{40 \times 12}{20 \text{ feet}} = 24$ cwt. on the support nearest to the weight.

WHEEL AND AXLE.

RULE.—As the radius of the wheel is to the radius of the axle, so is the effect to the power.

EXAMPLE.—A weight of 50 lbs. is exerted on the periphery of a wheel whose radius is 10 feet; required the weight raised at the extremity of a cord wound round the axle, the radius being 20 inches.

$$\frac{50 \text{ lbs.} \times 10 \text{ feet} \times 12 \text{ inches}}{20 \text{ inches.}} = 300 \text{ lbs., Ans.}$$

PULLEY.

RULE.—Divide the weight to be raised by twice the number of pulleys in the lower block; the quotient will give the power necessary to raise the weight.

EXAMPLE.—What power is required to raise 600 lbs., when the lower block contains six pulleys?

$$\frac{600}{6 \times 2} = 50 \text{ lbs., Ans.}$$

INCLINED PLANE.

RULE.—As the length of the plane is to its height, so is the weight to the power.

EXAMPLE.—Required the power necessary to raise 540 lbs. up an inclined plane, five feet long and two feet high.

As 5 : 2 :: 540 : 216 lbs., Ans.

WEDGE.

CASE 1.—*When two bodies are forced from one another by means of a wedge, in a direction parallel to its back.*

RULE.—As the length of the wedge is to half its back or head, so is the resistance to the power.

Example.—The breadth of the back or head of the wedge being three inches, and the length of either of its inclined sides 10 inches, required the power necessary to separate two substances with a force of 150 lbs.

As 10 : $1\frac{1}{2}$: : 150 : $22\frac{1}{2}$ lbs., Ans.

Case 2.—*When only one of the bodies is movable.*

Rule.—As the length of the weight is to its back or head, so is the resistance to the power.

Example.—The breadth, length, and force, the same as in the last example.

As 10 : 3 : : 150 : 45 lbs., Ans.

SCREW.

The screw is an inclined plane, and we may suppose it to be generated by wrapping a triangle, or an inclined plane, round the circumference of a cylinder. The base of the triangle is the circumference of the cylinder; its height, the distance between two consecutive cords or threads; and the hypothenuse forms the spiral cord or inclined plane.

Rule.—To the square of the circumference of the screw, add the square of the distance between two threads, and extract the square root of sum. This will give the length of the inclined plane; its height is the distance between two consecutive cords or threads.

When a winch or lever is applied to turn the screw, the power of the screw is as the circle described by the handle of the winch, or lever, to the interval or distance between the spirals.

Velocity is gained at the expense of power by the lever and the wheel and axle.

LEVER.

CASE.—*When the weight to be raised is at one end of the lever, the fulcrum at the other, and the power is applied between them.*

RULE.—As the distance between the power and the fulcrum is to the length of the lever, so is the weight to the power.

EXAMPLE.—The length of the lever being eight feet, and the weight at its extremity 60 lbs., required the power to be applied six feet from the fulcrum to raise it?

As 6 : 8 :: 60 : 80 lbs., Ans.

N. B.—Any other example may be computed by reversing any of the foregoing operations.

FRICTION.

WE have considered the effects of the first movers of machinery, and we must now direct our attention to the subject of Friction, which, as we have frequently noticed, tends to diminish these effects. On this subject it is not our intention to dwell long, as all the researches that have been hitherto made in this branch of mechanical science are not of such a nature as to furnish means of deducing satisfactory laws. The resistance arising from one surface rubbing against another is denominated friction; and it is the only force in nature which is perfectly inert—its tendency always being to destroy motion. Friction may thus be viewed as an obstruction to the power of man in the construction of machinery; but, like all the other forces in nature, it may, when properly understood, be turned to his advantage,—for friction is the chief cause of the stability of buildings or machinery, and without it animals could not exert their strength.

The friction of planed woods and polished metals, without grease, on one another, is about one-fourth of the pressure.

The friction does not increase on the increase of the rubbing surfaces.

The friction of metals is nearly constant.

The friction of woods seems to increase after they are some time in action.

The friction of a cylinder rolling down a plane, is inversely as the diameter of the cylinder.

The friction of wheels is as the diameter of the axle directly, and as the diameter of the wheel inversely. The following hints may be of use for the purpose of diminishing friction:

The gudgeons of pivots and wheels should be made of polished iron, and the bushes or collars in which they move should be made of polished brass. In small and delicate machines, the pivots or knife edges should rest on garnet. Oily substances diminish friction—swine's grease and tallow should be used for wood, but oil for metal. Black lead powder has been used with effect for wooden gudgeons. The ropes of pulleys should be rubbed with tallow.

As to the friction of the mechanic powers. The simple lever has no such resistance, unless the place of the fulcrum be moved during the operation. In the wheel and axle, the friction on the axis is nearly as the weight, the diameter of the axis, and the angular velocity—it is, however, very small. When the sheaves rub against the blocks, the friction of the pulley is very great. In most, if not in all screws, the friction of the screw is equal to the pressure—the square-threaded screw is the best.

In the inclined plane, the friction of a rolling body is far less than that of a sliding one.

To estimate the amount of the friction of a carriage upon a railway, we have,

$$P - \frac{P \times T}{t} = \text{friction},$$

in which rule P signifies the power that will keep

the wagon on the plane, independent of friction; T the time of descent without friction,—both of which are to be determined by the laws of the inclined plane given before: and t is the time of actual descent of the wagon or carriage.

There is a loaded carriage on a railroad 120 feet in length, having an inclination of one foot to the hundred. The carriage, together with its load, weighs 4500 lbs. Now, the height of the plane may be found by the principles of geometry, from the proportion of similar triangles.

$100 : 120 :: 1 : 1{\cdot}2 =$ the height of the plane; and by the laws of falling bodies, and the properties of the inclined plane,

$\sqrt{\frac{1{\cdot}2}{16}} \times 120 = {\cdot}2731 \times 120 = 32{\cdot}772 =$ the time in seconds in which the carriage would descend down the plane without friction—and by the properties of the inclined plane, $100 : 1 :: 4500 : 45 =$ the force that sustains the carriage, without friction, from rolling down the plane; wherefore, by the rule,

$45 - \frac{45 \times 32{\cdot}772}{60} = 20{\cdot}421 =$ the friction in pounds, which retards the carriage in rolling down the railway.

TABLE

Of Comparative Velocity of Driving Wheels to Pistons, the Circumference of the former taken as 1.

Half travel of Piston, in Inches.	Diameter of Wheels, in Feet.									
	3½	4	4½	5	5½	6	6½	7	7½	8
24	0·3638	0·3182	0·2830	0·2541	0·2315	0·2122	0·1958	0·1819	0·1691	0·1592
22	0·3334	0·2918	0·2593	0·2334	0·2122	0·1945	0·1796	0·1667	0·1556	0·1417
20	0·3031	0·2652	0·2393	0·2122	0·1929	0·1768	0·1632	0·1516	0·1414	0·1326
19	0·2880	0·2519	0·2273	0·2016	0·1832	0·1679	0·1550	0·1440	0·1343	0·1259
18	0·2728	0·2386	0·2151	0·1910	0·1736	0·1591	0·1468	0·1364	0·1272	0·1194
17	0·2577	0·2254	0·2034	0·1803	0·1640	0·1503	0·1387	0·1288	0·1202	0·1127
16	0·2425	0·2121	0·1914	0·1697	0·1543	0·1415	0·1305	0·1213	0·1131	0·1061
15	0·2273	0·1989	0·1795	0·1591	0·1447	0·1326	0·1224	0·1137	0·1060	0·0994
14	0·2122	0·1856	0·1675	0·1485	0·1350	0·1237	0·1141	0·1061	0·0990	0·0928
13	0·1971	0·1724	0·1555	0·1379	0·1254	0·1149	0·1061	0·0985	0·0919	0·0862
12	0·1819	0·1591	0·1436	0·1273	0·1157	0·1061	0·0979	0·0909	0·0848	0·0796

TABLE *of Gradients, and Resistance per Ton for each Gradient.*

Vertical Rise.		Gravity due to incline, per Ton.	Vertical Rise.		Gravity due to incline, per Ton.
Ratio,	Per Mile.		Ratio,	Per Mile.	
One in	Feet.	Lbs.	One in	Feet.	Lbs.
100	52·80	22·40	60	88·00	37·333
99	53·33	22·626	59	89·49	37·966
98	53·88	22·858	58	91·03	38·620
97	54·43	23·092	57	92·63	39·298
96	55·00	23·334	56	94·28	40·0
95	55·60	23·579	55	96·00	40·726
94	56·17	23·830	54	97·77	41·480
93	56·77	24·086	53	99·62	42·264
92	57·52	24·342	52	101·53	43·076
91	58·02	24·614	51	103·52	43·920
90	58·66	24·888	50	105·60	44·800
89	59·33	25·168	49	107·75	45·716
88	60·0	25·454	48	110·00	46·688
87	60·69	25·746	47	112·34	47·660
86	61·39	26·046	46	115·04	48·684
85·16	62·00	26·303	45	117·33	49·777
85	62·12	26·353	44	120·0	50·908
84	62·86	26·666	43	122·78	52·092
83	63·61	26·988	42	125·71	53·333
82	64·39	27·317	41	128·78	54·634
81	65·20	27·718	40	132·00	56·00
80	66·0	28·00	39	135·38	57·436
79	66·83	28·355	38	138·95	58·944
78	67·69	28·718	37	142·70	60·540
77	68·57	29·090	36	146·66	62·222
76	69·47	29·472	35	150·84	64·000
75	70·40	29·867	34	155·30	65·880
74	71·38	30·270	33	160·0	67·880
73	72·32	30·685	32	165·0	70·0
72	73·33	31·111	31	170·32	72·216
71	74·36	31·550	30	176·00	74·666
70	75·43	32·000	29	182·06	77·240
69	76·49	32·464	28	188·56	80·00
68	77·64	32·940	27	195·55	82·960
67	78·81	33·932	26	203·06	86·152
66	80·0	33·940	25	211·20	89·60
65	81·23	34·460	24	220·0	93·336
64	82·50	35·0	23	229·56	97·368
63	83·81	35·555	22	240	101·816
62	85·16	36·108	21	251·43	106·666
61	86·55	36·720			

TABLE OF TIME

Occupied in running One Mile, Speed in Feet per Minute, and Number of Revolutions of the Driving Wheels, or Double Strokes of the Piston, per Minute, at the following given speeds.

Speed per Hour.	Speed per Minute.	Time of running 1 mile.	Revolution of Wheels, per Minute—the Diameter of Wheels being in Feet.										
			3 feet.	3½ ft.	4 feet.	4½ feet.	5 feet.	5½ feet.	6 feet.	6½ feet.	7 feet.	7½ feet.	8 feet.
Miles.	Feet.	Min. Sec.	No.	No.	No.	No.	No.	No.	No.	No.	No.	No.	No.
10	880	6 00	93·37	80·	70·	62·25	56·02	50·93	46·68	43·09	40·	37·35	35·01
11	968	5 27	102·71	88·	77·	68·47	61·62	56·02	51·35	47·40	44·	41·08	38·51
12	1056	5 00	112·04	96·	84·	74·70	67·23	61·12	56·02	51·71	48·	44·82	42·02
13	1144	4 37	121·37	104·	91·	80·92	72·73	66·21	60·69	56·02	52·	48·55	45·52
14	1232	4 17	130·70	112·	98·	87·14	78·33	71·30	65·36	60·33	56·	52·29	49·
15	1320	4 00	140·06	120·	105·	93·37	84·03	76·40	70·03	64·64	60·	56·02	52·53
16	1408	3 45	149·39	128·	112·	99·69	89·63	81·50	77·70	68·95	64·	59·76	56·
17	1496	3 32	158·72	136·	119·	105·82	95·23	86·59	79·37	73·26	68·	63·49	59·5
18	1584	3 20	169·06	144·	126·	112·04	100·84	91·68	84·03	77·57	72·	67·23	63·
19	1672	3 09½	178·39	152·	133·	118·26	106·44	96·77	88·70	81·88	76·	70·96	66·5
20	1760	3 00	187·72	160·	140·	124·48	112·04	101·86	93·37	86·19	80·	74·70	70·
21	1848	2 51½	197·05	168·	147·	130·72	117·65	106·95	98·04	90·50	84·	78·43	73·5
22	1936	2 43½	206·38	176·	154·	136·94	123·25	112·04	102·71	94·81	88·	82·17	77·
23	2024	2 36½	215·71	184·	161·	143·17	128·85	117·14	107·38	99·12	92·	85·50	80·5
24	2112	2 30	225·05	192·	168·	149·40	134·45	122·24	112·05	103·43	96·	89·63	84·
25	2200	2 24	233·48	200·	175·	155·63	140·05	127·33	116·72	107·74	100·	93·37	87·5

26	2288	2	18⅔	242·77	208·	182·	161·85	145·65	132·42	121·39	112·05	104·	97·14	91·
27	2376	2	13⅓	255·74	216·	189·	168·07	151·26	137·52	126·05	116·36	108·	100·87	94·5
28	2464	2	08½	261·43	224·	196·	174·3	156·86	142·63	130·72	120·67	112·	104·57	98·
29	2552	2	04	270·78	232·	203·	180·52	162·47	147·74	135·38	124·98	116·	108·32	101·5
30	2640	2	00	280·11	240·	210·	186·74	168·08	152·85	140·04	129·30	120·	112·02	105·
31	2728	1	56	289·52	248·	217·	192·97	173·78	157·98	144·71	133·61	124·	115·75	108·5
32	2816	1	52½	298·79	256·	224·	199·20	179·39	163·	149·38	137·62	128·	119·5	112·
33	2904	1	49	308·12	264·	231·	205·42	185·	168·1	154·05	141·93	132·	123·23	115·5
34	2992	1	45⅝	317·46	272·	238·	211·64	190·60	172·99	158·72	146·24	136·	127·06	119·
35	3080	1	42⅝	326·80	280·	245·	217·13	196·21	177·29	163·33	150·85	140·	130·69	122·5
36	3168	1	40	336·13	288·	252·	224·09	201·82	182·4	168·	155·16	144·	134·42	126·
37	3256	1	37¼	345·47	296·	259·	230·32	207·42	187·5	172·67	159·41	148·	138·16	129·5
38	3344	1	34¾	354·81	304·	266·	236·54	213·03	192·6	177·34	163·72	152·	143·90	133·
39	3432	1	32⅓	364·15	312·	273·	242·77	218·63	197·95	182·05	168·03	156·	145·63	136·5
40	3520	1	30	373·57	320·	280·	252·72	224·24	203·76	186·72	172·40	160·	149·36	140·
42	3696	1	25¾	392·15	336·	294·	261·44	235·44	214·	196·05	181·02	168·	156·83	147·
45	3960	1	20	420·17	360·	315·	284·30	252·27	229·23	210·06	193·95	180·	168·03	157·5
48	4224	1	15	438·18	384·	336·	298·79	269·10	244·55	224·06	206·88	192·	179·23	118·
50	4400	1	12	446·85	400·	350·	315·90	280·30	254·75	233·70	215·50	200·	186·70	185·
55	4840	1	05½	513·54	440·	385·	347·49	308·33	280·17	256·74	237·05	220·	205·37	192·5
60	5280	1	00	560·23	480·	420·	379·08	336·36	305·64	280·5	258·6	240·	224·04	210·1
65	5720	0	55⅓	606·91	520·	455·	416·67	364·39	331·11	303·42	280·15	260·	242·71	227·5
70	6160	0	51⅜	653·59	560·	490·	442·19	392·42	356·58	326·76	301·70	280·	261·38	245·
75	6600	0	48	700·28	600·	525·	473·85	420·50	372·05	350·10	323·25	300·	280·05	262·5
80	7040	0	45	746·96	640·	560·	505·50	448·48	407·60	373·44	344·80	320·	298·72	280·
85	7480	0	42⅓	792·74	680·	595·2	528·38	476·50	433·25	396·77	346·35	340·	317·42	297·6
90	7920	0	40	840·34	720·	630·27	560·23	504·62	458·65	420·11	367·90	360·	336·	315·14

COMPARATIVE ELASTICITY OF WROUGHT AND CAST IRON.

An able work on tubular bridges gives the following as the comparative elasticity of wrought and cast iron:—

"The mean ultimate resistance of wrought iron to a force of compression, as useful in practice, is twelve tons per square inch, while the crushing weight of cast iron is forty-nine tons per square inch, but for a considerable range, under equal weights, the cast iron is twice as elastic, or compresses twice as much as the wrought iron.

"A remarkable illustration of the effect of intense strain on cast iron was witnessed by the author, at the works of Messrs. Easton & Amos. The subject of the experiment was a cast-iron cylinder ten and five-eighths inches thick, fourteen and a half inches high, the external diameter being eighteen inches. If requisite for a specific purpose to reduce the internal diameter three and a half inches, this was effected by the insertion of a smaller cast-iron cylinder into the centre of the large one; and to insure some initial strain, the large cylinder was expanded by heating it, and the internal cylinder being first turned too large, was thus powerfully compressed. The inner cylinder was partly filled with pewter, and a steel piston being fitted to the bore, a pressure of 972 tons was put on the steel piston. The steel was 'upset' by the pressure, and the internal diameter of the small cylinder was increased by full three-sixteenths of an inch; *i. e.* the diameter became $3\frac{11}{16}$ of an inch! A new piston was accordingly adapted to these dimensions—and in this state the cylinder continues to be used, and to resist the pressure; the external layer of the inner cylinder was thus permanently extended $3\frac{1}{15}$ of its length. In fact, it can only be regarded as loose packing, giving no additional strength to the cylinder. Under these high pressures, when confined mechanically, cast iron, as well as other metals, appears, like liquids, to exert an equal pressure in every direction in which its motion is opposed."

LOSS FROM RESISTANCES AGAINST THE PISTON,

Produced by imperfect action of the Valves.

This is a branch of the subject deserving especial consideration. Its importance, as referring to the economical working of steam-engines, may be profitably illustrated by a brief historical account of the consecutive alterations and improvements in the valve arrangements and mechanism of the locomotive engine, and of the results produced in the saving of fuel.

It may be premised that the same principles have

their application not only to the engines of other railways, making due allowances for difference in the gradients, and difference in the loads and dimensions of engines, and difference of speed, but also to fixed engines in general.

The history of the locomotive engine may, for the sake of convenient classification, be divided into two periods—the first a period of increasing, the second a period of decreasing consumption, as respects the article of fuel. Brief allusion may be made to the events of both periods, and a reference to the causes which retarded as well as to those which accelerated improvement.

During the first few years after the opening of railroads, the class of improvements comprising the gradual enlargement of dimensions, as necessary for maintaining higher rates of speed and the transport of heavy bodies, the better disposition and proportionment of the component parts, and the selection of suitable materials, capable of resisting heavy strains and various other causes of derangement and decay, demanded, in consequence of their direct influence upon the traffic of the companies, unremitting attention. The necessity of securing regularity in the transport of trains, whether of passengers or goods, was pressing and paramount, and afforded sufficient materials for thought and experiment. It is, therefore, a source of less surprise than regret, that little progress should have been made in diminishing the consumption of fuel. Trials of the consumption of different engines of similar size and power were made from time to time, and these agreeing pretty closely together, served to lull suspicion of unnecessary waste of fuel. As the engines increased in dimensions, the consumption of fuel increased also, which was considered a natural and inevitable consequence of the exertion of increased power.

The adoption, in 1836, for the passenger traffic, of what were termed short-stroked engines, was attended with the establishment of a quicker rate of travelling than had before been known, but, unfortunately, also with an extravagant increase in consumption of coke. This was erroneously referred to the mechanical disadvantage of the short stroke, an explanation which for a time was deemed satisfactory. Attention was directed to schemes of smoke-burning, by which the use of coal, as a much cheaper fuel than coke or wood, might be rendered possible. Hitherto all engines were furnished with the slide valve ordinarily used in high pressure engines, the mode of operation of which is well known to every practical mechanic. It will be remembered that the operations of admitting the fresh steam and releasing the waste steam are alternately performed by the same valve and by the same motion. The valve, being made to slide backwards and forwards upon the face of the ports, opens and closes the several passages in their turn. The two extreme ones, termed steam ports, communicate with either

Fig. 53.—Old Valve, $\frac{1}{16}$ Lap.

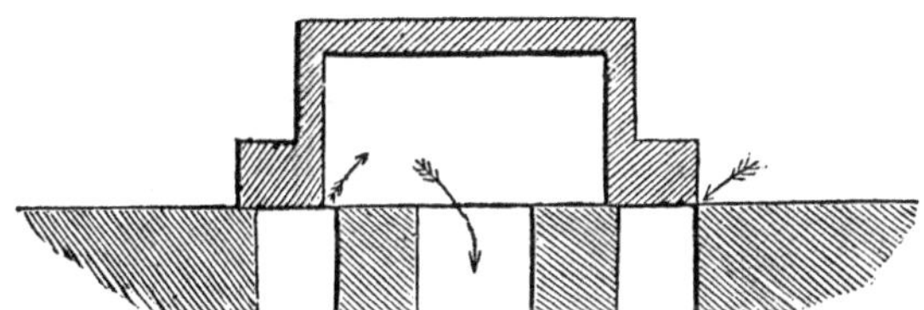

end of the cylinder. The middle one is termed the exhausting port, and its corresponding passage terminates in a pipe open to the atmosphere, and carried into the chimney. Steam is admitted freely into the steam-chest from the boiler. The valve is made of sufficient length to cover, when placed in the centre of the stroke, all the parts. In this position no steam can enter the cylinder; but as the valve moves on, one of the ports opens, and the arrangement of the valve-gearing is such, that when the piston is ready to begin its stroke, the steam-port begins to open. During the forward progress of the piston, the valve not only travels to the end of its stroke, but returns to the point from whence it set out. Its continued motion in the same direction finally closes the valve, and prevents any further admission of steam. The steam has now done its work, and must be removed. In the middle of the valve a hollow chamber is formed, of sufficient length to span between the ports. As soon as the edge of this chamber passes the edge of the steam-port, the pent-up steam finds vent, and rushing through the chamber into the exhausting passage, escapes into the chimney.

It will be observed, by referring to fig. 53, that the exhausting port opens when the steam-port closes, and both events happen as nearly as may be at the end of the stroke. The perfection of a slide valve consists, other things being supposed equal, in the degree of nicety with which its motion is timed relatively to the motion of the piston. The functions of the piston are absolutely dependent

Fig. 54. $\frac{3}{8}$ Lap.

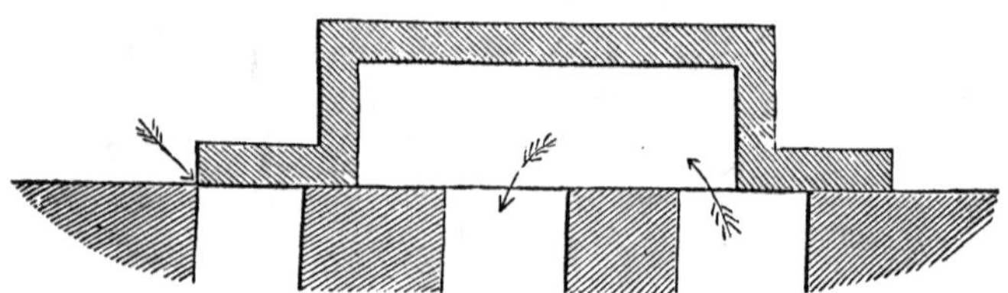

upon the proper timing of the admission and release of the steam. A most slight and apparently trifling error in the adjustment produces a most serious effect upon the consumption of fuel.

If from any cause the valve should open to admit steam for a fresh stroke before the preceding stroke is finished, it opens too soon, and an unnecessary resistance to the piston is produced.

If, on the other hand, the valve should delay its

opening until the piston has begun to return, it opens too late, because then the steam has uselessly to fill the space left vacant. Hence a waste of steam and loss of power. As far, then, as the admission of steam is concerned, it is a necessary condition that the steam-ports should open neither before nor after, but at the precise moment when the stroke commences. Some engineers, indeed, have recommended giving the valve "lead," as it is termed; that is to say, setting it so as to open a little before the completion of the foregoing stroke; but it seems very questionable whether the slightest advantage is gained by doing so to a greater extent than is necessary to compensate for any slackness in the parts of the valve-gearing, or for their expansion when hot; and about $\frac{1}{16}$ of an inch may be considered sufficient for this purpose in a well-constructed engine.

The valve shown in fig. 53 satisfies the conditions required in the admission of steam. It opens exactly at the right time. The steam begins to enter as the piston begins to move, and follows it steadily and effectively throughout its course. Whatever time the piston takes for its journey, the steam is allowed as much time to follow it. At first the opening is small; but then the motion of the piston is comparatively slow, and therefore the supply keeps pace with the demand.

As respects the release of the steam when the

stroke has been completed, the performance of this valve is altogether unsatisfactory, and here lurks the cause of the difference in the performances of the old and the late engines.

But it might be said the release does appear to take place at the right time, because it occurs just when the piston has finished the stroke; and if it were to occur before, a loss of power would ensue. This is a plausible view of the case, and one which undoubtedly delayed, for years, the saving of fuel which has since been effected.

Sufficient attention was not bestowed upon the processes going on in the interior of the cylinder, or upon the facts which might have indicated them. Alternately to fill and empty the cylinder of its contents are operations requiring time. The time allowed for the first operation—that of filling the cylinder with steam—necessarily corresponds with the duration of the stroke, whatever its duration may be. But this cannot be the case as regards the second operation—the emptying of the cylinder. This ought to be performed in an instant, in the minutest fraction of the duration of the stroke; otherwise the steam continues pent up when it ought to be liberated—when it ought to assume its minimum pressure, the pressure of the atmosphere—and exerts an injurious counter-pressure against the piston, tending to increase the resistance to be overcome.

To effect the free and rapid discharge, it is necessary not merely to open the communication to the exhausting pipe, but to open a wide passage, and to have this down by the time the piston recommences its motion. The valve alluded to cannot accomplish this. Its motion is gradual, not instantaneous. The passage only begins to open when the piston is in the turn, and it is not wide open until the piston has travelled through $\frac{1}{10}$th of its entire stroke. The steam in the cylinder is consequently restrained from escaping, being wire-drawn in the passage out, and consequently takes considerable time to assume the pressure of the atmosphere.

In the mean while the new stroke has begun, and been partially completed; and so far the piston has had to contend with a resistance altogether illegitimate—a resistance which, in many cases, and especially at high speeds, has been nearly equal to all the other resistances put together.

In the year 1838 the extent of the disease was first suspected, and a remedy attempted. It had before been observed that the giving of an engine "lead" tended to improve its speed when travelling already at a high speed, and with a light load. The circumstance was attributed to the opening of the steam-port being wide at the time of commencing the stroke, thereby increasing the facility for the entrance of the steam in following up the piston.

Its true explanation was found to be the earlier release of the waste steam, and consequent diminution of resistance. As sometimes ⅜ths of an inch, or even ½ an inch "lead" was given in passenger engines, it was decided to try the effect of opening the exhausting passage earlier by the same amount, while the steam-port should still be made to open only at the turn of the stroke. An engine was chosen for the experiment. Its original valve resembled fig. 53. Placing the valve on the ports, so as to allow the exhausting passage to be ⅜ths of an inch open, the steam-port would, at the same time, be ¼ inch open. This space, therefore, was closed by adding to the length of the valve, at each end, ¼ inch. The eccentric was, of course, shifted on the axle to correspond with the alteration, and the engine with the altered valve (Fig. 54) was again set to work. The amount by which the valve at each end overlaps the steam-ports, when placed exactly over them, is technically termed the *lap*. The lap of the valve being then ⅜ths of an inch, the exhausting passage was about ⅜ths of an inch open when the stroke was finished. The engine was made the subject of several experiments. With passenger trains the saving in fuel was very considerable, the consumption, while running, being only about 25 lbs. of coke per mile, with loads of five to eight cars, and the speed was considerably improved.

It here becomes necessary to refer to the consumption of the Liverpool and Manchester engines before and at the time we speak of, in order to form a just conception of the position arrived at.

In 1836 and 1837, larger engines were gradually introduced to replace the smaller class, which had become insufficient for maintaining the higher rate of speed then demanded; and their increased consumption of fuel was commensurate with their increase of size.

For an idea of the general effect attendant upon their introduction, the following table, showing the coke consumed in several consecutive years, may be consulted.

11,561 trips in 1836, 7,907 tons (gross) coke.
12,063 trips in 1837, 9,876 tons (gross) coke.
12,953 trips in 1838, 10,816 tons (gross) coke.

Thus, during three years, when the change went on, although the work done increased only in the proportion of 100 to 136, without material difference in the magnitude of the loads, in 1839 and 1840 the average consumption attained its maximum, being about 49 lbs. per mile, gross, with passenger trains averaging seven cars, and 54 lbs. per mile with freight trains averaging sixteen burthen cars.

40 lbs. net consumption with passenger trains,

was moderate for such an engine used for the experiment; and the performance of the engine when altered, being under 30 lbs. net, was naturally considered favourable. This result was evidently obtained from the earlier exhaustion of the steam.

Whereas previously the opening of the exhaustion passage was contemporaneous with the termination of the stroke; now it took place before, and was already $\frac{3}{8}$ths of an inch open at the end of the stroke. A portion of the steam could by that time escape, and the back pressure was diminished.

The valves of two engines, Nos. 10 and 12, were next altered to have $\frac{3}{8}$ths of an inch lap—No. 10 in January, No. 12 in June, 1841. During the last quarter of the year 1841, the gross consumption of No. 10 was $36\frac{1}{2}$ lbs. per mile, and that of No. 12 40 lbs. per mile, and the net consumption about 30 and 33 lbs.

No. 12 Valve, with $\frac{3}{8}$ths of an inch Lap.

Week ending		Coke. cwt.	qrs.	lbs.		Per Trip. cwt.	qrs.	lbs.	per mile.
Jan. 4, 1841,	12 trips of 30 miles,	130	0	0					
Jan. 11, 1841,	12 trips of 30 miles,	127	2	0					
	24	257	2	0	=	10	2	25	= 40·1

Valve with $\frac{3}{4}$ths of an inch Lap.

Week ending		cwt.	qrs.	lbs.		cwt.	qrs.	lbs.	per mile.
Feb'ry 9, 1841,	10 trips of 30 miles,	88	3	0					
March 7, 1841,	8 trips of 30 miles,	71	1	0					
March 21, 1841,	14 trips of 30 miles,	118	3	0					
March 28, 1841,	16 trips of 30 miles,	137	2	0					
	48 trips.	416	1	0	=	8	2	19	= 32·4
								Difference	7·7

DIMENSIONS OF PARTS OF LOCOMOTIVES.

Diameter of Cylinder.—In locomotive engines the diameter of the cylinder varies less than in either the land or the marine engine. In few of the locomotive engines at present in use is the diameter of the cylinder greater than 18 inches, or less than 12 inches. The length of the stroke of nearly all the locomotive engines at present in use is 18 inches, and there are always two cylinders, which are generally connected to cranks upon the axle, standing at right angles with one another. Outside cylinders, operating upon pins in the driving wheels, have latterly been largely introduced.

AREA OF INDUCTION PORTS.

RULE.—*To find the size of the steam-ports for the locomotive engine.*—Multiply the square of the diameter of the cylinder by ·068. The product is the proper size of the steam-ports in square inches.

Example.—Required the proper size of the steam-ports of a locomotive engine whose diameter is 15 inches. Here, according to the rule, size of steam-ports = $\cdot068 \times 15 \times 15 = \cdot068 \times 225 = 15\cdot3$ square inches, or between $15\frac{1}{4}$ and $15\frac{1}{2}$ square inches.

After having determined the area of the ports, we may easily find the depth when the length is given, or, conversely, the length when the depth is given. Then, suppose we know the length was 8 inches, then we find that the depth should be 15·3 ÷ 8 = 1·9125 inches, or nearly 2 inches; or suppose we knew the depth was 2 inches, then we would find that the length was 15·3 ÷ 2 = 7·65 inches, or nearly 7¾ inches.

Area of eduction ports.—The proper area for the eduction ports may be found from the following rule.

RULE.—*To find the area of the eduction ports.*—Multiply the square of the diameter of the cylinder in inches by ·128. The product is the area of the eduction ports in square inches.

Example.—Required the area of the eduction ports of a locomotive engine, when the diameter of the cylinders is 13 inches. In this example we have, according to the rule, area of eduction port $= \cdot128 \times 13^2 = \cdot128 \times 169 = 21\cdot632$ inches, or between 21½ and 21¾ square inches.

Breadth of bridge between ports.—The breadth of the bridges between the eduction port and the induction ports is usually between ¾ inch and 1 inch.

DIAMETER OF BOILER.

RULE.—*To find the inside diameter of the boiler.*—Multiply the diameter of the cylinder in inches by

3·11. The product is the inside diameter of the boiler in inches.

Example.—Required the inside diameter of the boiler for a locomotive engine, the diameter of the cylinders being 15 inches.

In this example we have, according to the rule, inside diameter of boiler = 15 × 3·11 = 46·65 inches, or about 3 feet 10⅝ inches.

Length of boiler.—In the Northern and Eastern Counties Railway the length of the boiler is 8 feet; while in the North Midland Counties Railway, in the Great Western Railway, and in the Hartlepool Railway, the length of the boiler is 8½ feet. In the Belgian railways the length of the boiler is 8 feet 2 inches. And in the Bordeaux and La Teste railway the length of the boiler is 8 feet 9 inches. In Stephenson's locomotive engines, the length of the boiler is between 11 and 12 feet. In this country the length is from 10 to 14 feet.

Diameter of steam dome inside.—It is obvious that the diameter of the steam dome may be varied considerably, according to circumstances; but the first indication is to make it large enough. It is usual, however, in practice, to proportion the diameter of the steam dome to the diameter of the cylinder; and there appears to be no great objection to this. The following rule will be found to give the diameter of the dome usually adopted in practice.

RULE.—*To find the diameter of the steam dome.*—Multiply the diameter of the cylinder in inches by 1·43. The product is the diameter of the dome in inches.

Height of steam dome.—The height of the steam dome may vary. Judging from practice, it appears that a uniform height of 2½ feet would answer very well.

Diameter of safety-valve.—In practice the diameter of the safety-valve varies considerably. The following rule gives the diameter of the safety-valve usually adopted in practice.

RULE.—*To find the diameter of the safety-valve.*—Divide the diameter of the cylinder in inches by 4. The quotient is the diameter of the safety-valve in inches.

Example.—Required the diameter of the safety-valves for the boiler of a locomotive engine, the diameter of the cylinder being 13 inches. Here, according to the rule, diameter of safety-valve = 13 ÷ 4 = 3¼ inches. A larger size, however, is preferable, as being less likely to stick.

Diameter of valve spindle.—The following rule will be found to give the correct diameter of the valve spindle. It is entirely founded on practice.

RULE.—*To find the diameter of the valve spindle.*—Multiply the diameter of the cylinder in inches by ·076. The product is the proper diameter of the valve spindle.

Example.—Required the diameter of the valve spindle for a locomotive engine whose cylinders' diameters are 13 inches.

In this example we have, according to the rule, diameter of valve spindle = 13 × ·076 = ·988 inches, or very nearly 1 inch.

Diameter of chimney.—It is usual in practice to make the diameter of the chimney equal to the diameter of the cylinder. Thus, a locomotive engine whose cylinders' diameters are 15 inches, would have the inside diameter of the chimney also 15 inches, or thereabouts. This rule has, at least, the merit of simplicity.

Area of fire-grate.—The following rule determines the area of the fire-grate usually given in practice. We may remark, that the area of the fire-grate in practice follows a more certain rule than any other part of the engine appears to do; but it is in all cases much too small, and occasions a great loss of power by the urging of the blast it renders necessary, and a rapid deterioration of the furnace plates from excessive heat. There is no good reason why the furnace should not be nearly as long as the boiler: it would then resemble the furnace of a marine boiler, and be as manageable.

Rule.—*To find the area of fire-grate.*—Multiply the diameter of the cylinder in inches by ·77. The product is the area of the fire-grate in superficial feet.

Example.—Required the area of the fire-grate of a locomotive engine, the diameters of the cylinders being 15 inches.

In this example we have, according to the rule, area of fire-grate $= \cdot 77 \times 15 = 11 \cdot 55$ square feet, or about $11\frac{1}{2}$ square feet. Though this rule, however, represents the usual practice, the area of the fire-grate should not be contingent upon the size of the cylinder, but upon the quantity of steam to be generated.

Area of heating surface.—In the construction of a locomotive engine, one great object is to obtain a boiler which will produce a sufficient quantity of steam with as little bulk and weight as possible. This object is admirably accomplished in the construction of the boiler of the locomotive engine. This little barrel of tubes generates more steam in an hour than was formerly raised from a boiler and fire occupying a considerable house. This favourable result is obtained simply by exposing the water to a greater amount of heating surface.

In the usual construction of the locomotive boiler it is obvious that we can only consider four of the six faces of the inside fire-box as effective heating surface, viz. the crown of the box, and the three perpendicular sides. The circumferences of the tubes are also effective heating surface; so that the whole effective heating surface of a locomotive boiler may be considered to be the four faces of the inside fire-box, plus the sum of the surfaces of the tubes. Understanding this to be the effective heating surface, the following rule determines the average amount of heating surface usually given in practice.

RULE.—*To find the effective heating surface.*—Multiply the square of the diameter of the cylinder in inches by 5; divide the product by 2. The quotient is the area of the effective heating surface in square feet.

Example.—Required the effective heating surface of the boiler of a locomotive engine, the diameters of the cylinders being 15 inches.

In this example we have, according to the rule, effective heating surface $= 15^2 \times 5 \div 2 = 225 \times 5 \div 2 = 1125 \div 2 = 562\frac{1}{2}$ square feet.

According to the rule which we have given for the fire-grate, the area of the fire-grate for this boiler would be about $11\frac{1}{2}$ square feet. We may suppose, therefore, the area of the crown of the box to be 12 square feet. The area of the three perpendicular sides of the inside fire-box is usually three times the area of the crown; so that the effective heating surface of the fire-box is 48 square feet. Hence the heating surface of the tubes $= 526{\cdot}5 - 48 = 478{\cdot}5$ square feet. The inside diameters of the tubes are generally about $1\frac{3}{4}$ inches; and therefore the circumference of a section of these tubes is 5·4978 inches. Hence, supposing the tube to be $8\frac{1}{2}$ feet long, the surface of one $= 5{\cdot}4978 \times 8\frac{1}{2} \div 12 = {\cdot}45815 \times 8\frac{1}{2} = 3{\cdot}8943$ square feet. And, therefore, the number of tubes $= 478{\cdot}5 \div 3.8943 = 123$ nearly.

Area of water-level.—This of course varies with the different circumstances of the boiler. The average area may be found from the following rule.

RULE.—*To find the area of the water-level.*—Multiply the diameter of the cylinder in inches by 2·08. The product is the area of the water-level in square feet.

Example.—Required the area of the water-level for a locomotive engine, whose cylinders' diameters are 14 inches.

In this case we have, according to the rule, area of water-level $= 14 \times 2{\cdot}08 = 29{\cdot}12$ square feet.

Cubical content of water in boiler.—This of course varies, not only in different boilers, but also in the same boiler at different times. The following rule is supposed to give the average quantity of water in the boiler.

RULE.—*To find the cubical content of the water in the boiler.*—Multiply the square of the diameter of the cylinder in inches by 9; divide the product by 40. The quotient is the cubical content of the water in the boiler in cubic feet.

Example.—Required the average cubical content of the water in the boiler of a locomotive engine, the diameters of the cylinders being 14 inches.

In this example we have, according to the rule, cubical content of water $= 9 \times 14^2 \div 40 = 44{\cdot}1$ cubic feet.

Content of feed-pump.—In the locomotive engine the feed-pump is generally attached to the cross-head, and consequently it has the same stroke as the piston. As we have mentioned before, the stroke of the locomotive engine is generally in practice 18 inches. Hence, assuming the stroke of the feed-pump to be constantly 18 inches, it only remains for us to determine the diameter of the ram. It may be found from the following rule.

RULE.—*To find the diameter of the feed-pump ram.*—Multiply the square of the diameter of the cylinder in inches by ·011. The product is the diameter of the ram in inches.

Example.—Required the diameter of the ram for the feed-pump for a locomotive engine whose diameter of cylinder is 14 inches.

In this example we have, according to the rule, diameter of ram $= {\cdot}011 \times 14^2 = {\cdot}011 \times 196 = 2{\cdot}156$ inches, or between 2 and $2\frac{1}{4}$ inches.

Cubical content of steam room.—The quantity of steam in the boiler varies not only for different boilers, but even for the same boiler in different circumstances. But when the locomotive is in motion, there is usually a certain proportion of the boiler filled with the steam. Including the dome and the steam-pipe, the content of the steam room will be found usually to be somewhat less than the cubical content of the water. But as it is desirable that it should be increased, we give the following rule.

RULE.—*To find the cubical content of the steam room.*—Multiply the square of the diameter of the cylinder in inches by 9; divide the product by 40. The quotient is the cubical content of the steam room in cubic feet.

Example.—Required the cubical content of the steam room in a locomotive boiler, the diameters of the cylinders being 12 inches.

In this example we have, according to the rule, cubical content of steam room $= 9 \times 12^2 \div 40 = 9 \times 144 \div 40 = 32.4$ cubic feet.

Cubical content of inside fire-box above fire-bars.— The following rule determines the cubical content of fire-box usually given in practice.

RULE.—*To find the cubical content of inside fire-box above fire-bars.*—Divide the square of the diameter of the cylinder in inches by 4. The quotient is the content of the inside fire-box above fire-bars in cubic feet.

Example.—Required the content of inside fire-box above fire-bars in a locomotive engine, when the diameters of the cylinders are each 15 inches.

In this example we have, according to the rule, content of inside fire-box above fire-bars $= 15^2 \div 4 = 225 \div 4 = 56\frac{1}{4}$ cubic feet.

Thickness of the plates of boiler.—In general the

thickness of the plates of the locomotive boiler is 9·32 inch, or No. 3 wire-gage.

Inside diameter of steam-pipe.—The diameter usually given to the steam-pipe of the locomotive engine may be found from the following rule.

RULE.—*To find the diameter of the steam-pipe of the locomotive engine.*—Multiply the square of the diameter of the cylinder in inches by ·03. The product is the diameter of the steam-pipe in inches.

Example.—Required the diameter of the steam-pipe of a locomotive engine, the diameter of the cylinder being 13 inches. Here, according to the rule, diameter of steam-pipe $= \cdot 03 \times 13^2 = \cdot 03 \times 169 = 5 \cdot 07$ inches; or a very little more than 5 inches. The steam-pipe is usually made too small in engines intended for high speeds.

Diameter of branch steam-pipes.—The following rule gives the usual diameter of the branch steam-pipe for locomotive engines.

RULE.—*To find the diameter of the branch steam-pipe for the locomotive engine.*—Multiply the square of the diameter of the cylinder in inches by ·021. The product is the diameter of the branch steam-pipe for the locomotive engine in inches.

Example.—Required the diameter of the branch steam-pipes for a locomotive engine, when the cylinders' diameter is 15 inches. Here, according to the rule, diameter of branch pipe $= \cdot 021 \times 15^2 = \cdot 021 \times 225 = 4 \cdot 725$ inches, or about $4\frac{3}{4}$ inches.

Diameter of top of blast-pipe.—The diameter of the top of the blast-pipe may be found from the following rule.

RULE.—*To find the diameter of the top of the blast-pipe.*—Multiply the square of the diameter of the cylinder in inches by ·017. The product is the diameter of the top of the blast-pipe in inches.

Example.—The diameter of a locomotive engine is 13 inches; required the diameter of the blast-pipe at top. Here, according to the rule, diameter of blast-pipe at top $= \cdot017 \times 13^2 = \cdot017 \times 169 =$ 2·873 inches, or between $2\frac{3}{4}$ and 3 inches; but the variable exhaust is now generally used.

Diameter of feed-pipes.—There appears to be no theoretical considerations which would lead us to determine exactly the proper size of the feed-pipes. Judging from practice, however, the following rule will be found to give the proper dimensions.

RULE.—*To find the diameter of the feed-pipes.*—Multiply the diameter of the cylinder in inches by ·141. The product is the proper diameter of the feed-pipes.

Example.—Required the diameter of the feed-pipes for a locomotive engine, the diameter of the cylinder being 15 inches.

In this example we have, according to the rule, diameter of feed-pipe $= 15 \times \cdot141 = 2\cdot115$ inches, or between 2 and $2\frac{1}{4}$ inches.

Diameter of piston-rod.—The diameter of the

piston-rod for the locomotive engine is usually about one-seventh the diameter of the cylinder. Therefore,

RULE.—*To find the diameter of the piston-rod for the locomotive engine.*—Divide the diameter of the cylinder in inches by 7. The quotient is the diameter of the piston-rod in inches.

Example.—The diameter of the cylinder of a locomotive engine is 15 inches, required the diameter of the piston-rod. Here, according to the rule, diameter of piston-rod = 15 ÷ 7 = $2\frac{1}{7}$ inches.

Thickness of piston.—The thickness of the piston in locomotive engines is usually about two-sevenths of the diameter of the cylinder. Therefore,

RULE.—*To find the thickness of the piston in the locomotive engine.*—Multiply the diameter of the cylinder in inches by 2; divide the product by 7. The quotient is the thickness of the piston in inches.

Example.—The diameter of the cylinder of a locomotive engine is 14 inches, required the thickness of the piston. Here, according to the rule, thickness of piston = 2 × 14 ÷ 7 = 4 inches.

Diameter of connecting-rods at middle.—The following rule gives the diameter of the connecting-rod at middle. The rule is entirely founded on practice.

RULE.—*To find the diameter of the connecting-rod at middle of the locomotive engine.*—Multiply the diameter of the cylinder in inches by ·21. The product is the diameter of the connecting-rod at middle in inches.

Example.—Required the diameter of the connecting-rods at middle for a locomotive engine, the diameter of the cylinders being 12 inches.

For this example we have, according to the rule, diameter of connecting-rods at middle $= 12 \times \cdot 21 = 2{\cdot}52$ inches, or $2\frac{1}{2}$ inches.

Diameter of ball on cross-head spindle.—The diameter of the ball on the cross-head spindle may be found from the following rule.

RULE.—*To find the diameter of the ball on cross-head spindle of a locomotive engine.*—Multiply the diameter of the cylinder in inches by ·23. The product is the diameter of the ball on the cross-head spindle.

Example.—Required the diameter of the ball on the cross-head spindle of a locomotive engine, when the diameter of the cylinder is 15 inches. Here, according to the rule, diameter of ball $= \cdot 23 \times 15 = 3{\cdot}45$ inches, or nearly $3\frac{1}{2}$ inches.

Diameter of the inside bearings of the crank-axle.—It is obvious that the inside bearings of the crank-axle of the locomotive engine correspond to the paddle-shaft journal of the marine engine, and to the fly-wheel shaft journal of the land engine. We may conclude, therefore, that the proper diameter of these bearings ought to depend jointly upon the length of the stroke and the diameter of the cylinder. In the locomotive engine the stroke is usually 18 inches, so that we may consider that the diameter of the bearing depends solely upon the diameter of the cylinder. The following rule will give the diameter of the inside bearing.

RULE.—*To find the diameter of the inside bearing for the locomotive engine.*—Extract the cube root of the square of the diameter of the cylinder in inches; multiply the result by ·96. The product is the proper diameter of the inside bearing of the crank-axle for the locomotive engine.

Diameter of plain part of crank-axle.—It is usual to make the plain part of crank-axle of the same sectional area as the inside bearings.

RULE.—*To determine the diameter of the plain part of crank-axle for the locomotive engine.*—Extract the cube root of the square of the diameter of the cylinder in inches; multiply the result by ·96. The product is the proper diameter of the plain part of the crank-axle of the locomotive engine in inches.

Diameter of the outside bearings of the crank-axle.—The crank-axle, in addition to resting upon the inside bearings, is sometimes also made to rest partly upon outside bearings. These outside bearings are added only for the sake of steadiness, and they do not need to be so strong as the inside bearings. The proper size of the diameter of these bearings may be found from the following rule.

RULE.—*To find the diameter of outside bearings for the locomotive engine.*—Multiply the square of the diameter of the cylinders in inches by ·396; extract the cube root of the product. The result is the diameter of the outside bearings in inches.

Diameter of crank-pin.—The following rule gives the proper diameter of the crank-pin. It is obvious that the crank-pin of the locomotive engine is not altogether analogous to the crank-pin of the marine or land engine, and, like them, ought to depend upon the diameter of the cylinder, as it is usually formed out of the solid axle.

RULE.—*To find the diameter of the crank-pin for the locomotive engine.*—Multiply the diameter of the cylinder in inches by ·404. The product is the diameter of the crank-pin in inches.

Example.—Required the diameter of the crank-pin of a locomotive engine whose cylinders' diameters are 15 inches.

In this example we have, according to the rule, diameter of crank-pin = 15 × ·404 = 6.06 inches, or about 6 inches.

Length of crank-pin.—The length of the crank-pin usually given in practice may be found from the following rule.

RULE.—*To find the length of the crank-pin.*—Multiply the diameter of the cylinder in inches by ·233. The product is the length of the crank-pins in inches.

The part of the crank-axle answering to the crank-pin is usually rounded very much at the corners, both to give additional strength and to prevent side play.

These, then, are the chief dimensions of locomotive engines, according to the practice most generally followed. The establishment of express trains and the general exigencies of steam locomotion are daily introducing innovations, the effect of which is to make the engines of greater size and power; but it cannot be said that a plan of locomotive engine has yet been contrived that is free from grave objections. The most material of these defects is the necessity that yet exists of expending a large proportion of the power in the production of a draft; and this evil is traceable to the inadequate area of the fire-grate, which makes an enormous rush of air through the fire necessary to accomplish the combustion of the fuel requisite for the production of the steam. To gain a sufficient area of fire-grate an entirely new arrangement of engine must be adopted; the furnace must be greatly lengthened, and perhaps it may be found that short upright tubes may be introduced with advantage. Upright tubes have been found to be more effectual in raising steam than horizontal tubes; but the tube-plate in the case of the upright tubes would be more liable to burn.

We here give the preceding rules in formulæ, in

the belief that those well acquainted with algebraic symbols prefer to have a rule expressed as a formulæ, as they can thus see at once the different operations to be performed. In the following formulæ we denote the diameter of the cylinder in inches by D.

Parts of the Cylinder.

Area of induction ports, in square inches = $\cdot 068 \times D^2$.

Area of eduction ports, in square inches = $\cdot 128 \times D^2$.

Breadth of bridge between ports between $\frac{3}{4}$ inch and 1 inch.

Parts of Boiler.

Diameter of boiler, in inches = $3.11 \times D$.

Length of boiler between 8 feet and 12 feet.

Diameter of steam dome inside, in inches = $1\cdot 43 \times D$.

Height of steam dome = $2\frac{1}{2}$ feet.

Diameter of safety-valve, in inches = $D \div 4$.

Diameter of valve-spindle, in inches = $\cdot 076 \times D$.

Diameter of chimney, in inches = D.

Area of fire-grate, in square feet = $\cdot 77 \times D$.

Area of heating-surface, in square feet = $5 \times D^2 \div 2$.

Area of water-level, in square feet = $2.08 \times D$.

Cubical content of water in boiler, in cubic feet = $9 \times D^2 \div 40$.

Diameter of feed-pump ram, in inches = $\cdot 011 \times D^2$.

Cubical content of steam room, in cubic feet $= 9 \times D^2 \div 40$.

Cubical content of inside fire-box above fire-bars, in cubic feet $= D^2 \div 4$.

Thickness of the plates of boiler $= \frac{3}{8}$ inch.

Dimensions of several Pipes.

Inside diameter of steam-pipe, in inches $= \cdot 03 \times D^2$.

Inside diameter of branch steam-pipe, in inches $= \cdot 021 \times D^2$.

Inside diameter of the top of blast-pipe $= \cdot 017 \times D^2$.

Inside diameter of the feed-pipes $= \cdot 141 \times D$.

Dimensions of several moving Parts.

Diameter of piston-rod, in inches $= D \div 7$.

Thickness of piston, in inches $= 2\,D \div 7$.

Diameter of connecting-rods at middle, in inches $= \cdot 21 \times D$.

Diameter of the ball on cross-head spindle, in inches $= \cdot 23 \times D$.

Diameter of the inside bearings of the crank-axle, in inches $= \cdot 96 \times \sqrt[3]{D^2}$.

Diameter of the plain part of crank-axle, in inches $= \cdot 96 \times \sqrt[3]{D^2}$.

Diameter of the outside bearings of the crank-axle, in inches $= \sqrt[3]{\cdot 396 \times D^2}$.

Diameter of crank-pin, in inches $= \cdot 404 \times D$.

Length of crank-pin, in inches $= \cdot 233 \times D$.

The following simple rules I have always made use of in the construction of locomotives, and the result of their performances proves most fully that my theory is correct, having never failed in one single instance in the performance of an engine, and having drawn the heaviest load ever drawn by a single locomotive in the world. The "Philadelphia" hauled a load of 1268 tons from Pottsville to Richmond—94 miles—158 coal cars, containing 750 tons of coal. The train was 2020 feet in length. The load was started and drawn through curves of 750 feet radius, at a rate of 10 miles per hour, the engine only weiging $15\frac{8}{10}$ tons. The engine was upon 6 wheels, with my patent flexible vibrating truck, coupled, 42 inch diameter, cylinder $14\frac{1}{2} \times 22$.

To find the capacity of boiler.—For every cubic inch of cylinder, make 13 square inches of fire surface, $\frac{1}{7}$th of which must be in fire-box, $\frac{6}{7}$ths in tubes.

For area of steam-ports on valve face.—Divide the area of cylinder by 12, which will be the required area, making the ports never less than 1 inch, nor more than $1\frac{1}{4}$.

For area of exhaust on valve face.—Multiply the area of steam-ports by 2·06. *For steam pipe* make it equal to area of steam-port. *For large steam pipe,* $1\frac{1}{2}$ the area of steam-port. *For exhaust,* make it equal to area of exhaust opening on face of cylinder. *For high speeds,* lap one inch, lead $\frac{1}{16}$th. *Slow speed freight engine,* lap $\frac{1}{2}$ inch, lead $\frac{3}{16}$ths.

General Features of the Boiler.

The boiler is the most important part of a locomotive engine, and the useful effect of the machine depends in a great degree on the boiler being capable of generating the requisite quantity of pure steam, without requiring the draught of air and flame through the fire and tubes to be accelerated or forced excessively. The fire-box is that part of the boiler in which the heat is generated and partially absorbed, the remaining absorption taking place in the flue tubes, which convey the products of combustion from the fire, through the water, to the smoke-box, whence they are dissipated in the atmosphere. Of course, the more nearly these products of combustion, at their entrance into the chimney, are found to have been cooled down to the temperature of the water in the boiler, the more economical in fuel the boiler will, *cæteris paribus*, be. To obtain the utmost economy in this way, the superficial surface of the tubes has been increased to the utmost extent, by enlarging the diameter and increasing the number and size of the tubes. The boiler of Bury's 14-inch* engine contains 92 tubes of $2\frac{1}{8}$ inches external diameter, and 10 feet 6

* This dimension is the diameter of cylinder, by which dimension locomotives are distinguished.

inches long; the boiler of Stephenson's 15-inch engine contains 150 tubes of $1\frac{5}{8}$ inch external diameter, and 13 feet 6 inches long. It will therefore be seen that the superficial surface in Bury's tubes is, comparatively, rather small, but yet the production of steam is found to be sufficiently copious, with a blast-pipe of rather more than the average diameter; on the other hand, notwithstanding its great surface, Stephenson's boiler is found to require a smaller blast-pipe than usual. It seems highly probable that the extra intensity of blast requisite in the latter case consumes so much power to produce it, as completely to countervail the economy of fuel consequent on the very complete abstraction of the heat, by the great length of tubes in proportion to their diameter.

In an experiment tried by Mr. Stephenson, the heating surface of the fire-box, where the heat is received by radiation, was found to be more effectual than the tube surface, where the heat is received by conduction, in the ratio of 1 to 3, and hence the heating surface of a locomotive is sometimes estimated as the surface of the furnace plus one-third that of the tubes.

The shell, which is cylindrical, is attached to the smoke-box and fire-box by angle-iron; the end of the shell next the smoke-box is closed entirely by the tube-plate, but at the smoke-box end the water has free access quite round the internal fire-box, one side of which forms the tube-plate. The shell, external fire-box, and the smoke-box are always of iron, the thickness of plate being $\frac{5}{16}$th in. in ordinary boilers of 3 feet 4 in. in diameter, though in some cases it is $\frac{3}{8}$ in.; the pitch of rivets is $1\frac{7}{8}$ in., and the diameter of rivets $\frac{11}{16}$th in. The shell is sometimes made with flush joints, a band of iron covering the joint attached by two rows of rivets. The boiler plates should have their fibres running round the boiler instead of in the direction of its length, as the plate is somewhat stronger in that direction. The boiler is secured endwise by longitudinal stays, which are fastened by cutters to jaws attached to the end plates.

The blast-pipe is the eduction pipe diminished in area at the mouth to such a degree as to cause the steam to issue with a great velocity, whereby a powerful draught through the fire is maintained by the steam rushing up the chimney. The area of the mouth of the blast-pipe varies in different engines, but an area of $\frac{1}{22}$d of the area of the cylinder is a common proportion. A variable blast-pipe, the orifice of which may be increased or diminished in area, is now much used. One arrangement for this purpose consists of the application of a regular plate at the top of the blast-pipe, with a hole through the centre of the plate, through which the nozzle of the blast-pipe passes. When this regulator plate is closed, the whole of the steam has to ascend through the central nozzle ; but when the regulator is open, or partly open, a part of the steam escapes through the holes in it. Another plan consists in the application of a movable plug within the blast-pipe, which may narrow the escape orifice to an annular space of small area, the plug being raised or lowered by a lever and rod. Stephenson's method of contracting the blast consists in making the nozzle of the pipe conical, and forming it to slide within the upright pipe, whereby an annular space is left for the escape of the steam around the nozzle when the nozzle is lowered.

The man-hole, or entrance into the boiler, consists of a circular or oval aperture of about 15 in. diameter, placed by Bury at the summit of his dome, and by Stephenson in the front part, a few inches above the cylindrical part of the boiler. The cover that closes this aperture in Bury's engine also contains the safety-valve seats, thus simplifying the construction by preventing the necessity of an independent aperture and cover for the safety-valves, as in Stephenson's engine, where the safety-valves are placed independently on the top of the dome. The steam-tight joint of the man-hole cover is made in Bury's engine by a single thickness of canvas, smeared with red-lead; and the joint is not liable to become defective or leaky, because the surfaces are turned true and smooth, both on the cover and its seat. When these surfaces have not been made true in this manner, it becomes requisite to use a number of thicknesses of canvas, or other material, to form the joint; and the action of the steam soon rotting away the soft substance, a leakage is caused through the joint, which makes repair indispensable. The small domes are of the same form as those used on the Grand Junction Railway, which are cylindrical vessels of about 20 in. diameter, and 2 feet in height, with a semi-globular top, are generally made of plate-iron, about $\frac{3}{8}$ in. thick, welded at the seam, and with the flange at the bottom turned out of the same piece. In some cases, domes of this form have been constructed of cast iron, about $\frac{3}{4}$ in. thick, but they have been found objectionable from their top weight, and they cannot be considered as altogether safe from explosion.

Fire-box.—Iron fire-boxes have been extensively tried by Bury and others, and in cases where the plate-iron of which they were formed has been of a peculiarly perfect texture, and not liable to laminate or crack under the action of the heat, they have been found to answer exceedingly well, and not only to be much cheaper than copper, but also to last at least twice as long before requiring renewal. If the materials be very carefully selected, the use of iron fire-boxes will be found productive of economy, if only used in situations where pure water is obtainable. The duration of ordinary copper fire-boxes depends in a great measure upon the original texture of the copper, which ought to be rather coarse-grained than rich and soft, and also particularly free from irregularity of structure and lamination. Considerable advantages have been found to arise from increasing the capacity of the fire-box, more especially its depth, which ought to be such as to allow of the requisite quantity of coke being placed within it without reaching above the mouths of the lower tubes, a fault which would cause the smaller pieces of coke to enter and block up the tubes, to the manifest deterioration of the draught, and diminution of the efficacy of the engine. The heating surface in the fire-box being of an extremely valuable and efficient nature, and the extensive area of fire-bar surface being very conducive to freedom of draught, we are induced to question whether the large square fire-box is not *pro tanto* preferable to the round one, which must necessarily be very small, except on the 7-feet gage, in which case the round fire-box offers decided advantages. The square fire-box is generally made of iron, $\frac{3}{8}$ in. to $\frac{1}{2}$ in. thick in every part except the tube-plate, which has been from $\frac{5}{8}$ in. to $\frac{3}{4}$ in.; but experience has shown considerable advantage in making the tube-plate $\frac{7}{8}$ in. thick, as this great strength prevents the spaces between the tubes from being compressed, and the tube holes rendered oval; in the processes of drifting and feruling the tubes, however, this evil will be found to exist, even with a $\frac{7}{8}$ in. tube-plate, if the tube holes be placed in too close contiguity, as has been found the case in several of Stephenson's engines; and, from practical observation, we find that ¾ in. should be the minimum distance between any two tubes. The sides, back, and front below the tubes, of the square fire-box, are stayed at intervals of 4½ in. to 5 in. with either copper or iron stays, screwed through the outer case into the fire-box, and securely riveted; but, as the riveting within the fire-box is found to decay rapidly, from the action of the heat, Mr. Dewrance, of the Liverpool and Manchester Railway, has adopted, with good results, stays formed with a large square head, and screwed from within the fire-box outwards, the square head projecting 2 in. into the flame. Iron stay-bolts for the fire-box are found to last nearly as long as copper, and, from their superior tenacity, are often considered preferable. Until lately, it had been supposed that round fire-boxes possessed such advantages in point of strength over square ones, owing to their arched form, that they were capable of resisting the pressure of the steam without the use of stays; but experience has shown that, whatever be the shape, a fire-box must be stayed more or less to render it safe, for the shell of the fire-box is liable to be wasted so much by the heat, that it is not safe to depend altogether upon the strength its form confers, especially as the form will be changed if the boiler be suffered to become short of water. In round fire-boxes, the sides near the crown part generally suffer most from waste: these portions are now provided with stays by Messrs. Bury, Curtis, and Kennedy, who are the main supporters of round fire-boxes; and with this provision the round fire-boxes are necessarily the stronger. The roofs of all fire-boxes require to be stayed by cross-bars; but the bars are required to be both stronger and more numerous for the square fire-boxes, and should always be carefully made of wrought-iron, and very carefully fitted before being bolted on. Stay-bars of cast-iron have been employed, on account of their cheapness; but, having led several times to accidents from explosion, they are now discarded. These bars are only in contact with the fire-box at the part around the rivets, and in all the other parts they permit the access of the water below them. It is advisable to bring these bars to an edge on the under side, so as to facilitate the escape of the steam. In Sharp and Robert's engines, the fire-box is made of three plates; the tube-plate and front plate have their edges bent over, and to these are attached a single plate which forms the crown and two sides of the furnace. The interior fire-box is joined at foot to the exterior by a Z-shaped iron, which forms the bottom of the water-space, and is preferred, inasmuch as it leaves a wide water-space, and is easily cleaned. The outer and inner fire-boxes are joined round the furnace door, which is double, to prevent inconvenient radiation. The external fire-box has sometimes a semi-cylindrical top, joined by turning over the sides like an arch, and sometimes a dome-shaped top.

The fire-bars have always been a source of much expense in the locomotive engine, as they burn out very rapidly, and have to be often renewed: from the rapid combustion going on over their upper surfaces, they become heated intensely throughout, causing them to throw off scale, and to bend under the weight of the fuel. The best remedy has been found to consist in making the bars very thin and deep, so as to keep their lower edges exposed to a cooling draught of air, and to diminish the area of metal conducting heat downwards from their heated upper edges. Thin fire-bars admit of being placed nearer together than thick ones, thus offering no increased impediment to free draught, while preventing the loss of small pieces of unburnt coke, which might otherwise drop through into the ash-box and be wasted. Fire-bars have given much satisfaction when made 4 inches deep, (parallel,) and full $\frac{5}{8}$ inch thick on the upper edge and $\frac{3}{8}$ inch on the lower edge. The frame carrying the fire-bars has often been made capable of being dropped on the instant, with its fire-bars and fire, into the ash-box, or upon the road, by means of catches drawn back by levers; but though the fire-bar frame is thus left unsupported, very often it will not drop, and even cannot be forced down out of its place, owing to the clinkers and tarry products of combustion forming an adhesive binding between its edge and the fire-box: it has accordingly been found best to support the fire-box frame permanently, and when any cause requires the sudden withdrawal of the fire, to lift the fire-bars singly out of place, by means of the ordinary dart. It is necessary to place the fire-bars with their upper surface about 3 inches higher than the bottom of the water-spaces, which, by this means, will be allowed to contain quiescent water, ready to retain without injury any deposite that subsides from the water; and the water-spaces should be periodically cleansed, by means of the mud-holes placed opposite the edge of each water-space in the lower part of the outer fire-box shell. These mud-holes are made water-tight by means of either a brass plug simply screwed in and with a slight taper, or by a door applied with a soft packing on its face, and screwed up with a bridge-piece and bolt, making the joint on the internal surface of the outer shell, the hole and door being made sufficiently oval to enable the door to be introduced into the water-space. The latter plan often gives rise to inconvenience, from the joint being found leaky when the steam is raised, rendering it necessary to drop the fire, and empty the boiler, before it can be renewed. In some very large square fire boxes, such as those used on the Great Western Railway, a diaphragm, or divisional 4-inch water-space, has been placed across the middle of the fire-box, with the view of obtaining increased heating surface. This diaphragm has its lower edge (in which deposite takes place) made straight, and about 2 inches below the general surface of the fire-bars, but its upper edge is of the form of an inverted arch, in order to promote the free delivery of the steam generated within it into the steam-dome. The sides of the fire-box, where the diaphragm is attached, are not cut away to form passages for the water and steam, but are pierced with a series of circular holes, 3 inches in diameter, to permit a due circulation without uselessly weakening the fire-box; but the uppermost hole of the series must be placed at the highest point of the diaphragm, otherwise an accumulation of steam, and consequent injury at that point, will ensue. The use of a diaphragm is found to be beneficial in the case of a very powerful engine, provided its upper edge be made sufficiently low to admit of the tubes being conveniently drifted over it, and to allow the dart to be used with facility in dropping the front set of fire-bars.

The ash-box consists of a plate-iron tray, placed below the fire-box, to receive the burning ashes that drop from between the fire-bars. In the earlier locomotives, no ash-boxes being used, the red-hot ashes were dispersed to a considerable distance by coming in contact with the wheels, and conflagrations were often thereby originated. The ash-box should be as large as convenient, and not less than 10 inches deep, otherwise it will materially impede the draught; but if of ample dimensions, and closed at the sides and back, it will increase the draught, particularly when running against a head wind, at which time a strong draught is required. A hanging shutter to open or close the front of the ash-box forms a good damper. The bottom of the ash-box is placed about 9 inches above the level of the rails, and should on no account be nearer than 6 inches, otherwise the engine cannot pass safely over stones or similar objects lying accidentally between the rails.

Tubes.—The tubes are generally formed of brass; the ferules by which they are secured are for the most part made of steel at the furnace end, and of malleable iron at the smoke-box end, and the holes in the tube-plates are tapered, so that the tubes bind them together. Great care should be taken in securing the tubes, as any neglect will be productive of much inconvenience. The ferules are found to be very injurious to freedom of draught, particularly in very small tubes; and to overcome this objection the methods we have mentioned, and many others, have been tried for fastening the tubes in by riveting over or screwing into the tube-plates; but hitherto no method, except that of internal tube-rings, has been found to answer in the case of brass tubes; but we think it likely that, with wrought-iron tubes, internal tube-rings will be ultimately abandoned. Stephenson has frequently adopted iron tubes of late, in preference to brass, on the score of their greater cheapness and durability; and in some cases, where unusual attention has been paid to them, and pure water used, they have been found to answer very well. A common internal diameter of tubes is $1\frac{5}{8}$ in. If made very small, the tubes are liable to be choked by pieces of coke, and the sectional area will be inconveniently contracted, while, if made much larger, the heating surface will be unduly diminished. The number of tubes varies considerably in different boilers; in one species of locomotive in extensive use the number is 134, and the pitch $2\frac{1}{4}$ in. Sufficient space is left below the tubes for deposite, that it may not be in contact with the tubes and cause them to be burned: the extreme tube of the widest row is about the diameter of a tube from the boiler shell. In the long-boiler engines of Stephenson, from the volume of water contained in them, considerable time is required to get up the steam, even so much as three and a half hours where the ordinary engines take two hours, and they require great care in firing and feeding to prevent the steam running low.

Smoke-box and chimney.—The smoke-box door of many engines is hinged at the bottom, and is kept shut by means of handles and catches; but the position of the door when open is in that case inconvenient, as it prevents ready access to the tubes. In some of Stephenson's engines, the smoke-box door is in two leaves, which open like the doors of a house, overlapping at the centre, where they are closed by a bar, and at the top and bottom by handles and catches. This door admits of the easy examination of the cylinders and valves. A small door is usually left near the bottom of the smoke-box, by which the accumulated cinders may be removed. The bottom of the smoke-box should not be below the ash-pan, or be much nearer the level of the rails than 18 inches, else the waste-water cocks of the cylinder projecting through it, would be liable to injury from objects lying on the line. The smoke-box is lower in freight engines than in passenger engines, on account of the driving wheels being smaller; and, being coupled with the other wheels, the cylinder has frequently to be inclined to let the moving parts work clear of the front axle.

The chimney must not stand more than 14 feet high above the rails. The sectional area of the chimney is about 1-10th of the area of fire-grate. The chimney is usually provided with a damper, similar to the disk throttle-valve of an ordinary engine; this is generally hung off the centre, and a hole is made in it for the top of the blast-pipe, which projects through it when it is closed. Another damper has been applied by Messrs. Rennie at the smoke-box end of the tubes, consisting of a sliding-plate perforated with holes, which, when opposite the ends of the tubes, will give a free current, and may be made to close them completely if required. Another kind of damper consists of an arrangement of thin bars similarly disposed to the laths of a Venetian blind; the plates being so hinged, that when placed with their edges to the tube-plate, they leave the flow of air through the tubes unimpeded, and when hanging down they close up the tubes, or they partially close the tubes in any intermediate position. By either of these arrangements, the hot air is retained for a longer period in contact with the tubes than if a simple damper were used, as each tube is virtually furnished with a hanging bridge which keeps in the hottest air and lets only the coldest flow out. An inconvenient degree of heat in the smoke-box is also prevented. The smoke-box is usually made of $\frac{1}{4}$th plate; the chimney of $\frac{1}{8}$th plate; the blast-pipe of $\frac{1}{8}$th copper, and the steam-pipe of $\frac{3}{16}$th copper.

Framing.—In some engines the side-frames consist of oak, with iron plates riveted on each side. The guard-plates are in these cases of equal length, the frames being curved upwards to pass over the driving-axle. Hard cast-iron blocks are riveted between the guard-plates, to serve as guides for the axle-bushes. The side-frames are connected across at the ends, and cross-stays are introduced beneath the boiler to stiffen the frames sidewise, and prevent the ends of the connecting or eccentric rods from falling down, if they should be broken. The springs are of the ordinary carriage kind, with plates, connected at the centre, and allowed to slide on each other at their ends. The upper plate terminates in two eyes, through each of which passes a pin, which also passes through the jaws of a bridle, connected by a double-threaded screw to another bridle, which is jointed to the framing: the centre of the spring rests on the axle-box. Sometimes the springs are placed between the guard-plates and below the framing, which rests upon their extremities. One species of spring which has gained a considerable introduction consists of a number of flat steel plates, with a piece of metal or other substance interposed between them at the centre, leaving the ends standing apart.

A common mode of connecting the engine and tender, is by means of a rigid bar with an eye at each end, through which pins are passed. Between the engine and tender, however, buffers should always be interposed, as their presence contributes greatly to prevent oscillation and other irregular motions of the engine. A bar is strongly attached to the front of the carriage on each side, and projects perpendicularly downwards to within a short distance of the rail, to clear away stones or other obstructions that might occasion accidents if the engine ran over them. The axles bear only against the tops of the axle boxes, which are generally of brass; but a plate extends beneath the bearing, to prevent sand from being thrown upon it. The upper part of the box in most engines has a reservoir of oil, which is supplied to the journal by two tubes and siphon wicks. Stephenson uses cast-iron axle boxes with brasses, and grease instead of oil, which is fed by the heat of the bearing melting the grease, and causing it to flow down through a hole in the brass. All the engines with outside bearings have inside bearings also; they are supported by longitudinal bars, which serve also in some cases to support the piston guides: these bearings are sometimes made so as not to touch the shaft, unless in the event of its breaking.

Steam-dome pipes and regulator.—The steam-dome, or separator, from the upper part of which the supply of steam is obtained, is now generally placed over the fire-box; and in Bury's and Stephenson's engines it forms a part of the external shell of the fire-box; whilst in the engines used on the Grand Junction Railway, it consists of an independent cylindrical vessel, attached to the low roof of the fire-box. Either plan, this latter or Bury's, is perfectly safe and strong, without the addition of stay-rods; but Stephenson's dome presents a large extent of flat surface, from the roof of the internal fire-box up to the arched roof of the external fire-box; and this flat surface requires to be powerfully stayed by angle-irons and tension-rods. We remember an instance in which the accidental omission of one of the numerous tension-rods led to the forcing out and partial explosion of the side of the fire-box, showing how much depends on the circumstances of these rods, with their joints and pins, remaining sound and uninjured from corrosion or other source of injury or decay. In this respect the round fire-box, with its dome, has the advantage of superior strength and safety. A large steam-dome is found to be the most efficacious mode yet tried for preventing the evil of priming or damp steam; but no height of dome will entirely prevent it if there be not space enough left above the tubes in the cylindrical part of the boiler to allow the free passage of the steam along to the fire-box and dome, while an excessive height of dome is also found to produce an unsteady motion of the engine, by causing the machine to be top-heavy. A height of about 2 feet 6 inches above the cylindrical part of the boiler is found to give satisfactory results in practice, and to lead to the production of as pure steam as any greater altitude could secure. In some engines the steam is withdrawn from a dome placed at the smoke-box end of the boiler, into which the steam-pipe rises. It is thought that the ebullition being less violent at this point, the steam will thus be more effectually dried. The steam-pipes are made either of iron or copper; and of these, iron best withstands the high temperature of the smoke-box and the impact of the cinders, but it is liable to internal corrosion. The steam-pipe, after entering the smoke-box, divides into two branches, one passing down each side of the smoke-box so as to leave a free space for cleaning the tubes, and also to avoid as much as possible the impact of the hot air and cinders; but in some engines the steam-pipe descends vertically, which is somewhat inconvenient in practice. The area of the steam-pipe is one-sixth to one-eighth of the area of cylinder, and the branch steam-pipes are each about one-tenth of the area of cylinder.

The admission of the steam from the boiler to the cylinders is regulated by a valve or regulator, which is generally placed immediately above the internal fire-box, and is connected with two copper pipes, one conducting steam from the highest point of the dome down to it, and the other conducting the steam that has passed through it along the boiler to the upper part of the smoke-box. Regulators may be divided into two sorts, viz. those with sliding valves and steam ports, and those with conical valves and seats, of which the latter kind are the best. The former kind have for the most part hitherto consisted of a circular valve and face, with radial apertures, the valve resembling the outstretched wings of a butterfly, and being made to revolve on its central pivot, by connecting links between its outer edges or by a central spindle. In some of Stephenson's engines with variable expansion geer, the regulator consists of a slide-valve covering a port on the top of the valve-chests. A rod passes from this valve through the smoke-box below the boiler, and, by means of a lever parallel to the starting lever, is brought up to the engineer's reach. Cocks were at first used as regulators, but were given up, as they were found liable to stick fast. A gridiron slide-valve has been used by Stephenson, which consists of a perforated square plate moving upon a face with an equal number of holes. This plan of a valve with a small movement gives a large area of opening. In Bury's engines a sort of conical plug is used, which is withdrawn by turning the handle in front of the fire-box; a spiral groove of very large pitch is made in the valve-spindle, in which fits a pin fixed to the boiler, and by turning the spindle an end motion is given to it which either shuts or opens the steam passage according to the direction in which it is turned. The best regulator would probably be a valve of the equilibrium description, such as is used in the Cornish engines.

Safety-valves and fusible plugs.—The safety-valves are placed upon the dome, in Bury's and Stephenson's engines; but it has been found much better to place them on the cylindrical part of the boiler, because when an engine commences to prime, the water projected from the blast-pipe generally causes an unusual generation of steam, which escapes at the safety-valve, and in its passage of course accumulates and lifts the surface-water and foam at whatever point of the boiler the safety-valves are situated; thus the further they are placed from the steam-dome the better, as they will then diminish the evil of priming, which, if placed upon the steam-dome, they would only aggravate. Indeed, if the safety-valves are properly situated, an engineman has the great advantage of being able to check or stop the priming of the boiler on the instant, by causing his safety-valves to blow off strongly. It is requisite to place the safety-valves upon a tubular pillar, of such altitude as to prevent the escaping cloud of steam from obscuring the look-out of the engineman. Bury's 14-inch engine contains a pair of safety-valves of 2¼ inches diameter, exclusive of the mitre; and Stephenson's 15-inch engine contains a pair of 4-inch diameter. The latter dimension is preferable, as large safety-valves are much less liable to adhere to their seats than small ones. Safety-valves require to be tested occasionally; and the best method consists in attaching the valve joint-pin to one end of an ordinary pair of scales, when the overbalancing weight at the reverse end will indicate the real pressure upon the valve, which exceeds the nominal pressure by the weight and friction of the lever, with its joints and spring balance, and the adhesion of the valve to its seat. To bring this adhesion to a minimum, it is a good plan to make the lip of the valve-seat somewhat flatter than a mitre, that is, at a less angle than 45° with the horizon: 30° answers very well.

Fig. 55.

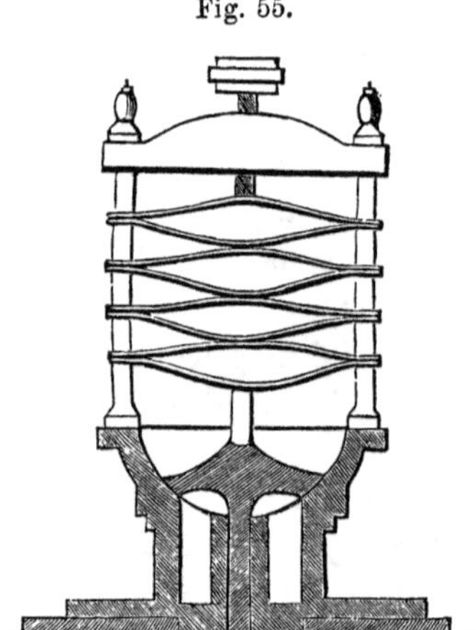

The safety-valve is pressed down by means of a lever, and a screw at its extremity is attached to a spiral spring balance. To find the pressure per square inch, multiply the weight indicated on the scale, by the ratio of the two arms of the lever, and divide the product by the number of square inches in the area of the valve; but to save the trouble of calculation, the ratio of the arms of the lever is made so as to be expressed by the number which represents the area of the valve, so that the weight marked on the balance is the pressure per square inch upon the valve. Some allowance must be made for the weight of the valve itself, and part of that of the lever. It is expedient to put a stop upon the screw by which the lever is screwed down or the tension of the spring increased, so as to prevent the pressure from exceeding a safe amount. Lock-up valves, which were intended as a precaution against the recklessness or neglect of the engineer, have fallen into disfavour, as from such valves being inaccessible and seldom being required to act, they became fixed in their seats; but it is an easy thing to make a valve which can be raised, but cannot be forced down by the engineer, and such valves are in general use in steam vessels. In the engines of Cave, Hick, and Jackson, one of the valves is permanently loaded a little above the usual pressure, and enclosed in a chest; it is usually made with bent, flat, steel springs, pressing against one another, and guided by standards screwed to the valve-seat. One of these valves is shown by fig. 55.

A plug of lead is usually fixed in the furnace crown, which melts if the boiler becomes short of water, and gives notice of the danger. In some engines a cock is attached to the top of the steam-dome, against which a small disk of fusible metal is retained by a ring of brass bolted to the cock, and which is intended as an antidote to explosions. When the cock is opened, the steam has access to the under side of the fusible plate, which when melted is forced through the small hole in the retaining plate; and the engineer being thus warned of the undue pressure, can shut the cock and take measures to reduce the pressure. This, however, is altogether a futile expedient, for the steam would be too much cooled in passing through this cock and small pipe to melt the metal: and even if that defect were remedied, the objections still remain, as applying to all fusible plugs, and the danger is increased by leading the engineer to trust to a measure of safety that is inoperative in the hour of danger. Steam gages have not been applied hitherto to locomotives, on account of the inconvenient height of the column of mercury requisite to balance the steam. But it would be an easy thing to make a steam gage of moderate dimensions, by making the tube, whether straight or siphon, of glass, closed at the top, so that the mercury in its ascent would have to compress the air above it; and the graduations would be equal, or nearly so, if the tube were made taper.

Cylinders and valves.—The cylinders are made of cast iron, about three-quarters of an inch thick, and should be of hard metal, so as to have but little tendency to wear oval from the weight and friction of the piston. The ends of the cylinder are made about one inch thich, and both ends are very generally made removable. At each end of the cylinder there is generally about half an inch of clearance. The valve is invariably of the three-ported description: it is made of brass, and is not pressed upon by the valve-casing, as it is necessary in the absence of cylinder escape-valves that the steam-valve should be capable of leaving the face to enable the steam or air shut within the cylinder to escape when the train is carried on by its momentum, and also to afford an escape for the water carried over by the steam when priming takes place. The operation of priming upon the cylinders and valves is very injurious, as the grit and sediment then carried over with the steam wears the pistons, cylinders, and valve faces very rapidly; so that if the water be sandy and the engine addicted to priming, the pistons and valves may be worn out and the cylinders require reboring in the course of a few months.

The valve-casing is sometimes cast on the cylinder: the face of the cylinder on which the valve works is raised a little, so that any foreign matters deposited upon it may be pushed off to the less elevated parts by the valve. The area of the steam-ports is in some cases one-ninth, and in others one-twelfth or one-thirteenth of the area of the cylinder; and the eduction one-sixth to one-eighth of the area of the cylinder,—proportions which allow at mean speeds of twenty-five to thirty miles per hour, a pressure little different from that of the steam in the steam-pipes; for higher speeds the ports should be larger in proportion. The valve-casing is covered with a door, which can be removed to inspect the valves or the cylinder face. Some valve-casings have covers upon their front end as well as their top, which admits of the valve and valve bridle being more readily removed.

A cock is placed at each end of the cylinder to allow the water to be discharged which accumulates there from priming and condensation. The four cocks of the two cylinders are connected, so that by working a handle the whole are opened or shut at the same time. In Stephenson's engines with variable expansion, there is but one cock, which is on the bottom of the valve chest.

The valve lever is usually longer than the eccentric lever, to increase the travel of the valve. The pins of the eccentric lever wear quickly. Stephenson puts a ferule of brass on these pins, which being loose and acting as a roller, facilitates the throwing in and out of gear, and when worn can easily be replaced; so that there need be no material derangement of the motion of the valve from play in this situation. The starting lever travels between two iron segments, and can be fixed at the dead point or for the forward or backward motions. This is done by a small catch or bell crank jointed to the bottom of the handle at the end of the lever, and coming up by the side of the handle, but pressed out from it by a spring. The smaller arm of this bell crank is jointed to a bolt which shoots into notches made in one of the segments between which the lever moves. By pressing the bell crank against the handle of the lever, the bolt is withdrawn, and the lever may be shifted to any other point; when the spring being released, the bolt flies into the nearest notch.

The pistons which consist of a single ring and tongue piece, or of two single rings set one above the other so as to break joint, are preferable to those which consist of many pieces. In Stephenson's pistons, the screws are liable to work slack and the springs to break. The piston-rods are made of steel, the diameter being from one-seventh to one-eighth of the diameter of the cylinder. They are tapered into the piston, and secured there with a cutter. The top of the piston-rod is secured by a cutter into a socket with jaws, through the holes of which a cross-head passes, which is embraced between the jaws by the small end of the connecting-rod, while the ends of the cross-head move in guides. Between the piston-rod clutch and the guide blocks, the feed-pump rod joins the cross-head in some engines. The guides are formed of steel plates attached to the framing, between which work the guide blocks, fixed on the ends of the cross-head, and which have flanges bearing against the inner edges of the guides. Steel or brass guides are better than iron ones. Stephenson and Hawthorn attach their guides at one end to a cross-stay,—at the other to lugs upon the cylinder cover; and they are made stronger in the middle than at the ends. Stout guide-rods of steel encircled by stuffing-boxes on the ends of the cross-head would probably be found superior to any other arrangement. The stuffing-boxes might contain conical bushes cut spirally, in addition to the packing; and a ring cut spirally might be sprung upon the rod and fixed in advance of the stuffing-box with lateral play, to wipe the rod before entering the stuffing-box, and prevent it from being scratched by the adhesion of dust.

Feed apparatus.—The feed-pumps are made of brass, but the plungers are sometimes made of iron, and are generally attached to the piston-rod cross-head, though in Stephenson's engines they are worked by rods attached to eyes on the eccentric hoops. There is a ball valve between the pump and the tender, and two usually in the pipe leading from the pump to the boiler, besides a cock close to the boiler, by which the pump may be shut off from the boiler in the case of accident to the valves. The ball valves are guided by four branches which rise vertically and join at top in a hemispherical form, as shown in fig. 56. The shocks of the ball against this have in some cases broken it after a week's

Fig. 56.

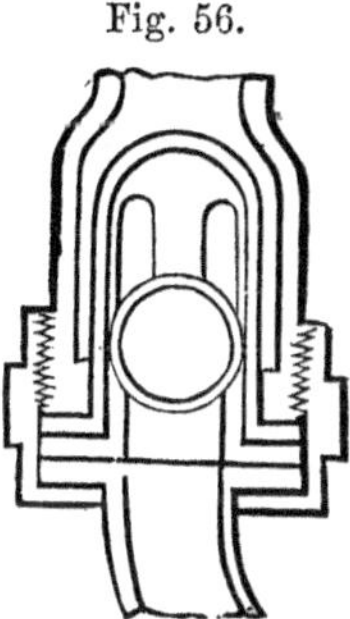

work, from the top of the cage having been made flat, and the branches not having had their junction at top properly filleted. These valve guards are attached in different ways to the pipes; when one occurs at the junction of two pieces of pipe it has a flange, which, along with the flanges of the pipes and that of the valve seat, are held together by a union joint. It is sometimes formed with a thread at the under end, and screwed into the pipe. The balls are cast hollow, to lessen the shock as well as to save metal: in some cases, where the feed-pump plunger has been attached to the cross-head, the piston-rod has been bent by the strain; and that must in all cases occur if the communication between the pump and boiler be closed when the engine is started, and there be no escape valve for the water. Spindle valves have in some cases been used instead of ball valves, but they are more subject to derangement. Slide valves might easily be applied, and would probably be found preferable to either of the other expedients. The pipes connecting the tender with the pumps should allow access to the valves and free motion to the engine and tender.

The feed-pipe of many engines enters the boiler near the bottom, and about the middle of its length. In Stephenson's, the water is let in at the smoke-box end of the boiler, a little below the water level. By this means, the heat is more effectually extracted from the escaping smoke; but the arrangement is of questionable applicability to engines of which the steam-dome and steam-pipe are at the smoke-box end, as in that case the entering cold water would condense the steam.

Wheels.—The driving wheels are made large to increase the speed; the bearing wheels also are easier on the road when large. In freight engines, the driving wheels are smaller than in passenger engines, and are generally coupled together. Wheels are made in various ways; they are frequently made with cast-iron naves, and with the spokes and rim of wrought-iron. The spokes are forged out of flat bars with T-formed heads; these are arranged radially in the founder's mould, while the cast-iron centre is poured around them; the ends of the T heads are then welded together to constitute the periphery of the wheel or inner tire, and little wedge-form pieces are inserted where there is any deficiency of iron. In some cases, the arms are hollow, though of wrought-iron, the tire of wrought-iron, and the nave of cast-iron; and the spokes are turned where they are fitted into the nave, and are secured in their sockets by means of cutters. Hawthorn makes his wheels with cast-iron naves, and wrought-iron rims and arms, but instead of welding the arms together, he makes palms on their outer end, which are attached by rivets to the rim. These rivets, however, unless very carefully formed, are apt to work loose; and we think it would be an improvement if the palms were to be slightly indented into the rim, in cases in which the palms do not meet one another at the ends. When the rim is turned, it is ready for the tire, which is now often made of steel. The materials for wheel tires are first swaged separately, and then welded together under the heavy hammer at the steel-works, after which they are bent to the circle, welded, and turned to certain gauges. The tire is now heated to redness in a circular furnace; during the time it is getting hot, the iron wheel, previously turned to the right diameter, is bolted down upon a face-plate or surface; the tire expands with the heat, and when at a cherry-red, it is dropped over the wheel, for which it was previously too small, and it is also hastily bolted down to the surface-plate; the whole load is quickly immersed by a swing crane into a tank of water about five feet deep, and hauled up and down until nearly cold; the tires are not afterwards tempered. It is not indispensable that the whole tire should be of steel, but a dovetail groove turned out of the tire at the place where it bears most on the rail, and fitted with a band of steel, which may be put in in pieces, is sometimes adopted, though at the risk of being thrown off in working. The steel, after being introduced, is well hammered, which expands it sideways, until it fills the dovetail groove, but it has sometimes come out. The tire is attached to the rim by rivets with countersunk heads, and the wheel is then fixed on its axle. The tire is turned somewhat conical, to facilitate the passage of the engine round curves—the diameter of the outer wheel being virtually increased by the centrifugal force, and that of the inner wheel correspondingly diminished, whereby the curve is passed without the resistance which would otherwise arise from the inequality of the spaces passed over by wheels of the same diameter fixed upon the same axle. The rails, moreover, are not set quite upright, but are slightly inclined inwards, in consequence of which the wheels must either be conical or slightly dished, to bear fairly upon them. One benefit of inclining the rails in this way and coning the tires is, that the flange of the wheel is less liable to bear against the side of the rail, and with the same view the flanges of all the wheels are made with large fillets in the corners. Wheels have been tried loose upon the axle, but they have less stability, and are not now much used.

In all locomotives there is a very material loss of power from the contraction of blast-pipe necessary to maintain the blast; at high speeds one-half of the power of the engine is lost by the inadequate area of the steam passages, of which the greatest loss is that arising from the contraction of the blast-pipe. Tenders are now made larger, to obviate the necessity of so many fuel and water stations. Tenders can be put on any number of wheels, so that inconvenience is not likely to arise from their size and weight.

Cranked axle.—The cranked axle is made of wrought-iron, with two cranks forged upon it, towards the middle of its length, at a distance from each other answerable to the distance between the cylinders; bosses are made on the axle for the wheels to be keyed upon, and there are bearings for the support of the framing. The axle is usually forged in two pieces, which are then welded together. Sometimes the pieces for the cranks are put on separately, but those so made are liable to give way. In engines with outside cylinders the axles are straight, the crank-pins being inserted in the naves of the wheels. The bearings to which the connecting-rods are attached are made with very large fillets in the corners, so as to strengthen the axle in that part, and to obviate side play in the connecting-rod. In engines which have been in use for some time, however, there is generally a good deal of end play in the bearings of the axles themselves, and this slackness contributes to make the oscillation of the engine more violent.

Connecting-rods.—It is very desirable that the length of the connecting-rod should remain invariable, in spite of the wear of the brasses, for there is a danger of the piston striking against the cover of the cylinder, if it be shortened, as the clearance is left as small as possible, in order to economize steam. In some engines the strap encircling the crank-pin is fixed immovably to the connecting-rod by dovetailed keys, as shown in fig. 58, and a bolt passes through the keys, rod, and strap, to prevent the dovetail keys from working out. The brass is tightened by a gib and cutter, which is kept from working loose by three pinching screws, and a cross-pin or cutter through the point. The effect of this arrangement is to lengthen the rod, but at the cross-head end of the rod the elongation is neutralized, by making the strap loose, so that in tightening the brass the rod is shortened by an amount equal to its elongation at the crank-pin end. The tightening here is also effected by a gib and cutter, which is kept from working loose by two pinching screws pressing on the side of the cutter. Both journals of the connecting-rod are furnished with oil-cups, having a small tube in the centre, with siphon wicks. The connecting-rod, represented in figs. 58, 57, is a thick flat bar, with its edges rounded. Stephenson's connecting-rod is

Fig. 58. Fig. 57.

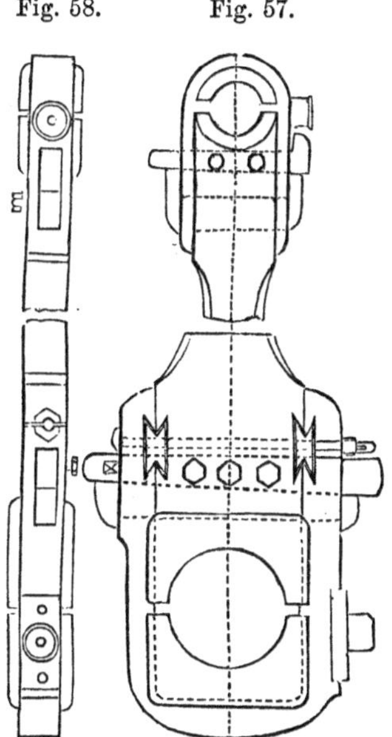

made at the crank end; a strap of round iron passes over both brasses, and is attached to the T end of the connecting-rod by means of nuts upon the ends of the bent iron, which is made thickest in the middle, to resist the strain. This plan has the defect of shortening the connecting-rod when the brasses are screwed up, and the brasses require to be very strong and heavy. Hawthorn's connecting-rod has a strap at each end, tightened by a gib and cutter; but, to obviate the tendency to shorten the rod, the piston-rod end is furnished with a cutter for tightening the brass outwards. The point of the cutter is screwed, and goes through a lug attached to the gib, and is tightened by a nut. It would be preferable to attach the lug to the cutter and the screw to the gib, as the projection of the screw, when the cutter is far in, would not then be so great. In the engines on the Rouen Railway the piston-rod end of the connecting-rod has neither strap nor brass, but simply embraces the cross-head, while the crank end is hollowed out to admit brasses, which are tightened by a gib and cutter. The length of the connecting-rod varies from four times the length of the crank to seven times. The long connecting-rod has the advantage of diminishing the friction upon the slides.

Eccentrics and eccentric-rod.—The eccentrics are made of cast iron; and when set on the axle between the cranks, they are put on in two pieces held together by bolts, as shown in figs. 59, 60: but in straight-axle engines they are cast in a piece, and are secured on the shaft by means of a key. The eccentric, when in two pieces, is retained at its proper angle on the shaft by a pinching-screw, which is provided with a jam-nut to prevent it from working loose. A piece is left out of the eccentric in casting it, to allow of the screw being inserted, and the void is afterwards filled by inserting a dovetailed piece of metal. Stephenson and Hawthorn leave holes in their eccentrics on each side of the central arm, and they apply pinching-screws in each of these holes. The screws sometimes slacken and allow the eccentric to shift, unless they are provided with jam-nuts. In the Rouen engines with straight axles, the four eccentrics are cast in one piece.

Fig. 60. Fig. 59.

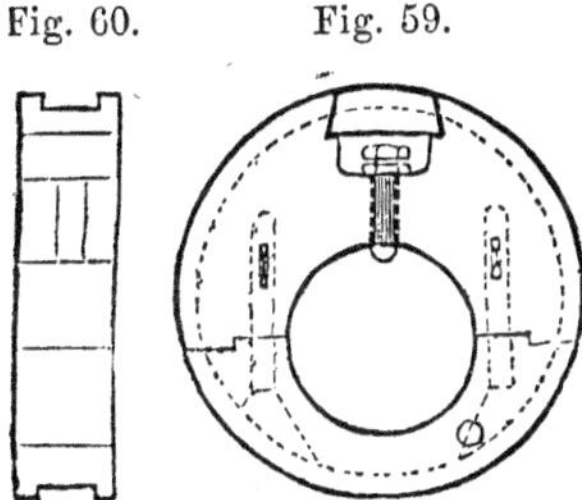

Eccentric straps are best made of wrought iron, as inconvenience arises from the frequent breakage of brass ones. When made of malleable iron, one-half of the strap is forged with the rod, the other half being secured to it by bolts, nuts, and jam-nuts. Pieces of brass are in some cases pinned within the malleable iron hoop, but it appears to be preferable to put brasses within the strap to encircle the eccentric, as in the case of any other bearing.

When brass straps are used, the lugs have generally nuts on both sides, so that the length of the eccentric-rod may be adjusted; but it is better for the lugs of the hoops to abut against the necks of the screws, and if any adjustment is necessary from the wear of the straps, washers can be interposed. In some engines the adjustment is effected by screwing the valve-rod, and the cross-head through which it passes has a nut on either side of it by which its position upon the valve-rod is determined. The forks of the eccentric-rod are steel. The length of the eccentric-rod is the distance between the centre of the crank axle and the centre of the valve-shaft.

Valve motions.—In locomotives the eccentrics are now always fixed upon the axle, and two are used, one for the forward, the other for the backward motion: the loose pulleys have been given up on account of their liability to get out of order from the shocks to which they were subjected by sudden change of direction when worked at a quick speed. The arrangement whereby the motion of the eccentric is transmitted to the valve, is either direct or indirect. In cases of indirect attachment the motion is given through the intervention of levers, and there is some variety in the arrangements by which the reversing is accomplished. Alcard and Buddicome use a pair of eccentrics at the end of the axle, which is straight; the reversing shaft is placed below the level of the piston-rod, and to a lever keyed upon it are attached links of unequal length, connected at their upper extremities with the ends of the eccentric-rods, one of which is above and one below the studs on the lever of the valve-shaft, so that the upper eccentric-rod, being in gear, gives the forward motion, and the lower gives the backward motion. In other engines, forks are situated above and below the stud of the eccentric levers; the forward eccentric-rod is lifted up out of gear by a link depending from the lever on the reversing shaft, and by the same movement the backing eccentric is lifted into gear by a longer link connecting it to a lever, not upon the reversing shaft, but upon a shaft below it. Stephenson and Hawthorn have both used a similar arrangement, but admitting of the eccentric-rods being both under the studs of the lever on the valve-shaft, so that there is no danger, in the event of a disengaged rod falling down, or of any part of the gearing being bent or twisted by both rods being in gear at the same time. The motion of the eccentrics is now frequently transmitted directly to the valves. In Pauwel's arrangement of valve gearing, the valve works on the side of the cylinder, and the valve-rod is prolonged in the form of a deep flat blade of a lozenge section, on each side of which a stud is fixed,—one being intended for the notch of the forward eccentric-rod, and the other for that of the reversing eccentric. Above them is fixed the reversing shaft, from a lever on which depend two links of unequal length, which are jointed to the ends of the eccentric-rods. By working this lever up or down, the eccentric-rods will be alternately engaged and disengaged, and will communicate their respective motions to the valve; or if the lever be kept in its mid position, both eccentrics will be out of gear, and the valve of course will remain stationary. Pauwel's engines are difficult to work, and are subject to shocks from going suddenly into gear: this arises from the whole weight of levers and rods being on the front of the reversing shaft, but the evil might be remedied by attaching a counterbalance to the shaft. Valves situated upon the sides of the cylinders are in many cases more easily connected with the eccentric, but they require springs to keep them up to the face, so that it appears preferable to make the faces of the two cylinders inclined to one another rather than upright, if valves on the sides of the cylinders are preferred. Stephenson's link motion is the most elegant, and one of the most eligible modes of connecting the valve with the eccentric yet introduced. The nature of this arrangement will be made plain by a reference to fig. 61, where *e* is the valve-rod which is attached by a pin to an open curved link connected at the one end with the driving eccentric-rod *d*, and at the other with the backing eccentric-rod *d'*. The link with the eccentric-rods is capable of being moved up or down by the rod *f* and bell crank *f''*, situated on the shaft *g*, while the valve-rod remains in the same

Fig. 61.

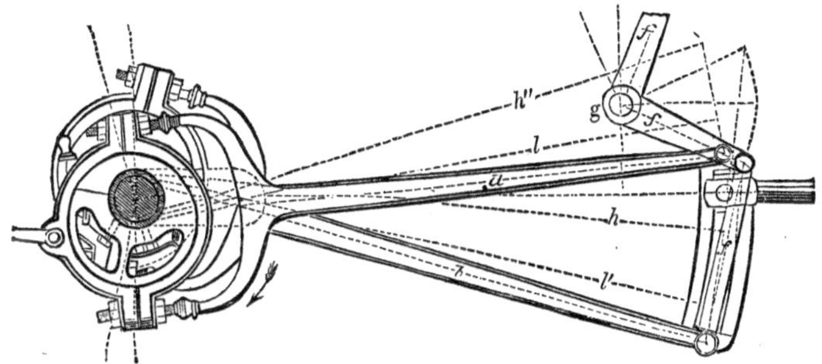

horizontal plane. It is very clear that each end of the link must acquire the motion of the eccentric-rod in connection with it, whatever course the central part of the link may pursue, and the valve-rod will partake most of the motion of the eccentric-rod that is nearest to it. When the link is lowered down, the valve-rod will acquire the motion of the upper eccentric-rod, which is that proper for going ahead; when raised up, the valve-rod will acquire the motion of the reversing eccentric, while in the central position the valve-rod will have no motion, or almost none. The link motion therefore obviates the necessity of throwing the eccentric-rod out of gear; it also enables the engine to be worked to a certain extent expansively, though as a contrivance for working expansively, we cannot hold it as de serving of much commendation. The dead point of the link motion is where the line of the valve-rod bisects the angle formed by the eccentric-rods. The maximum forward motion is when the rods are as figured, and the maximum backward motion when the rods *d* and *d′* are in the position *h″* and *h′*. The best forms of the link motions have side studs, to which the eccentric-rods are connected, and these are placed so that at the greatest throw, whether

Fig. 62.

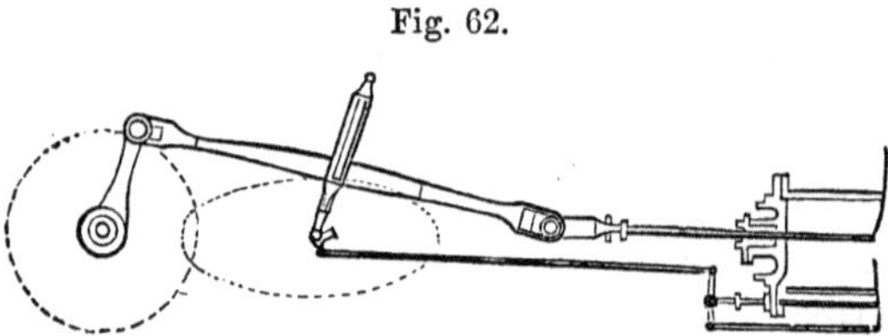

backward or forward, the valve-rod and eccentric-rod are in the same straight line, and the valve receives the full throw of the eccentric. A counterweight is also attached to the shaft to balance the weight of the link and rods. The second eccentric and eccentric-rod of the link motion might, it appears to us, be beneficially dispensed with by placing the shaft *g* in the plane of the valve-rod, and attaching a pin to the centre of the link, which would work in the eye of the horizontal arm of the lever *f*. This lever would in such case require to be made much stronger than at present, as it would have to withstand the thrust of the eccentric, and the link would then virtually be a double-ended lever with a movable centre. Where more convenient, the pin in the centre of the link might be moved in vertical or curved guides, instead of being attached to the lever *f*. The act of raising the link, and with it the eccentric-rod, would in effect alter the position of the eccentric on the shaft, and, if the eccentric-rod were properly proportioned in length, would make the lead right on the reversing side.

How to set the valves of locomotives.—When the cylinder is horizontal, the crank is horizontal at the ends of the stroke; but it is not vertical when the piston is at the middle of its stroke, owing to the deviation from parallelism introduced from the connecting-rod being compelled to move at one of its extremities in a straight line. When the piston is at the end of the bottom stroke, and is gradually advanced towards the middle of the stroke, the end of the connecting-rod is carried round by the crank in a curve opposed to that which it would naturally describe round the cross-head as centre; but when the piston has approached the end of the top stroke, the curvature of the path in which the end of the connecting-rod is moved by the crank is in the same direction as that of the circle which it would describe round the cross-head, and these curves would coincide if the connecting-rod were equal in length to the crank: it will be easily seen, therefore, that at the top stroke the piston-rod requires but a small movement to enable the end of the connecting-rod to traverse a large portion of the circle of the crank, while at the bottom stroke the piston has to travel farther to allow of an equal arc being described by the crank. From these considerations it follows, that the motion of the crank being nearly uniform, there must be considerable inequalities in the speed of the piston; and more than a half circle will be described by the crank during the top half of the stroke, and less than a half circle in the bottom half of the stroke. The length of the connecting-rod is the distance from the cross-head at half stroke to the centre of the shaft; and it is clear, therefore, that at mid-stroke the crank cannot be vertical. The motion of the valve partakes of the same species of irregularity; but as the eccentric-rod is much longer in proportion to the radius of the eccentric than the connecting-rod, that inequality only may be noted which arises from the relation between the circumference of a circle and its diameter. The irregularity arising from the angle of the connecting-rod also affects the valve, but not to an injurious extent in ordinary cases. In fig. 63 we have shown the direct connection, as used in some of Stephenson's locomotives, A E B F representing the crank circle, and the inner circle that of the eccentric. Supposing, now, that the total length of the valve face were equal to the distance between the extreme edges of the steam ports, the valve would be without *lap;* and leaving the question of *lead* out of consideration for the present, that is, supposing that the steam were admitted exactly at the ends of the stroke, the eccentric would be fastened upon the shaft at right angles to the crank; in other words, the small crank which constitutes the eccentric would be at right angles to the large crank, which is attached to the piston-rod. In this way, the valve would be in the middle of its stroke when the piston was at either end of its stroke, so as to close both the steam and eduction passages, and to be ready with the slightest possible advance to open both for the return stroke of the piston. It has been found advantageous, however, to make the valve face longer than the distance between the extreme edges of the steam ports, so that when it is in the middle of its stroke it projects or overlaps the ports at both ends; and hence it requires to move through a space equal to the overlap before it is in a condition to open the steam port for the return stroke of the piston. To effect this, it is only necessary to move the eccentric forward in its path, until, at the end of the stroke of the piston, the valve is on the edge of the steam port, ready, as before, upon the slightest farther advance, to admit the steam to the cylinder. Now, as the valve is thus required to move through a part of its travel or throw equal to the overlap at each end, and as the throw is equal to the diameter of the circle which the eccentric describes, it follows that, to give the requisite advance, that distance must be measured upon the diameter of the circle, and the corresponding position of the centre of the eccentric is that of which we are in search.

Fig. 63.

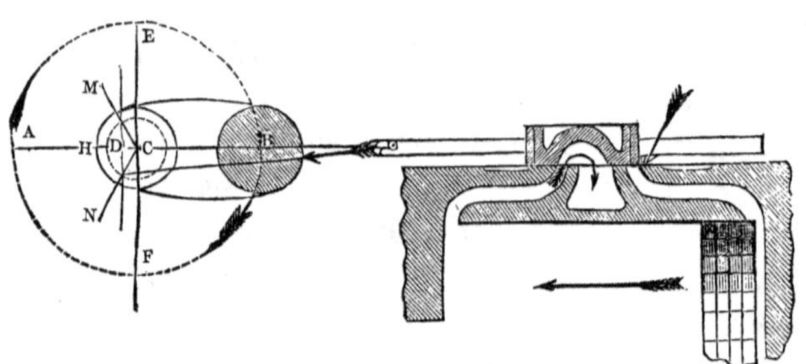

On the remote side of the centre of the crank-shaft, and on the line of centres, mark off D C, the amount of overlap at each end of the valve, and draw a line parallel to E F, the vertical centre line of the crank-shaft; the arc of the eccentric circle intercepted between these parallel lines is that through which the eccentric must move, in order to draw the valve through a portion of its stroke equal to the overlap D C; and the point in which the line intersects the circle of the eccentric is, therefore, the position which the centre of the eccentric should occupy when the piston is at the end of its down-stroke, and on the very point of beginning its up-stroke. In practice, however, the valve is not so set as to open simultaneously with the commencement of the stroke of the piston, but is set so that the steam commences to flow into the cylinder a very little before the beginning of the stroke; and hence, when the piston actually commences its stroke, the valve has already partially opened the port. To make this adjustment, an additional advance must be given to the valve, and of course in the same direction; and the amount of *lead*, or opening, which the port has at the commencement of the stroke of the piston, must be added to the *lap*, their sum from C to D being treated the same in every respect as if the whole were *lap;* and so, for the sake of brevity, we may treat it.

Let us suppose now that it was required to find the length that the eccentric-rod should be:—Place the crank horizontal, so that it may have the piston at the bottom of its stroke; bring round the eccentric to the corresponding position which we find it should occupy, and measure the distance from that point to the centre of the joint by which the eccentric-rod is to be attached to the valve-rod; this will be the length of the eccentric-rod. When the length of the eccentric-rod is known, either the valve or eccentric may be put in its proper place, if one of them be already set: thus, if the valve be set, as in the drawing, and the eccentric-rod connected also with the eccentric, it will bring the latter into its place, where it may be fixed; but if the valve could not be conveniently set, it would then be necessary to take the following method, which requires the knowledge of the amount of lap, and the length of the eccentric-rod. Find, as before, the position of the eccentric, attach the rod, and the valve must come into connection in the proper position. In practice, the most convenient method of finding the position of the eccentric with a given lap is to draw a circle, such as H K, representing the crank-shaft, upon a board or a piece of sheet-iron, and another equal to the circle of the eccentric, and draw two diameters perpendicular to each other; mark off from the centre of the crank-shaft, and upon one diameter, the amount of lap C D; through this point draw a line parallel to E F, the other diameter; the points in which this line cuts the circle of the eccentric are the positions of the forward and backward eccentrics. Through these points, and from the centre of the crank-shaft, draw lines C M, C N, which will intersect the circumference of the crank-shaft; upon this circumference measure with a pair of compasses the chord of the arc intercepted between either point of intersection and that of the vertical diameter E F; and the lines of diameters being first drawn upon the shaft itself, then, by transferring with the compasses the distance found upon the diagram, the proper position of the eccen tric at the end of the stroke of the piston is at once determined; and this being marked upon the shaft, the eccentric can at any time be set, by bringing it round to that mark. Before leaving this figure, we may remark, that as the valve in Stephenson's locomotives of this kind is on the side of the cylinder, the cylinder face should be towards us in the drawing. As this arrangement, however, would have afforded a less easy explanation, we have adopted the present one. It will also be observed that the crank-shaft and cylinder are too close, and are not in a line with each other; but this, while it could not be easily avoided, is at the same time of no importance in considering the respective motions of the piston and valve, crank and eccentric, which are shown in their true relative positions. The crank is upon the centre, and the piston, consequently, at the end of the bottom stroke; the eccentric and valve being put in advance of the piston by the lap, have shut off the steam before the end of the stroke, and have also opened the eduction in readiness for the up-stroke; whereas, without lap, the valve would shut off the steam at one end, and open the eduction at the other, simultaneously with the termination of the stroke of the piston.

In fig. 64 we have a different kind of valve-gearing, there being levers which reverse the direction of the motion; that is, while the eccentric-rod and lever are moving in one direction, the valve-rod and lever, being on the opposite side of the weigh-bar shaft, are moving in the opposite direction. In the former case there were no levers, and therefore no

Fig. 64.

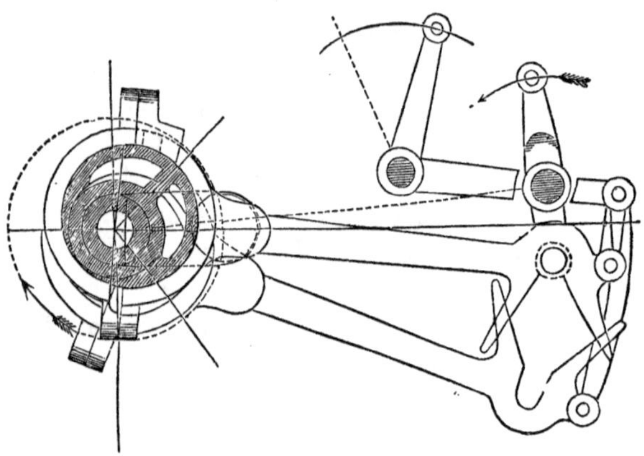

reversal of the motion. Hence, in order to give the valve the same motion as before, in relation to the crank, it is necessary to throw the eccentric to the opposite side of the crank-shaft, so that its motion may be in the revérse direction, to compensate for the reversing action of the levers. For whereas, when upon one side of the shaft they caused the valve to move in the same direction as themselves by means of the eccentric-rods, now that the levers are introduced, the eccentrics must themselves move in an opposite direction, to give the valves the same motion as heretofore. And this can only be done by putting the eccentrics on the opposite side of the crank centre, round which they move, and, of course, in an opposite direction.

Fig. 65.

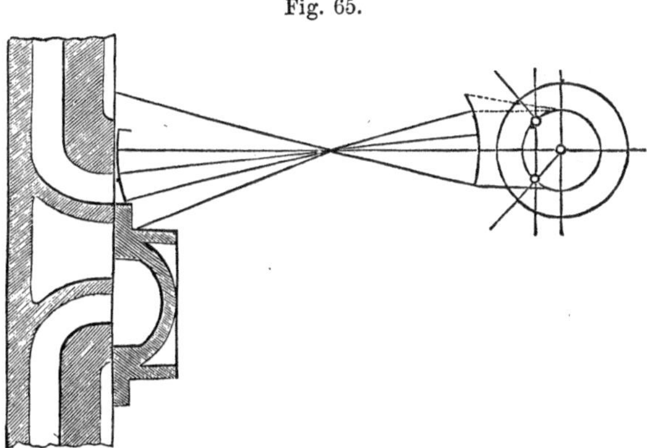

Fig. 65 is intended to illustrate the valve connection of the common locomotive, in which the motion of the eccentric is communicated through levers to the valve, and generally with an increase of throw. In this figure we have the cylinder face, with the valve upon it, at one end of its travel. Measure off the length of the valve throw, from the end of the valve face, in the direction of its travel. The throw of the valve may best be found by adding the lap to the breadth of the steam-port, and doubling their sum. If there were no levers intervening between the valve and eccentric, the line thus measured, which is the throw of the valve, would be the diameter also of the circle described by the centre of the eccentric pulley; but the use of levers interferes with this proportion unless the levers be made of equal length. The effect of levers of unequal length, in making a proportional inequality between the throw of the valve and of the eccentric, will be readily seen by reference to a diagram. From the centre A of the diameter, representing the throw of the valve, draw a line perpendicular to the valve face; and from the same point measure off, upon that line, the length of the lever A B, which is to be attached to the valve-rod, and which, for distinction, we shall call the valve lever. From the point B thus found as a centre with the radius B A, describe a portion of a circle intersecting perpendiculars drawn from C and D, the extremities of the line which represents the throw of the valve; from those points in the circumference of the circle produce lines through the centre B. On either side of the centre line A E, and at a distance from it equal to the radius of the eccentric, draw a parallel line. From B as a centre, with the distance from the centre B to the points H K,—in which the parallels intersect the produced lines of the lever, as radius,—describe an arc of a circle; the radius of this circle is the length which the eccentric lever must be, in order to give the requisite throw to the valve. It will be evident from the inspection of this diagram, that if it be desired to give a smaller throw to the valve than that of the eccentric, it is necessary to make the valve lever shorter than the eccentric lever; and if it were desired to make the valve throw greater than the eccentric throw, it is indispensable that the valve lever should be made proportionally longer than the eccentric lever. If, for example, the throw of the valve is to be made twice the throw of the eccentric, then this can only be accomplished by making the valve lever twice the length of the eccentric lever. Hence the relations between these quantities are expressed by simple proportion; and any three being given, we can readily find the remaining one. For the sake of clearness, we shall state the various forms which the proportion will assume.

First.—Given the throw of the valve, the throw of the eccentric, and the length of the lever attached to the valve-rod, to find the length of the eccentric lever; we have then the proportion:—

RULE.—As the throw of the valve is to the throw of the eccentric, so is the length of the valve lever to the length of the eccentric lever.

If we represent the throw of the valve by T, that of the eccentric by t, the valve lever by L, and the eccentric lever by l, we will have the proportion in a condensed algebraic form, thus,—$T : t :: L : l$; or taking the actual dimensions in inches of the engine before us, $4{\cdot}5 : 3 :: 9 : 6$.

Secondly.—Given the throw of the valve, the throw of the eccentric, and the length of the eccentric lever, to find the length of the valve lever. Then,

Rule.—As the throw of the eccentric is to the throw of the valve, so is the length of the eccentric lever to the length of the valve lever:

Or, algebraically, $t : T :: l : L$; or, as before in actual dimensions, $3 : 4{\cdot}5 :: 6 : 9$.

Thirdly.—Given the throw of the valve and the lengths of the levers, to find the throw of the eccentric.

Rule.—As the valve lever is to the eccentric lever, so is the valve throw to the eccentric throw;

Or thus, $L : l :: T : t$; or, $9 : 6 :: 4{\cdot}5 : 3$.

Fourthly.—Given the eccentric lever, the valve lever, and the eccentric throw, to find the valve throw.

Rule.—As the eccentric lever is to the valve lever, so is the eccentric throw to the valve throw;

Or, $l : L :: t : T$; or, $6 : 9 :: 3 : 4{\cdot}5$.

We formerly explained how the reversing action of the levers rendered it necessary to set the eccentric on that side of the crank-shaft centre nearest to the cylinder; whereas, in the case of the direct valve connection, it was set on the side remote from the cylinder. Having now found the means of ascertaining the lengths of the levers to be employed with a given throw of valve and eccentric, the next step necessary is to determine the true position of the eccentric upon the shaft, in reference to the crank.

Place the crank-pin in the dead point nearest the cylinder; that is, place the centres of the crank-shaft and crank-pin in a line with the centre line of the piston-rod. Upon this line of centres A G, raise a perpendicular L M, through the point F. From F draw a circle, the diameter of which is equal to the throw of the eccentric, and another equal to the cranked axle. If the levers are equal, mark off from F, upon the line of centres and on the cylinder side, the amount of lap, and draw a line parallel to L M, cutting the eccentric circle in the points N O. From F draw lines through N and O to the circumference of the cranked axle. The points N and O are the positions of the centres of the eccentric pulleys for the forward and backward gear, only one of which is necessary for going one way. In practice it is convenient to make marks at P R, as the points N and O are inaccessible. If there were no lap upon the valve, there would be nothing to set off from the centre line L M, and therefore that line would give the positions of the eccentrics.

The intersections of the perpendicular A G would give the positions of the eccentrics on the shaft if the connecting-rod were infinitely long; but inasmuch as the shortness of the connecting-rod introduces irregularity, the true position of the crank at the middle of the stroke of the piston must be taken.

If the lengths of the levers be unequal, the throws of the eccentric and valve will also be unequal; and if the valve lever be the longer, as in the case we have taken, the eccentric throw is less than the valve throw in the same proportion as the eccentric lever is less than the valve lever; and therefore, since the eccentric throw is thus less than the valve throw, by reason of the levers, it follows that the lap, which we set off from F, and which is part of the valve throw, must also be diminished in the same proportion as the whole throw, in order to set off the proper quantity from F. The simplest way of accomplishing this is, by marking off the lap from the line of centres, fig. 65, at the point A, at the same end as we formerly marked off half the valve throw. This distance will be from A to the edge of the port, that being the overlap; then from the edge of the port draw a parallel to A G; and from the point in which this parallel cuts the arc of the longer lever, draw a line through the centre B, and produce it till it cuts the arc K H; the perpendicular from this point to the line E A is the reduced amount of lap, which is to be set off from point F.

Another useful problem is the method of finding the length of the eccentric-rod, the positions of the crank-shaft, and the weigh-bar shaft, and the length of the eccentric lever being given. From the centre of the weigh-bar shaft, with the length of the eccentric lever as radius, describe an arc; draw a tangent from this to the centre of the crank-shaft; from the centre of the weigh-bar shaft drop a perpendicular to the tangential line; the distance from the point of intersection to the centre of the crank-shaft is the length of the eccentric-rod, and the perpendicular is the line of the eccentric lever, when the valve lever is perpendicular to the line of the valve-rod: this gives, therefore, the positions in which these levers must be keyed upon the weigh-bar shaft.

In fig. 65 the mid-line of the eccentric-rod was the same as the line of the piston-rod; but in fig. 64 it is thrown down below that of the piston-rod, forming an angle with it, the vertex of which is the centre of the crank-shaft. In this case the centres of the eccentric pulleys must, consequently, be moved downwards as many degrees as the central line. In order to facilitate this adjustment, we may briefly explain, that every circle is supposed to have its circumference divided into 360 equal parts, called degrees; and if two diameters be drawn in it at right angles to each other, they will divide the circumference into four equal parts, each of which contains 90 degrees. This, therefore, is the means by which the angle is measured; nor will it matter, although the circle be of any size whatever, for it is still equally divided by the two diameters. Hence, if the number of degrees contained in the angle which the mid-line of the eccentric-rod makes with the line of the piston-rod, be measured upon any circle described from the centre of the crank-shaft, and the angle be laid down upon a board, and if from the vertex of the angle a circle be described equal to the diameter of the crank-shaft, the chord of the arc of this circle intercepted between the lines containing the angle, is the distance to be transferred upon the crank-shaft, and through which the eccentric pulley must be moved round, in order to compensate for the obliquity of the eccentric-rod. In the example, fig. 64, the mid-line of the eccentric-rod, when in gear, lies at an angle of five degrees with the line of the piston-rod; and in all such cases this line is to be taken when reference is made to the valve motion; and the piston-rod line is to be taken when reference is made to the motion of the piston. In the case of fig. 65, these lines were made to coincide, for the sake of simplicity.

Miscellaneous remarks respecting locomotives.—The tractive force requisite for drawing carriages over well-formed and level common roads is about $\frac{1}{36}$ of the load, at low speeds. On railways, the tractive force has generally been rated at about $\frac{1}{300}$ of the load, or $7\frac{1}{2}$ pounds per ton, at low speeds; but in well-formed railways the tractive force is probably less than this, to keep the train moving slowly. The resistance of railway trains, however, increases rapidly with the speed, on account of the resistance of the atmosphere; and the resistance occasioned by the atmosphere may be taken at 15 pounds per ton, with an ordinary passenger train moving at the rate of 30 miles an hour. The friction of the engine and the resistance of the rails vary simply as the velocity, if the power of the engine remains the same; but the resistance of the atmosphere varies as the square of the velocity, and the power requisite for overcoming that resistance as the cube of the velocity: so that by doubling the speed of a train, by diminishing the load without increasing the power, the friction is doubled, the atmospheric resistance is made four times greater than before, and the power requisite to overcome that resistance eight times greater. This shows the extravagance of high speeds, even if the power were as economically produced at high speeds, which is by no means the case. In moderately light trains, upwards of 50 per cent. of the power is expended in overcoming atmospheric resistance, in speeds of about 35 miles per hour; and the loss will be greater if the trains be very light, and present a large frontage.

We have already stated that in low-pressure condensing engines the evaporation of one cubic foot of water from the boiler may be taken to represent a horse power. In high-pressure engines, working without expansion, the mechanical efficacy of a cubic foot of water raised into steam will be somewhat less, on account of the resistance to the motion of the piston, occasioned by the pressure of the atmosphere; but in locomotive engines, where the working pressure is very high, the resistance due to the pressure of the atmosphere becomes relatively nearly as small as the resistance due to the rare vapor within the condenser of a condensing-engine; and it will not, therefore, be a material deviation from the truth if, in locomotive engines, working without priming, we reckon a cubic foot of water evaporated per hour as equivalent to a horse power. An engine evaporating 200 cubic feet of water per hour, and therefore exerting about 200-horse power, draws about 110 tons at thirty miles an hour; but if there were no loss from the resistance of the atmosphere, or of the blast-pipe, and no increased friction upon the engine from the increased power requisite for high speeds, the tractive force, if taken at 8 pounds per ton, would only require to be 70·4-horse power for 110 × 8 × 2640, the number of feet travelled per minute at 30 miles an hour, ÷ 33000 = 70·4-horse power. The friction of the train, however, at 30 miles an hour, including that of an engine of

200-horse power, cannot be taken at much less than 10 pounds per ton; for the friction of an engine increases with the power exerted, which determines the pressure upon its moving parts; and the friction of the carriages is also increased at high speeds, in consequence of the draw-bars being attached below the centre of effort of the frontage exposed to the wind, whereby the carriages are pressed down more firmly on the rails. If the traction be taken at 10 pounds per ton, then the power requisite for propulsion of a train, setting aside the resistance of the atmosphere, will be about 90-horse power, and the remaining 110-horse power is absorbed in overcoming the resistance of the atmosphere and of the blast-pipe. If the speed be increased from 30 to 60 miles an hour, about 200-horse power will be required for overcoming the friction of the train, and 880-horse power will be required to overcome the atmospheric resistance; making 1080-horse power, which will be necessary to propel a train of 110 tons at 60 miles an hour. The evaporation of a locomotive boiler is greatest when the speed is at its maximum, as the blast-pipe then produces its greatest effect; and the power of the engine varies nearly as the rate of evaporation, provided the blast-pipe be not unduly contracted. At ordinary railway speeds, the power of the boiler is seven or eight times greater than it would be without the blast, though, indeed, such a comparison hardly holds, as without the blast the fire of a locomotive boiler would not draw at all. At a speed of 20 miles an hour, a locomotive boiler boils off from 10 pounds to 14 pounds of water per square foot of heating-surface, and the rate of evaporation varies nearly as the √ of the speed.

The adhesion of the wheels upon the rails is about one-fifth of the weight when the rails are clean, and either perfectly wet or perfectly dry; but when the rails are half wet or greasy, the adhesion is not more than one-tenth or one-twelfth of the weight. The weight of locomotive engines varies from 15 to 20 tons. A powerful locomotive engine and tender, such as is suitable for high speeds, will weigh about 25 tons. The consumption of power by the locomotive itself is very great at high speeds, chiefly in consequence of the resistance occasioned by the blast-pipe to the free escape of the steam. Mr. Stephenson considers that, at ordinary railway speeds, a locomotive engine will absorb as much power as 15 loaded carriages, weighing 60 tons; so that in a train of 15 carriages, half the power is consumed by the engine. These determinations, however, are all very indefinite, and experiments are yet wanting to show the power produced and consumed by locomotives under different circumstances. Locomotive engines in England cost from $9,000 to $11,000 each. They run, on an average, about 130 miles a day, at a cost for repairs of about

5 cents per mile; and the cost of locomotive power, including repairs, wages, oil, and tallow, and coke, may be taken at 12 cents per mile, on economically managed railways. This does not include a sinking fund for the renewal of engines which may be worn out, and which may be taken at 10 per cent. on the original cost of the locomotives. On second class railways, the expense of locomotives, and workshops, and tools for repairing them, may be set down at $10,000 per mile.

Economy of fuel in locomotives is materially promoted by working expansively; but all attempts at economizing fuel in locomotives should begin with an increase in the area of the fire-grate, so that the power of the engine may not suffer so large a diminution by the creation of the necessary draft.

Every locomotive engine should be furnished with efficient expansion apparatus of some kind or other; as, setting aside the economy of fuel accomplishable by expansion, it is clear that expansion acts beneficially by diminishing the weight of the boiler, which may be made smaller at every increase of the. efficiency of the steam. When the draft is strong, a great loss of effect is caused by opening the furnace door, from the refrigeration due to the large volume of air admitted; and it would be a material improvement if the furnace could be fed by some such mechanism as the revolving grate. The use of sediment-collectors in locomotive boilers also appears expedient, as, if judiciously applied, they will effectually prevent the formation of scale upon the tubes, and will also operate as an antidote to priming in many cases. The form of collector best adapted for a locomotive boiler, will depend in a great measure upon the peculiar structure of the boiler; but generally any form will answer which communicates with the water level, and contains water within it in a tranquil state. The V-shaped cuts for establishing the communication between the exterior and interior of the vessel, have been found preferable to holes of any other form; for a subsiding particle, so soon as it falls in a slight degree, gets behind the case of the collecting vessel, and cannot afterwards escape.

A very important appendage to a locomotive, which I have never seen. and one which I consider indispensable, is a vacuum valve, to prevent the leakage of the tubes and an undue strain upon the boiler. No one would suppose the enormous pressure that is brought to bear upon the tubes when the boiler is blown out and a vacuum formed inside. For example, a tube is generally 10 feet long and 2 inches diameter, which equals in surface 753 square inches: now multiply that number by the pressure of the atmosphere on a square inch, which is 15 pounds, and we have the enormous pressure of 11,293 pounds; deduct one-half as not being a perfect vacuum, we have a pressure on each tube of 5,647 pounds, sufficient to start the joints and brazing. A simple valve opening inwards and held in its place by a spiral wire spring, will remedy the evil; as the vacuum is formed, the atmosphere will press the valve inwards and the atmosphere fill the boiler. I consider it highly important to have it on all locomotive boilers.

THE END.

THE ARTS OF TANNING AND CURRYING

Theoretically and Practically considered in all their details. Being a full and comprehensive Treatise on the Manufacture of the various kinds of Leather. Illustrated by over two hundred Engravings. Edited from the French of De Fontenelle and Malapeyere. With numerous Emendations and Additions, by CAMPBELL MORFIT, Practical and Analytical Chemist. Complete in one Volume, octavo..$5.00

This important Treatise will be found to cover the whole field in the most masterly manner, and it is believed that in no other branch of applied science could more signal service be rendered to American Manufacturers.

The publisher is not aware that in any other work heretofore issued in this country, more space has been devoted to this subject than a single chapter; and in offering this volume to so large and intelligent a class as American Tanners and Leather Dressers, he feels confident of their substantial support and encouragement.

THE PRACTICAL COTTON-SPINNER AND MANUFACTURER; Or, The Manager's and Overseer's Companion.

This works contains a Comprehensive System of Calculations for Mill Gearing and Machinery, from the first moving power through the different processes of Carding, Drawing, Slabbing, Roving, Spinning, and Weaving, adapted to American Machinery, Practice, and Usages. Compendious Tables of Yarns and Reeds are added. Illustrated by large Working-drawings of the most approved American Cotton Machinery. Complete in One Volume, octavo..$3.50

This edition of Scott's Cotton-Spinner, by OLIVER BYRNE, is designed for the American Operative. It will be found intensely practical, and will be of the greatest possible value to the Manager, Overseer, and Workman.

THE PRACTICAL METAL-WORKER'S ASSISTANT,

For Tin-Plate Workers, Brasiers, Coppersmiths, Zinc-Plate Ornamenters and Workers, Wire Workers, Whitesmiths, Blacksmiths, Bell Hangers, Jewellers, Silver and Gold Smiths, Electrotypers, and all other Workers in Alloys and Metals. By CHARLES HOLTZAPPFEL. Edited, with important additions, by OLIVER BYRNE. Complete in One Volume, octavo............$4.00

It will treat of Casting, Founding, and Forging; of Tongs and other Tools; Degrees of Heat and Managemnet of Fires; Welding; of Heading and Swage Tools; of Punches and Anvils; of Hardening and Tempering; of Malleable Iron Castings, Case Hardening, Wrought and Cast Iron. The management and manipulation of Metals and Alloys, Melting and Mixing. The management of Furnaces, Casting and Founding with Metallic Moulds, Joining and Working Sheet Metal. Peculiarities of the different Tools employed. Processes dependent on the ductility of Metals. Wire Drawing, Drawing Metal Tubes, Soldering. The use of the Blowpipe, and every other known Metal-Worker's Tool. To the works of Holtzappfel, OLIVER BYRNE has added all that is useful and peculiar to the American Metal-Worker.

THE MANUFACTURE OF IRON IN ALL ITS VARIOUS BRANCHES:

To which is added an Essay on the Manufacture of Steel, by FREDERICK OVERMAN, Mining Engineer, with one hundred and fifty Wood Engravings. A new edition. In One Volume, octavo, five hundred pages......................................$5.00

We have now to announce the appearance of another valuable work on the subject which, in our humble opinion, supplies any deficiency which late improvements and discoveries may have caused, from the lapse of time since the date of "Mushet" and "Schrivenor." It is the production of one of our transatlantic brethren, Mr. Frederick Overman, Mining Engineer; and we do not hesitate to set it down as a work of great importance to all connected with the iron interest; one which, while it is sufficiently technological fully to explain chemical analysis, and the various phenomena of iron under different circumstances, to the satisfaction of the most fastidious, is written in that clear and comprehensive style as to be available to the capacity of the humblest mind, and consequently will be of much advantage to those works where the proprietors may see the desirability of placing it in the hands of their operatives.—*London Morning Journal.*

A TREATISE ON THE AMERICAN STEAM-ENGINE.

Illustrated by numerous Wood Cuts and other Engravings. By OLIVER BYRNE. In One Volume. (In press.)

PROPELLERS AND STEAM NAVIGATION:

With Biographical Sketches of Early Inventors. By ROBERT MACFARLANE, C. E., Editor of the "Scientific American." In One Volume, 12mo. Illustrated by over Eighty Wood Engravings..75 cts.

The object of this "History of Propellers and Steam Navigation" is twofold. One is the arrangement and description of many devices which have been invented to propel vessels, in order to prevent many ingenious men from wasting their time, talents, and money on such projects. The immense amount of time, study, and money thrown away on such contrivances is beyond calculation. In this respect, it is hoped that it will be the means of doing some good.—*Preface.*

A TREATISE ON SCREW-PROPELLERS AND THEIR STEAM-ENGINES.

With Practical Rules and Examples by which to Calculate and Construct the same for any description of Vessels. By J. W. NYSTROM. Illustrated by thirty-two large working Drawings. In one Volume, octavo...................................$3.50

PRACTICAL SERIES.

THE AMERICAN MILLER AND MILLWRIGHT'S ASSISTANT. $1.
THE TURNER'S COMPANION. 75 cts.
THE PAINTER, GILDER, AND VARNISHER'S COMPANION. 75 cts.
THE DYER AND COLOUR-MAKER'S COMPANION. 75 cts.
THE BUILDER'S COMPANION. $1.
THE CABINET-MAKER'S COMPANION. 75 cts.
A TREATISE ON A BOX OF INSTRUMENTS. BY THOMAS KENTISH. $1.
THE PAPER-HANGER'S COMPANION. BY J. ARROWSMITH. 75 cts.
THE ASSAYER'S GUIDE. BY OSCAR M. LIEBER. 75 cts.
THE COMPLETE PRACTICAL BREWER. BY M. L. BYRN. $1.
THE COMPLETE PRACTICAL DISTILLER. BY M. L. BYRN. $1.
THE BOOKBINDER'S MANUAL.
THE PYROTECHNIST'S COMPANION. BY G. W. MORTIMER. 75 cts.
WALKER'S ELECTROTYPE MANIPULATION. 75 cts
COLBURN ON THE LOCOMOTIVE ENGINE. 75 cts.

THE AMERICAN MILLER AND MILLWRIGHT'S ASSISTANT:

By WILLIAM CARTER HUGHES, Editor of "The American Miller," (newspaper,) Buffalo, N. Y. Illustrated by Drawings of the most approved Machinery. In One Volume, 12mo.........$1

The author offers it as a substantial reference, instead of speculative theories, which belong only to those not immediately attached to the business. Special notice is also given of most of the essential improvements which have of late been introduced for the benefit of the Miller.—*Savannah Republican.*

The whole business of making flour is most thoroughly treated by him.—*Bulletin*

A very comprehensive view of the Millwright's business.—*Southern Literary Messenger.*

THE TURNER'S COMPANION:

Containing Instructions in Concentric, Elliptic, and Eccentric Turning. Also, various Plates of Chucks, Tools, and Instruments, and Directions for using the Eccentric Cutter, Drill, Vertical Cutter, and Circular Rest: with patterns and Instructions for working them. Illustrated by numerous Engravings. In One Volume, 12mo...75 cts.

The object of the Turner's Companion is to explain in a clear, concise, and intelligible manner, the rudiments of this beautiful art.—*Savannah Republican.*

There is no description of turning or lathe-work that this elegant little treatise does not describe and illustrate.—*Western Lit. Messenger.*

THE PAINTER, GILDER, AND VARNISHER'S COMPANION:

Containing Rules and Regulations for every thing relating to the arts of Painting, Gilding, Varnishing, and Glass Staining; numerous useful and valuable Receipts; Tests for the detection of Adulterations in Oils, Colours, &c., and a Statement of the Diseases and Accidents to which Painters, Gilders, and Varnishers are particularly liable; with the simplest methods of Prevention and Remedy. In one vol. small 12mo., cloth. 75cts.

Rejecting all that appeared foreign to the subject, the compiler has omitted nothing of real practical worth.—*Hunt's Merchant's Magazine.*

An excellent *practical work*, and one which the practical man cannot afford to be without.—*Farmer and Mechanic.*

It contains every thing that is of interest to persons engaged in this trade. —*Bulletin.*

This book will prove valuable to all whose business is in any way connected with painting.—*Scott's Weekly.*

Cannot fail to be useful.—*N. Y. Commercial.*

THE BUILDER'S POCKET COMPANION:

Containing the Elements of Building, Surveying, and Architecture; with Practical Rules and Instructions connected with the subject. By A. C. Smeaton, Civil Engineer, &c. In one volume, 12mo. $1.

Contents:—The Builder, Carpenter, Joiner, Mason, Plasterer, Plumber, Painter, Smith, Practical Geometry, Surveyor, Cohesive Strength of Bodies, Architect.

It gives, in a small space, the most thorough directions to the builder, from the laying of a brick, or the felling of a tree, up to the most elaborate production of ornamental architecture. It is scientific, without being obscure and unintelligible, and every house-carpenter, master, journeyman, or apprentice, should have a copy at hand always.—*Evening Bulletin.*

Complete on the subjects of which it treats. A most useful practical work. —*Balt. American.*

It must be of great practical utility.—*Savannah Republican.*

To whatever branch of the art of building the reader may belong, he will find in this something valuable and calculated to assist his progress.—*Farmer and Mechanic.*

This is a valuable little volume, designed to assist the student in the acquisition of elementary knowledge, and will be found highly advantageous to every young man who has devoted himself to the interesting pursuits of which it treats.—*Va. Herald.*

THE DYER AND COLOUR-MAKER'S COMPANION:

Containing upwards of two hundred Receipts for making Colors, on the most approved principles, for all the various styles and fabrics now in existence; with the Scouring Process, and plain Directions for Preparing, Washing-off, and Finishing the Goods. In one volume, small 12mo., cloth. 75 cts.

This is another of that most excellent class of practical books, which the publisher is giving to the public. Indeed we believe there is not, for manufacturers, a more valuable work, having been prepared for, and expressly adapted to their business.—*Farmer and Mechanic.*

It is a valuable book.—*Otsego Republican.*

We have shown it to some practical men, who all pronounced it the completest thing of the kind they had seen—*N. Y. Nation.*

THE CABINET-MAKER AND UPHOLSTERER'S COMPANION:

Comprising the Rudiments and Principles of Cabinet Making and Upholstery, with familiar instructions, illustrated by Examples, for attaining a proficiency in the Art of Drawing, as applicable to Cabinet Work; the processes of Veneering, Inlaying, and Buhl Work; the art of Dyeing and Staining Wood. Ivory, Bone, Tortoise-shell, etc. Directions for Lackering, Japanning, and Varnishing; to make French Polish; to prepare the best Glues, Cements, and Compositions, and a number of Receipts particularly useful for Workmen generally, with Explanatory and Illustrative Engravings. By J. Stokes. In one volume, 12mo., with illustrations. Second Edition. 75 cts.

THE PAPER-HANGER'S COMPANION:

In which the Practical Operations of the Trade are systematically laid down; with copious Directions Preparatory to Papering; Preventions against the effect of Damp in Walls; the various Cements and Pastes adapted to the several purposes of the Trade; Observations and Directions for the Panelling and Ornamenting of Rooms, &c. &c. By James Arrowsmith. In One Volume, 12mo. 75 cts.

THE ANALYTICAL CHEMIST'S ASSISTANT:

A Manual of Chemical Analysis, both Qualitative and Quantitative, of Natural and Artificial Inorganic Compounds; to which are appended the Rules for Detecting Arsenic in a Case of Poisoning. By FREDERIK WŒHLER, Professor of Chemistry in the University of Göttingen. Translated from the German, with an Introduction, Illustrations, and copious Additions, by OSCAR M. LIEBER, Author of the "Assayer's Guide." In one Volume, 12mo. $1.25.

RURAL CHEMISTRY:

An Elementary Introduction to the Study of the Science, in its relation to Agriculture and the Arts of Life. By EDWARD SOLLEY, Professor of Chemistry in the Horticultural Society of London. From the Third Improved London Edition. 12mo. $1.25.

THE FRUIT, FLOWER, AND KITCHEN GARDEN.

By PATRICK NEILL, L.L.D.

Thoroughly revised, and adapted to the climate and seasons of the United States, by a Practical Horticulturist. Illustrated by numerous Engravings. In one volume, 12mo. $1.25.

HOUSEHOLD SURGERY; OR, HINTS ON EMERGENCIES.

By J. F. SOUTH, one of the Surgeons of St. Thomas's Hospital. In one volume, 12mo. Illustrated by nearly fifty Engravings. $1.25.

HOUSEHOLD MEDICINE.

In one volume, 12mo. Uniform with, and a companion to, the above. (In immediate preparation.)

THE COMPLETE PRACTICAL BREWER;

Or, Plain, Concise, and Accurate Instructions in the Art of Brewing Beer, Ale, Porter, &c. &c., and the Process of Making all the Small Beers. By M. LAFAYETTE BYRN, M. D. With Illustrations, 12mo. $1.

THE COMPLETE PRACTICAL DISTILLER;

By M. LAFAYETTE BYRN, M. D. With Illustrations, 12mo. $1.

THE ENCYCLOPEDIA OF CHEMISTRY, PRACTICAL AND THEORETICAL:

Embracing its application to the Arts, Metallurgy, Mineralogy, Geology, Medicine, and Pharmacy. By JAMES C. BOOTH, Melter and Refiner in the United States Mint; Professor of Applied Chemistry in the Franklin Institute, etc.; assisted by CAMPBELL MORFIT, author of "Chemical Manipulations," etc. Complete in one volume, royal octavo, 978 pages, with numerous wood cuts and other illustrations. $5.

It covers the whole field of Chemistry as applied to Arts and Sciences. * * * As no library is complete without a common dictionary, it is also our opinion that none can be without this Encyclopedia of Chemistry.—*Scientific American.*

A work of time and labour, and a treasury of chemical information.—*North American.*

By far the best manual of the kind which has been presented to the American public.—*Boston Courier.*

PERFUMERY; ITS MANUFACTURE AND USE:

With Instructions in every branch of the Art, and Receipts for all the Fashionable Preparations; the whole forming a valuable aid to the Perfumer, Druggist, and Soap Manufacturer. Illustrated by numerous Wood-cuts. From the French of Celnart, and other late authorities. With Additions and Improvements by CAMPBELL MORFIT, one of the Editors of the "Encyclopedia of Chemistry." In one volume, 12mo., cloth. $1.50

A TREATISE ON A BOX OF INSTRUMENTS,

And the SLIDE RULE, with the Theory of Trigonometry and Logarithms, including Practical Geometry, Surveying, Measuring of Timber, Cask and Malt Gauging, Heights and Distances. By THOMAS KENTISH. In One Volume, 12mo. $1.

THE LOCOMOTIVE ENGINE:

Including a Description of its Structure, Rules for Estimating its Capabilities, and Practical Observations on its Construction and Management. By ZERAH COLBURN, 12mo..............75 cts.

SYLLABUS OF A COMPLETE COURSE OF LECTURES ON CHEMISTRY:

Including its Application to the Arts, Agriculture, and Mining, prepared for the use of the Gentlemen Cadets at the Hon. E. I. Co.'s Military Seminary, Addiscombe. By Professor E. SOLLY, Lecturer on Chemistry in the Hon. E. I. Co.'s Military Seminary. Revised by the Author of "Chemical Manipulations." In one volume, octavo, cloth. $1.25.

THE ASSAYER'S GUIDE;

Or, Practical Directions to Assayers, Miners, and Smelters for the Tests and Assays, by Heat and by Wet Processes, of the Ores of all the principal Metals, and of Gold and Silver Coins and Alloys. By OSCAR M. LIEBER, late Geologist to the State of Mississippi. 12mo. With Illustrations. 75 cts.

THE BOOKBINDER'S MANUAL.

Complete in one Volume, 12mo. (in press.)

ELECTROTYPE MANIPULATION:

Being the Theory and Plain Instructions in the Art of Working in Metals, by Precipitating them from their Solutions, through the agency of Galvanic or Voltaic Electricity. By CHARLES V. WALKER, Hon. Secretary to the London Electrical Society, etc Illustrated by Wood-cuts. A New Edition, from the Twenty-fifth London Edition. 12mo. 75 cts.

PHOTOGENIC MANIPULATION:

Containing the Theory and Plain Instructions in the Art of Photography, or the Productions of Pictures through the Agency of Light; including Calotype, Chrysotype, Cyanotype, Chromatype, Energiatype, Anthotype, Amphitype, Daguerreotype, Thermography, Electrical and Galvanic Impressions. By GEORGE THOMAS FISHER, Jr., Assistant in the Laboratory of the London Institution. Illustrated by wood-cuts. In one volume, 24mo., cloth. 62 cts.

MATHEMATICS FOR PRACTICAL MEN:

Being a Common-Place Book of Principles, Theorems, Rules, and Tables, in various departments of Pure and Mixed Mathematics, with their Applications; especially to the pursuits of Surveyors, Architects, Mechanics, and Civil Engineers, with numerous Engravings. By OLINTHUS GREGORY, L. L. D. $1.50.

Only let men awake, and fix their eyes, one while on the nature of things, another while on the application of them to the use and service of mankind. —*Lord Bacon*

EXAMINATIONS OF DRUGS, MEDICINES, CHEMICALS, &c.

As to their Purity and Adulterations. By C. H. PEIRCE, M.D., Translator of "Stöckhardt's Chemistry," Examiner of Medicines for the Port of Boston, &c. &c. 12mo, cloth.................$1.25

SHEEP-HUSBANDRY IN THE SOUTH:

Comprising a Treatise on the Acclimation of Sheep in the Southern States, and an Account of the different Breeds. Also, a Complete Manual of Breeding, Summer and Winter Management, and of the Treatment of Diseases. With Portraits and other Illustrations. By HENRY S. RANDALL. In One Volume, octavo...$1.25

ELWOOD'S GRAIN TABLES:

Showing the value of Bushels and Pounds of different kinds of Grain, calculated in Federal Money, so arranged as to exhibit upon a single page the value at a given price from *ten cents to two dollars* per bushel, of any quantity from *one pound to ten thousand bushels.* By J. L. ELWOOD. A new Edition. In One Volume, 12mo...$1

To Millers and Produce Dealers this work is pronounced by all who have it in use, to be superior in arrangement to any work of the kind published—and *unerring accuracy in every calculation may be relied upon in every instance.*

☞ A reward of Twenty-five Dollars is offered for an error of one cent found in the work.

MISS LESLIE'S COMPLETE COOKERY.

Directions for Cookery, in its Various Branches. By MISS LESLIE. Forty-seventh Edition. Thoroughly Revised, with the Addition of New Receipts. In One Volume, 12mo, half bound, or in sheep...$1

In preparing a new and carefully revised edition of this my first work on cookery, I have introduced improvements, corrected errors, and added new receipts, that I trust will on trial be found satisfactory. The success of the book (proved by its immense and increasing circulation) affords conclusive evidence that it has obtained the approbation of a large number of my countrywomen; many of whom have informed me that it has made practical housewives of young ladies who have entered into married life with no other acquirements than a few showy accomplishments. Gentlemen, also, have told me of great improvements in the family table, after presenting their wives with this manual of domestic cookery, and that, after a morning devoted to the fatigues of business, they no longer find themselves subjected to the annoyance of an ill-dressed dinner.—*Preface.*

MISS LESLIE'S TWO HUNDRED RECEIPTS IN FRENCH COOKERY.

A new Edition, in cloth...25 cts.

THE DYER'S INSTRUCTOR,

Comprising Practical Instructions in the Art of Dyeing Silk, Cotton, Wool and Worsted and Woollen Goods, &c., containing nearly 800 Receipts, to which is added the Art of Padding and the Printing of Silk Warps, Skeins, and Handkerchiefs, and the various Mordants and Colours for the different styles of such work. By David Smith, Pattern Dyer, 1 vol. 12mo, (just published)..$1.50

TWO HUNDRED DESIGNS FOR COTTAGES AND VILLAS, &c. &c.

Original and Selected. By Thomas U. Walter, Architect of Girard College, and John Jay Smith, Librarian of the Philadelphia Library. In Four Parts, quarto........................$10

GUIDE FOR WORKERS IN METALS AND STONE.

Consisting of Designs and Patterns for Gates, Piers, Balcony and Cemetery Railing, Window Guards, Balustrades, Staircases, Verandas, Fanlights, Lamps and Lamp Posts, Palisades, Monuments, Mantles, Gas Fittings, Stoves, Stands, Candlesticks, Silver and Plated Ware, Chandeliers, Candelabras, Potters' Ware, &c. &c. By T. U. Walter, Architect, and John Jay Smith, 4 vols. 4to, plates..$10

FAMILY ENCYCLOPEDIA

Of Useful Knowledge and General Literature; containing about Four Thousand Articles upon Scientific and Popular Subjects. With Plates. By John L. Blake, D. D. In One Volume, 8vo, cloth extra..$3.50

THE PYROTECHNIST'S COMPANION;

Or, A Familiar System of Recreative Fire-Works. By G. W. Mortimer. Illustrated by numerous Engravings. 12mo. 75 cts

STANDARD ILLUSTRATED POETRY.

THE TALES AND POEMS OF LORD BYRON:

Illustrated by Henry Warren. In One Volume, royal 8vo with 10 Plates, scarlet cloth, gilt edges.................................$5
Morocco extra...$7

It is illustrated by several elegant engravings, from original designs by Warren, and is a most splendid work for the parlour or study.—*Boston Evening Gazette.*

CHILDE HAROLD; A ROMAUNT BY LORD BYRON:

Illustrated by 12 Splendid Plates, by Warren and others. In One Volume, royal 8vo., cloth extra, gilt edges...................$5
Morocco extra...$7

Printed in elegant style, with splendid pictures, far superior to any thing of the sort usually found in books of this kind.—*N. Y. Courier.*

THE FEMALE POETS OF AMERICA.

By Rufus W. Griswold. A new Edition. In One Volume, royal 8vo. Cloth, gilt...$2.50
Cloth extra, gilt edges...$3
Morocco super extra...$4.50

The best production which has yet come from the pen of Dr. Griswold, and the most valuable contribution which he has ever made to the literary celebrity of the country.—*N. Y. Tribune.*

THE LADY OF THE LAKE:

By Sir Walter Scott. Illustrated with 10 Plates, by Corbould and Meadows. In One Volume, royal 8vo. Bound in cloth extra, gilt edges...$5
Turkey morocco super extra...$7

This is one of the most truly beautiful books which has ever issued from the American press.

LALLA ROOKH; A ROMANCE BY THOMAS MOORE:

Illustrated by 13 Plates, from Designs by Corbould, Meadows, and Stephanoff. In One Volume, royal 8vo. Bound in cloth extra, gilt edges...$5
Turkey morocco super extra...$7

This is published in a style uniform with the "Lady of the Lake."

THE POETICAL WORKS OF THOMAS GRAY:

With Illustrations by C. W. Radcliff. Edited with a Memoir, by Henry Reed, Professor of English Literature in the University of Pennsylvania. In One Volume, 8vo. Bound in cloth extra, gilt edges..$3.50
Turkey morocco super extra......................................$5.50
In One Volume, 12mo, without plates, cloth..................$1.25
Do. do. do. cloth, gilt edges....$1.50

We have not seen a specimen of typographical luxury from the American press which can surpass this volume in choice elegance.—*Boston Courier.*

It is eminently calculated to consecrate among American readers, (if they have not been consecrated already in their hearts,) the pure, the elegant, the refined, and, in many respects, the sublime imaginings of Thomas Gray.—*Richmond Whig.*

THE POETICAL WORKS OF HENRY WADSWORTH LONGFELLOW:

Illustrated by 10 Plates, after Designs by D. Huntingdon, with a Portrait. Ninth Edition. In One Volume, royal 8vo. Bound in cloth extra, gilt edges......................................$5
Morocco super extra..$7

This is the very luxury of literature—Longfellow's charming poems presented in a form of unsurpassed beauty.—*Neal's Gazette.*

POETS AND POETRY OF ENGLAND IN THE NINETEENTH CENTURY.

By Rufus W. Griswold. Illustrated. In One Volume, royal 8vo. Bound in cloth..$3
Cloth extra, gilt edges..$3.50
Morocco super extra..$5

Such is the critical acumen discovered in these selections, that scarcely a page is to be found but is redolent with beauties, and the volume itself may be regarded as a galaxy of literary pearls.—*Democratic Review.*

THE TASK, AND OTHER POEMS.

By William Cowper. Illustrated by 10 Steel Engravings. In One Volume, 12mo. Cloth extra, gilt edges..................$2
Morocco extra..$3

"The illustrations in this edition of Cowper are most exquisitely designed and engraved."

THE FEMALE POETS OF GREAT BRITAIN.

With Copious Selections and Critical Remarks. By FREDERIC ROWTON. With Additions. Illustrations. 8vo, cloth......$2.50
Cloth extra, gilt edges..$3.00
Turkey morocco, super..$4.50

Mr. ROWTON has presented us with admirably selected specimens of nearly one hundred of the most celebrated female poets of Great Britain, from the time of Lady Juliana Berners, the first of whom there is any record, to the Mitfords, the Hewitts, the Cooks, the Barretts, and others of the present day.—*Hunt's Merchants' Magazine.*

SPECIMENS OF THE BRITISH POETS.

From the time of Chaucer to the end of the Eighteenth Century. By THOMAS CAMPBELL. In One Volume, royal 8vo. (In press.)

THE POETS AND POETRY OF THE ANCIENTS:

By WILLIAM PETER, A. M. Comprising Translations and Specimens of the Poets of Greece and Rome, with an elegant engraved View of the Coliseum at Rome. Bound in cloth......$3
Cloth extra, gilt edges..$3.50
Turkey morocco super extra..$5

It is without fear that we say that no such excellent or complete collection has ever been made. It is made with skill, taste, and judgment.—*Charleston Patriot.*

THE POETICAL WORKS OF N. PARKER WILLIS.

Illustrated by 16 Plates, after designs by E. LEUTZE. In One Volume, royal 8vo. A new Edition. Bound in cloth extra, gilt edges..$5
Turkey morocco super extra..$7

This is one of the most beautiful works ever published in this country.—*Courier and Inquirer.*

Pure and perfect in sentiment, often in expression, and many a heart has been won from sorrow or roused from apathy by his earlier melodies. The illustrations are by LEUTZE,—a sufficient guarantee for their beauty and grace. As for the typographical execution of the volume, it will bear comparison with any English book, and quite surpasses most issues in America.—*Neal's Gazette.*

The admirers of the poet could not have his gems in a better form for holiday presents.—*W. Continent.*

MISCELLANEOUS.

JOURNAL OF ARNOLD'S EXPEDITION TO QUEBEC, IN 1775.

By ISAAC SENTER, M. D. 8vo, boards.........................62 cts

---

ADVENTURES OF CAPTAIN SIMON SUGGS;

And other Sketches. By JOHNSON J. HOOPER. With Illustrations. 12mo, paper..50 cts.
Cloth..75 cts.

AUNT PATTY'S SCRAP-BAG.

By Mrs. CAROLINE LEE HENTZ, Author of "Linda." 12mo.
Paper covers..50 cts.
Cloth..75 cts.

BIG BEAR OF ARKANSAS;

And other Western Sketches. Edited by W. T. PORTER. In One Volume, 12mo, paper..50 cts.
Cloth..75 cts.

COMIC BLACKSTONE.

By GILBERT ABBOT A' BECKET. Illustrated. Complete in One Volume. Cloth..75 cts.

GHOST STORIES.

Illustrated by Designs by DARLEY. In One Volume, 12mo, paper covers..50 cts.

MODERN CHIVALRY; OR, THE ADVENTURES OF CAPTAIN FARRAGO AND TEAGUE O'REGAN.

By H. H. BRACKENRIDGE. Second Edition since the Author's death. With a Biographical Notice, a Critical Disquisition on the Work, and Explanatory Notes. With Illustrations, from Original Designs by DARLEY. Two volumes, paper covers 75cts.
Cloth or sheep..$1.00

COMPLETE WORKS OF LORD BOLINGBROKE·

With a Life, prepared expressly for this Edition, containing Additional Information relative to his Personal and Public Character, selected from the best authorities. In Four Volumes, 8vo. Bound in cloth..$7.00
In sheep..8.00

CHRONICLES OF PINEVILLE.

By the Author of "Major Jones's Courtship." Illustrated by DARLEY. 12mo, paper..50 cts.
Cloth ....75 cts.

GILBERT GURNEY.

By THEODORE HOOK. With Illustrations. In One Volume, 8vo., paper..50 cts.

MEMOIRS OF THE GENERALS, COMMODORES, AND OTHER COMMANDERS,

Who distinguished themselves in the American Army and Navy, during the War of the Revolution, the War with France, that with Tripoli, and the War of 1812, and who were presented with Medals, by Congress, for their gallant services. By THOMAS WYATT, A. M., Author of "History of the Kings of France." Illustrated with Eighty-two Engravings from the Medals. 8vo.
Cloth gilt $2.00
Half morocco...$2.50

GEMS OF THE BRITISH POETS.

By S. C. HALL. In One Volume, 12mo., cloth...........$1.00
Cloth, gilt $1.25

VISITS TO REMARKABLE PLACES:

Old Halls, Battle Fields, and Scenes Illustrative of striking passages in English History and Poetry. By WILLIAM HOWITT. In Two Volumes, 8vo, cloth......................................$4.00

NARRATIVE OF THE ARCTIC LAND EXPEDITION.

By CAPTAIN BACK, R. N. In One Volume, 8vo, boards...$2.00

THE MISCELLANEOUS WORKS OF WILLIAM HAZLITT.

Including Table-talk; Opinions of Books, Men, and Things; Lectures on Dramatic Literature of the Age of Elizabeth; Lectures on the English Comic Writers; The Spirit of the Age, or Contemporary Portraits. Five Volumes, 12mo., cloth......$5.00
Half calf..$6.25

FLORAL OFFERING

A Token of Friendship. Edited by FRANCES S OSGOOD. Illustrated by 10 beautiful Bouquets of Flowers In One Volume, 4to, muslin, gilt edges..$3.50
Turkey morocco super extra...................................$5.50

THE HISTORICAL ESSAYS,

Published under the title of "Dix Ans D'Etude Historique," and Narratives of the Merovingian Era; or, Scenes in the Sixth Century. With an Autobiographical Preface. By AUGUSTUS THIERRY, Author of the "History of the Conquest of England by the Normans." 8vo., paper..$1.00
Cloth $1 25

BOOK OF THE SEASONS;

Or, The Calendar of Nature. By WILLIAM HOWITT. One Volume, 12mo, cloth...$1
Calf extra...$2

PICKINGS FROM THE "PORTFOLIO OF THE REPORTER OF THE NEW ORLEANS PICAYUNE."

Comprising Sketches of the Eastern Yankee, the Western Hoosier, and such others as make up Society in the great Metropolis of the South. With Designs by DARLEY. 18mo., paper...50 cts.
Cloth...75 cts.

NOTES OF A TRAVELLER

On the Social and Political State of France, Prussia, Switzerland, Italy, and other parts of Europe, during the present Century. By SAMUEL LAING. In One Volume, 8vo., cloth.....$1.50

HISTORY OF THE CAPTIVITY OF NAPOLEON AT ST. HELENA.

By GENERAL COUNT MONTHOLON, the Emperor's Companion in Exile and Testamentary Executor. One Volume, 8vo., cloth, $2.50
Half morocco..$3.00

MY SHOOTING BOX.

By FRANK FORRESTER, (Henry Wm. Herbert, Esq.,) Author of "Warwick Woodlands," &c. With Illustrations, by DARLEY.
One Volume, 12mo., cloth..75 cts.
Paper covers..50 cts.

MYSTERIES OF THE BACKWOODS:

Or, Sketches of the South-west—including Character, Scenery, and Rural Sports. By T. B. THORPE, Author of "Tom Owen, the Bee-Hunter," &c. Illustrated by DARLEY. 12mo, cloth, 75 cts.
Paper.. 50 cts.

NARRATIVE OF THE LATE EXPEDITION TO THE DEAD SEA.

From a Diary by one of the Party. Edited by EDWARD P. MONTAGUE. 12mo, cloth..$1

MY DREAMS:

A Collection of Poems. By Mrs. LOUISA S. MCCORD. 12mo, boards ....75 cts

---

AMERICAN COMEDIES.

By JAMES K. PAULDING and WM. IRVING PAULDING. One Volume, 16mo, boards...50 cts.

RAMBLES IN YUCATAN;

Or, Notes of Travel through the Peninsula: including a Visit to the Remarkable Ruins of Chi-chen, Kabah, Zayi, and Uxmal. With numerous Illustrations. By B. M. NORMAN. Seventh Edition. In One Volume, octavo, cloth.................................$2

THE AMERICAN IN PARIS.

By JOHN SANDERSON. A New Edition. In Two Volumes, 12mo, cloth..$1.50

This is the most animated, graceful, and intelligent sketch of French manners, or any other, that we have had for these twenty years.—*London Monthly Magazine.*

ROBINSON CRUSOE.

A Complete Edition, with Six Illustrations. One Volume, 8vo, paper covers..$1.00
Cloth, gilt edges...$1.25

SCENES IN THE ROCKY MOUNTAINS,

And in Oregon, California, New Mexico, Texas, and the Grand Prairies; or, Notes by the Way. By RUFUS B. SAGE. Second Edition. One Volume, 12mo, paper covers ....50 cts.
With a Map, bound in cloth...75 cts.

THE PUBLIC MEN OF THE REVOLUTION:

Including Events from the Peace of 1783 to the Peace of 1815. In a Series of Letters. By the late Hon. WM. SULLIVAN, LL. D. With a Biographical Sketch of the Author, by his son, JOHN T. S. SULLIVAN. With a Portrait. In One Volume, 8vo. cloth$2.50

ACHIEVEMENTS OF THE KNIGHTS OF MALTA.

By ALEXANDER SUTHERLAND. In One Volume, 16mo, cloth, $1.00
Paper...75 cts.

ATALANTIS.

A Poem. By WILLIAM GILMORE SIMMS. 12mo, boards, 50 cts.

LIVES OF MEN OF LETTERS AND SCIENCE.

By HENRY LORD BROUGHAM. Two Volumes, 12mo, cloth, $1 50
Paper $1.00

THE LIFE, LETTERS, AND JOURNALS OF LORD BYRON.

By THOMAS MOORE. Two Volumes, 12mo, cloth.............. $2

THE BOWL OF PUNCH.

Illustrated by Numerous Plates. 12mo, paper............50 cts

CHILDREN IN THE WOOD.

Illustrated by HARVEY. 12mo, cloth, gilt..................50 cts.
Paper ....25 cts.

TOWNSEND'S NARRATIVE OF THE BATTLE OF BRANDYWINE.

One Volume, 8vo, boards...$1.

THE POEMS OF C. P. CRANCH.

In One Volume, 12mo, boards..................................37 cts.

THE WORKS OF BENJ. DISRAELI.

Two Volumes, 8vo, cloth $2
Paper covers...$1

NATURE DISPLAYED IN HER MODE OF TEACHING FRENCH.

By N. G. DUFIEF. Two Volumes, 8vo, boards..................$5

NATURE DISPLAYED IN HER MODE OF TEACHING SPANISH.

By N. G. DUFIEF. In Two Volumes, 8vo, boards............ $7

FRENCH AND ENGLISH DICTIONARY.

By N. G. Dufief. In One Volume, 8vo, sheep..................$5

FROISSART BALLADS AND OTHER POEMS.

By Philip Pendleton Cooke. In One Volume, 12mo, boards..50 cts.

THE LIFE OF RICHARD THE THIRD.

By Miss Halsted. In One Volume, 8vo, cloth...........$1.50

THE LIFE OF NAPOLEON BONAPARTE.

By William Hazlitt. In Three Volumes, 12mo, cloth......$3
Half calf..$4

TRAVELS IN GERMANY, BY W. HOWITT.

EYRE'S NARRATIVE. BURNE'S CABOOL.

In One Volume, 8vo, cloth......................................$1.25

CAMPANIUS HOLMES'S ACCOUNT OF NEW SWEDEN.

8vo, boards..$1.50

IMAGE OF HIS FATHER.

By Mayhew. Complete in One Volume, 8vo, paper....25

SPECIMENS OF THE BRITISH CRITICS.

By Christopher North (Professor Wilson) 12mo, cloth. $1.00

A TOUR TO THE RIVER SAUGENAY, IN LOWER CANADA.

By Charles Lanman. In One Volume, 16mo, cloth....62 cts
Paper.. 50 cts

TRAVELS IN AUSTRIA, RUSSIA, SCOTLAND, ENGLAND AND WALES.

By J. G. Kohl. One Volume, 8vo. cloth....................$1 25

LIFE OF OLIVER GOLDSMITH.

By James Prior. In One Volume, 8vo, boards............... .2

OUR ARMY AT MONTEREY.

By T. B. Thorpe. 16mo, cloth.................................62 cts.
Paper covers..50 cts.

OUR ARMY ON THE RIO GRANDE.

By T. B. Thorpe. 16mo, cloth.................................62 cts.
Paper covers..50 cts.

LIFE OF LORENZO DE MEDICI.

By William Roscoe. In Two Volumes, 8vo, cloth..........$3

MISCELLANEOUS ESSAYS OF SIR WALTER SCOTT.

In Three Volumes, 12mo, cloth..............................$3.50
Half morocco..$4.25

SERMON ON THE MOUNT.

Illuminated. Boards..$1.50
" Silk..$2.00
" Morocco super..$3.00

MISCELLANEOUS ESSAYS OF THE REV. SYDNEY SMITH.

In Three Volumes, 12mo, cloth..............................$3.50
Half morocco..$4.25

MRS. CAUDLE'S CURTAIN LECTURES...............12½ cts.

SERMONS BY THE REV. SYDNEY SMITH.

One Volume, 12mo, cloth.......................................75 cts.

MISCELLANEOUS ESSAYS OF SIR JAMES STEPHEN.

One Volume, 12mo, cloth.......................................$1.25

THREE HOURS; OR, THE VIGIL OF LOVE.

A Volume of Poems. By Mrs. Hale. 18mo, boards...75 cts

TORLOGH O'BRIEN:

A Tale of the Wars of King James. 8vo, paper covers 12½ cts
Illustrated...37½ cts

AN AUTHOR'S MIND.

Edited by M. F. Tupper. One Volume, 16mo, cloth....62 cts.
Paper covers...50 cts.

HISTORY OF THE ANGLO-SAXONS.

By Sharon Turner. Two Volumes, 8vo, cloth...........$4.50

PROSE WORKS OF N. PARKER WILLIS.

In One Volume, 8vo, 800 pp., cloth, gilt....................$3.00
Cloth extra, gilt edges.......................................$3.50
Library sheep...$3.50
Turkey morocco backs...$3.75
" extra...$5.50

MISCELLANEOUS ESSAYS OF PROF. WILSON.

Three Volumes, 12mo, cloth.......................................$3.50

WORD TO WOMAN.

By Caroline Fry. 12mo, cloth.......................................60 cts.

WYATT'S HISTORY OF THE KINGS OF FRANCE.

Illustrated by 72 Portraits. One Volume, 16mo, cloth...$1.00
Cloth, extra gilt...$1.25

www.ingramcontent.com/pod-product-compliance
Lightning Source LLC
LaVergne TN
LVHW020215110826
845151LV00003B/726

* 9 7 8 1 4 2 5 5 3 3 6 3 2 *